Limited Classical Reprint Library

SABBATH MORNING

READINGS

ON THE

OLD TESTAMENT.

BY

THE REV. JOHN CUMMING, D.D., F.R.S.E.,

MINISTER OF THE SCOTTISH NATIONAL CHURCH, CROWN COURT,
COVENT GARDEN.

Book of Deuteronomy.

Foreword by
Dr. Cyril J. Barber

Klock & Klock Christian Publishers, Inc.
2527 Girard Avenue North
Minneapolis, Minnesota 55411

Originally published by
John Farquhar Shaw
London, 1856

0-86524-088-4

Printed by Klock & Klock in the U.S.A.
1982 Reprint

FOREWORD

While sitting in a faculty meeting a few years ago, one of my learned colleagues made the following admission: "When I read the Old Testament I am forced to think that there may be something to dispensationalism after all. I cannot preach from the Old Testament, for the God of the Old Testament is a God of wrath and judgment. Only in the New Testament do we find Christ revealing God as a God of grace."

My colleague was wrong in his view of dispensationalism as well as in his view of the Old Testament. The Book of Deuteronomy repeats over and over again that God will do different things for His people Israel, *because He loves them*. Deuteronomy is essentially a book illustrating, by means of precept as well as practice, the love of God.

In this fifth book of Moses we have the essence of what God revealed to Moses at Horeb. His *love* lies at the heart of the message Moses now communicates to Israel. To be sure there are warnings, but these are the cautions of a loving Father. The path of blessing, then as now, lies in obedience.

The demonstration of the love of God in freeing Israel from the Egyptians, leading them through the trackless wilderness, providing for their needs through forty years in the desert, and now in bringing them to the borders of the Promised Land, is designed to elicit a response from the nation. They are to respond to His love with obedience to His laws. Then He will bless them. Israel's response, however, had almost without exception been deficient (*cf.*, Deuteronomy 10:20-22). They had not given God their wholehearted devotion. They had not loved Him with their entire being--heart, mind, soul, strength (*cf.*, Deuteronomy 6:5). Consequently their conduct was also deficient.

But the Book of Deuteronomy is more than a treatise on the love of God. It is about a new community as well--a community of people living in a relationship! Both verticle and horizontal relationships are important, and the latter is dependent upon the former.

In his messages, therefore, Moses was also preparing the people for a new life. The hardships of the wilderness were now behind them. The Promised Land was before them. The people, however, needed a new committment of themselves to God. There was also a need for a fresh understanding of the nature of their relationship to one another.

The love of God and the sense of community are, therefore, the primary foci of this book. And to show that the Old Testament can be preached and is relevant to our lives today, John Cumming (1807-1881), Scottish-born preacher and, for many years minister of the National Scottish Church, London, expounds Moses' last treatises with an unction that was characteristic of all that was best in the era in which he lived.

Nor are readers today "cheated" due to the fact that Form Criticism had not developed and was an unknown discipline to Dr. Cumming, for in our day a "New Criticism" (or *Werkinterpretation*) is replacing the old *Formgeschichte*. This "New Criticism," while not quite the same as the literal interpretation of the Bible used by evangelicals of all persuasions, is nevertheless refreshing, stressing instead the need for the acceptance of the books of the Old Testament as finished products. This new movement in biblical interpretation accepts the extant form of the text rather than engaging in a search for possible sources. And so, having come almost full circle, modern scholarship is slowly coming back to the position from which capable men of God of a generation past expounded the text.

Because the Book of Deuteronomy corrects many of our misconceptions regarding God, because it stresses the basics whereby people may live together in community (or fellowship), and because it is so vital to a proper understanding of much of the New Testament, it is hoped that the republication of this Old Testament commentary will contribute toward a better grasp of the teaching of the Bible as a whole.

Cyril J. Barber, D. Lit.
Author, *The Minister's Library*

PREFACE.

DEUTERONOMY means the repetition of the law already revealed. It closes the Pentateuch. It dwells less on the ritual and ceremonial, and more upon the moral and spiritual requirements of God.

It was uttered by Moses in circumstances of great solemnity; it was to be engraven on stones; the king in future ages was to write out for himself a copy of it; at the feast of tabernacles it was to be read in public. It is therefore historically as well as intrinsically a book of permanent excellence. Our blessed Lord quoted it in the temptation, and repelled by its words the wicked one. It is full of explicit predictions of the sins and sufferings of the Jews, their desolation by the Roman eagle, their dispersion into all lands. The prophecy of the Shiloh, the hope of Israel, is in this book clear and emphatic.

What a wonderful work is the Pentateuch; appearing in an age of darkness, and ignorance, and idolatry, and, by its purity, and morality, and glory, vindicating to earth the proof of its transmission from the skies.

I do believe, without assuming any credit, that in such familiar expositions, more light is cast on the wondrous works and ways of God, than in works of far greater bulk and learning; and if any derive as great profit from reading them, as the author has from arranging and writing them, he will feel he has had ample reward.

CONTENTS.

CHAPTER I.

CHAPTER II.

CHAPTER III.

CHAPTER IV.

CHAPTER V.

CONTENTS.

CHAPTER VI.

CHAPTER VII.

CHAPTER VIII.

CHAPTER IX.

CHAPTER X.

CHAPTER XI.

CHAPTER XII.

CHAPTER XIII.

CHAPTER XIV.

CHAPTER XV.

CHAPTER XVI.

CHAPTER XVII.

CHAPTER XVIII.

CHAPTER XIX.

CHAPTER XX.

CHAPTERS XXI.—XXV.

CHAPTER XXVI.

CHAPTER XXVII.

CHAPTER XXVIII.

CHAPTER XXIX.

CHAPTER XXX.

CHAPTER XXXI.

CHAPTER XXXII.

CHAPTER XXXIII.

CHAPTER XXXIV.

SABBATH MORNING READINGS

ON THE

Book of Deuteronomy.

CHAPTER I.

EXCELLENCE OF DEUTERONOMY. EXPOSITORY. ITS NAME. OUR
LORD'S QUOTATION FROM IT AS SCRIPTURE. THE LAST
CHAPTER AND ITS EXPLANATION. THE PRAYER OF MOSES.
JUDICIAL IMPARTIALITY. THE SPIES. THEIR REPORT.
ENCOURAGEMENT OF MOSES.

THE book, the opening chapter of which we have
now read, is by far perhaps the most interesting and
instructive of the Five Books of Moses, constituting
what is commonly called the Pentateuch. The other
books are more historical; this is expository—directly
instructive. It bears somewhat the same relationship
to the previous books of the Pentateuch, that the
Gospel of St. John seems to bear to the previous three
Gospels—dealing less with the outward history of
God's people, and relating more to their inward experience as believers in his name, and expectants of
an entrance into the everlasting and blessed rest.
Hence in this book we find countless instructive

B

lessons, addresses of the most touching and beautiful description, precious doctrines, and weighty maxims, fitted to convey to us, on whom the ends of the world are come, lessons no less valuable and applicable than they conveyed to the pilgrims of Israel in the midst of the desert on their way to Canaan.

In making some remarks upon this book, it is proper to explain that the name Deuteronomy is derived from the Greek, or given to this book in what is called the Septuagint Greek Bible; or the translation of the Old Testament out of Hebrew into Greek, executed by Alexandrian Jews about three hundred years before the birth of our Lord; and in that version it is called Deuteronomy, from two Greek words, which mean "a second law," or "the law repeated again;" which is the fact, only in variety of expression, and under difference of illustration. But in the original Hebrew it is not called so. As has been stated in our Readings on the previous Books of the Pentateuch, the Jews called a book of the Bible by its initial words. For instance, the initial words of Deuteronomy are, "These be the words." Hence when a Jew quotes Deuteronomy, he says, "You will find in such a section of "These be the words." The Hebrew for "These be the words," אֵלֶּה הַדְּבָרִים, (eleh hadebarim,) is the name of this book among the Jews to this day; and by which it is still called by the Jews as often as it is read in their synagogues, or in their families, as part and parcel of the word of God.

It is worthy of notice, in reference to this book, that the laity are specially enjoined to read it; the kings are instructed to write out a copy of it; it was to be engraven and imprinted also upon the stones as they crossed the Jordan; and was to be as frontlets before their eyes, so that its records might be near to them, remembered in their lying down and their rising up. Our blessed Lord expressly quotes this book as part of holy Scripture, when he was tempted in the desert, for he exclaimed, " It is written, Thou shalt not tempt the Lord thy God;" in which words he referred to this book, and thus quoted it as part and parcel of the sacred canon. Indeed, it never was denied at any time, or by any, that this book is inspired, and is therefore a portion of the sacred record. The Samaritans even accepted the Pentateuch, or the Five Books of Moses; and this with the others as one of the five. The Jews always accepted it. And when the translation was executed into Greek, three hundred years before the Christian era, you have the evidence in that translation of the existence of it; and though there be defects in that translation, yet it reflects with great accuracy on the whole the sentiments and truths of the sacred penmen. The only objection that has ever been urged against this book, by persons of a sceptic mind, seeking for objections to its authenticity rather than for evidences of its inspiration, is what we find recorded in the last chapter of it, where we read an account of the death of Moses. And they ask, and ask very naturally, If this book be written by Moses, how can you account for the fact, that in the 34th chapter he says, " Moses went up from the plains of Moab unto the mountain of Nebo. And the Lord showed him all the land of Gilead;" and afterwards, " So Moses the servant of the Lord died there in the land of Moab, according to the word of the Lord?" Now it is quite plain that Moses could not record these things respecting himself, and therefore that he cannot have written that chapter; whilst it may be contended, and contended properly, that he wrote the rest. The fact is, it does seem that either by some carelessness, or by some other misapprehension, the first chapter of Joshua has been transferred to the close of Deuteronomy, and what we call the 34th chapter of Deuteronomy ought really and truly to be the first chapter of Joshua; and then you will see that it falls in naturally with the opening chapter of Joshua. It is evidently a section cut off from the one book and appended as a closing remark to the records contained in the other and previous book. There is, therefore, no reason from that to infer that the book as a whole was not written by Moses. The Jews always accepted it as such; and I may add, too, what will in some degree justify what I have said, that the division of the Bible into chapters was not originally so. The Jews divided it into larger and lesser sections; and one can easily see how a portion might be transferred from the Book of Joshua, descriptive of Moses' death, and appended to that book which Moses had left, the last inspired part of the five books constituting the Pentateuch.

The chapter we have read is the recapitulation on the part of Moses, at the end of the fortieth year in the desert, of all that had transpired in the course of their marchings through the desert, as recorded at greater length in the Book of Numbers. He tells them that God has fulfilled to them the ancient promise that he made to their patriarchal father, that he would make his children countless as the stars in heaven, or as the sands by the sea-shore. And with

all the beneficence of a Christian man, about to retire
from his great mission, and to close his days upon
Mount Nebo, he prays that this promise may be
more and more fulfilled, and that "the Lord may
make you a thousand times as many more as ye are."
He then states to them how—and appeals to them
as if it were his last and his dying declaration to
them—when he felt the burden of responsibility
too heavy, he selected men from the tribes, and made
them heads over them, and charged them as judges
among them to settle every matter between man and
man, and between brother and stranger in the midst
of the land. And he gave them instructions worthy
of the most enlightened times under the influence of
the Christian dispensation; namely, that as judges
"ye shall not respect persons in judgment;" that is,
you shall deal impartially; you shall hear the small,
the obscure, the weak, and the friendless orphan, just
as attentively as you shall listen to the greatest and
the most powerful in the land. And also, "the cause
that is too hard for you, bring it unto me;" not unto
me as a priest professing to pronounce infallibly, but
as a legislator and a ruler, selected by God, and knowing more, and more experienced probably than you.

He then appeals to them how they departed from
Horeb after they had received officers, and arranged
to send the spies; not spies in our sense of the word,
persons criminally and deceitfully engaged, but messengers, inspectors, as they might very properly be
translated, to examine the land, and to give an idea
what this land was that was the burden of so many
promises, and the object of so bright hopes. A difference comes out here. In Numbers it seems as if God

appointed the spies or inspectors to go ; but here, where the matter is recorded at greater length, it appears that the people themselves asked to have inspectors ; and that God permitted them to go, rather than arranged in his sovereignty that they should go. These inspectors, or spies, came back, with two single exceptions, with the most depressing and deplorable accounts.   They said, " It is all over with you; there is no chance of your ever seeing Canaan.   Tremendous fortifications and powerful batteries are there ; men also that are Anakim and giants, and that will drive you out of the land.   And therefore you have nothing to do but to give up the thing in despair, and sit down and die in the desert."   Now nothing could have been more criminal than this.   If a course be the path of duty, it would have been the duty of the spies to say, " You have great difficulties before you, that is plain enough ; but then a brave heart must nerve itself for a great crisis ; and the greater the difficulties the more you should bestir yourselves, and the more earnestly you must look for support and strength to Him in whose work you are engaged, and in whose favour you are ever to approach the borders of the long-promised land."   If we cannot encourage, it is very useless to discourage ; it may do great harm, it cannot possibly do good.   To conceal matters would be wrong; but to depress the hearts of them that take a part in them would seem to be no less unwarranted.   And therefore these inspectors came back with very solemn faces, with very heavy hearts, and they told the people to give up the whole thing, and not to make an attempt to contend with such Anakim as were there, and to take by storm the cities, that were walled not in the ordinary way, but in their exaggerated language, walled up to the heavens. And then he tells them, But alas, ye yourselves did not believe the Lord your God, and gave ear to the testimony and the lugubrious reports of the spies. "Then I said unto you, Dread not, neither be afraid of them." Now why? He did not say, "The Anakim are shorter than the spies have represented them;" he did not say, "The cities have feebler walls than they have said." That might have been wrong: at all events, this was not the source of strength that Moses wished his people to refer to. But he said, Here it is: "The Lord your God which goeth before you, he shall fight for you, according to all that he did for you in Egypt before your eyes." In other words, he said, "Your cause is a righteous one; you are engaged in a work in which you can ask heaven's blessing; and however strong the walls, however formidable the foe, you are to go forward, believing that in his own cause God will fight for you; and that a few with a righteous cause behind them, are stronger than all that can be against them." And on the other hand, he told them that when they proposed to go where God had not sent them, "The Lord said unto me, Say unto them, Go not up, neither fight; for I am not among you."

One can learn from the whole of this chapter this great lesson—that our first inquiry about everything in which we are engaged should not be, Are there great difficulties? Is there great opposition? Shall we encounter much trouble? Shall we meet many losses? But the first inquiry should be, Is this a right cause? Is it sustained by justice, by faithfulness, by truth? If so, we may expect what in prayer we may ask—God's presence in the midst of us; and then, if the Lord be for us, who can be against us?

CHAPTER II.

THE WAY. PRINCIPLE. DEALING WITH ESAU AND MOAB.
NATIONAL LIFE. HARDENING THE HEART. HABIT.

I STATED in the course of my introductory remarks
to the reading of this interesting book, that it consists
less of historical details, recorded as details, and more
of practical and instructive reflections upon all the
facts as uttered by the mouth of Moses, according as
he was taught and inspired by the Holy Spirit of God.
This chapter, like the first one, and indeed the next
chapter also, is a sort of recapitulation of events which
we have already read in the Book of Numbers, with
some reflections upon them, calculated to show the
children of Israel that the Lord their God had been
with them; that they had nothing to fear in the
future, that they had much to be thankful for in the
past; and that all that had passed before them must
only bind them to God in greater gratitude, and thankfulness, and praise. In this chapter Moses begins by
stating, "We turned, and took our journey into the
wilderness by the way of the Red sea, as the Lord
spake unto me." The route they pursued was not
what their own judgment selected, but, as you will
recollect, what the pillar of fire that preceded them by
night, and the pillar of cloud that went before them
by day, the mark and symbol of a present God, indi-

cated and pointed out to them. And, therefore, though they might have selected routes that were more near, yet these near routes geographically, would have been morally, and for all practical purposes, more distant. It is our right course in this great desert, which the world still is, not to take the route that seems most expedient, but to take always that route that is just and right in the sight of God, for expediency is always on the side of right; right is not always what seems to be expedient.

We read that when they came to the people of Mount Seir—namely, the descendants of Esau, a people that had been very sinful in the sight of God, alike in themselves and in the person of their great forefather, God would nevertheless have them to regard them, enemies, persecuting enemies as they had been, yet God wished them to regard them as brethren—" Your brethren the children of Esau." And he says to them that they were not to meddle with them; that is, they were not to wage an offensive war, or to invade their borders, or to appropriate their cattle or their goods; but to act like honest and honourable men, by buying food of them to eat, and buying water from them to drink. And upon this ground they were to obey God—that he had blessed them in all the works of their hands, that he had known their wanderings through the desert, and that he had been with them. In other words, Moses insists upon their obedience to God for the future, on the ground that God had done so much for them in the past. And we shall always find that the noblest acts of devotedness have their foundation in the deepest impressions of love and gratitude to God who commands these acts.

We next read that they came over Seir through the land of the Moabites; and the very same law which was to regulate their conduct in dealing with Esau, was also to be adopted by them in going through the land of the Moabites. He speaks of those that dwelt there—the Emims, and the Anakims, and the Horims; all words that denoted the character of these people—savages, a people who had lost the knowledge of the true God, and lived in the practice of what was evil in his sight.

He states the melancholy fact that all the men who had left Egypt, and marched through the desert to enter into Canaan, had been wasted out among them; a whole generation had passed away chiefly under the judgments of God; and in fact eight-and-thirty years' wandering in the desert are almost passed over in silence, and only the leading events at the commencement, and the leading triumphs at the close, are recorded by Moses in this and in the preceding book.

We next read of their passing through the other nations—the Avims, the Hazerims, and the Caphtorims, "a nation which came forth out of Caphtor, and destroyed them, and dwelt in their stead." And the succession of tribes or nations indicated in the chapter is a very remarkable feature; showing that not only individuals pass away like a shadow, or are like the grass that groweth up, but nations also. There is not a nation at this moment inhabited by the people that dwelt in it fifteen or sixteen hundred years ago. The people in Rome are less like the ancient Romans than we are; the inhabitants of Athens are not the legitimate and lineal descendants of the ancient Greeks. And who knows not that our country has successively been invaded by Saxon, and by Norman, and by Norwegian, and by Dane; and that Britain, which we look upon as our home, has been successively peopled by different nations? As if God would teach the nations of the earth, as well as the units that compose them, that here we have no continuing city, no fixed place of abode; that we are nationally and individually pilgrims and strangers; and if Christians, we shall be looking for a better country, a city that hath foundations, whose builder and maker is God.

We read next how Moses acted with some of those whose territories he passed through; with Sihon, king of Heshbon, to whom he sent messengers, asking him to permit them to pass through. We then read of the conduct of Sihon, the king of Heshbon; and also what seems to us an infliction of wrong: "The Lord thy God hardened his spirit, and made his heart obstinate." Now we never can suppose that God will make any man's heart hard, and then when that heart cannot dictate conduct that is right, punish that man for it: that cannot be. But there is one way in which God deals with men in this world. When a person has long resisted the influence of truth, and has put off from his conscience its appeals, God gives up that person to judicial blindness, and hardens his heart. In that there is nothing inconsistent with the character of God; because if you have had opportunities and means enough in number and in force to lead you to embrace the truth, and if you have trodden

out every spark of life, and gone in your own way,
and walked after your own heart, and openly, and
long, and obstinately acted against God, then there
are two courses that God may pursue. He may either
cut you off as cumbering the ground, and bring you
to the judgment-seat, and assign you your eternal
doom; or he may do what is the same thing, judicially
harden your heart, and not cut you down as a tree
that cumbers the ground, but leave you as a withered
trunk, that others may see how sinful it is to depart
from the living God. If Sihon, the king of Heshbon,
had long and obstinately resisted duty, rejected truth,
and trodden out that truth, for God then to harden
his heart and his spirit, and to make it obstinate, was
simply a judicial infliction : and his guilt would lie
not in what he did after his heart was hardened, but
in what he did previous to that process; for there, and
there only, was his responsibility and his guilt in the
sight of God. And therefore I can see no grounds of
objection to what is said respecting God hardening
this king's heart, or hardening the heart of Pharaoh,
king of Egypt, if you view the hardening as a judicial
sentence inflicted after sins and crimes that had
brought it on.

But there is another way in which some have explained this, and there is no objection to it—namely,
that God is very often said to do things directly which
he does indirectly. For instance, God hardens a
heart in the year 1855, not by putting forth his omnipotent power upon that heart, but by constantly
bringing before that heart the claims, the obligations,
the duties, the hopes of the gospel. And it is a law
that we are all conscious of, that every time you reject

duty you become more able to reject it; every time you refuse the truth you become next time more able to refuse it; so that he that hears duties and responsibilities to-day and rejects them, will be far more able, with less struggle, less compunction, to reject the same duties and responsibilities next Sunday. And hence there is a process of hardening going on in every man that hears the truth, and makes up his mind to reject that truth, till he becomes case-hardened and insensible; such hear as God's people hear, come to the sanctuary as God's people come, but their hearts go after their covetousness. Now God does it indirectly through this process; but then God is not responsible for that; he permits it here, not inflicts it. In fact, this law runs through all nature. The same sun, for instance, that melts one substance by his beams, hardens and consolidates another substance; the same gospel that melts one heart, hardens and indurates another heart; the same gospel that is the savour of life to one, is the savour of death to another. But the blame does not rest with God, the blame rests with you; and the lesson to be learned and the inference to be gathered is never to trifle with obligations, with duties, with truth; to receive it in its simplicity, in the love of it, and to live it; for at least the habit of hearing, hearing, hearing, but never allowing what is heard to drop into the heart and influence it, is of all habits the most mischievous. By a law that we ourselves know, if you sit by a clock that you hear regularly strike, you cease ultimately to hear it. If you live by a mill-wheel going all night, at first you cannot sleep, by-and-by you sleep soundly, and by-and-by you cannot sleep without it. It has been noticed that the blacksmith's dog will lie amid the sparks that fly in showers from the anvil, not in the least disturbed. A sailor will sleep in the shrouds. Habit becomes a second nature; things we could not listen to with ease before, we come to regard as part and parcel of our existence. It is the same with preaching the gospel; first, you are startled, moved, influenced: but you come Sunday after Sunday, you hear sermon after sermon; and at last, sermons that would have thrilled through your hearts with electric effect, cease to have any power at all; and you most composedly say, it is the preacher's preaching that has lost its power, while it is your heart that has become more hardened in insensibility.

CHAPTER II.

" For the Lord thy God hath blessed thee in all the works of
thy hand : he knoweth thy walking through this great
wilderness : these forty years the Lord thy God hath
been with thee ; thou hast lacked nothing."—Ver. 7.

I HAVE selected these words less for the exposition
of each clause in detail, and more as the basis of some
remarks on a doctrine indicated in them, and extremely
important, very often misunderstood, if not denied—
namely, the special providence of God. This doctrine
is implied, or stated with great individuality, if I may
so speak, " The Lord thy God hath blessed *thee*," each
individual of the two millions and a half of the pilgrims
of the desert—"in all the works of *thy* hand; he
knoweth *thy* walking "—the walking of each individual
man, and woman, and child, "through this great
wilderness ; these forty years the Lord thy God hath
been with," not the hosts of Israel in mass, but " with
thee," an individual in detail. " And thou," whatever
your own imagination may be, " hast lacked nothing ; "
according to the inference of the Psalmist David, " The

Lord is my shepherd, and therefore I shall not want." Now the doctrine that God is concerned in the case, the individual case, of the humblest personage in the realm, seems so difficult to some, and so perplexing to others, and so impossible to many, that it needs some special illustration and exposition of difficulties, in order to obviate those objections that may occur to thinking minds on a subject so interesting and yet so difficult. Is it then true that God sees me just as if I were the only individual in the intense light of heaven, moving, thinking, acting, speaking, under the very eye, and in the closest and nearest presence of the great God, the searcher of all hearts? It is difficult for you and me to conceive this; but we have never formed a right apprehension of the providential, the special providential government of God till we have arrived at this point— that God sees me as clearly as if he had nobody else to look after; that he understands my heart, all its mechanism, all its workings, all its impulses, all its motives, all its ends and aims, just as thoroughly as if there were no other being in his universe; and that, however lowly I may be, however obscure my circumstances, there is not a want that pierces my heart that God does not see; there is not a grief that leaps from the deep springs of my heart that God does not recognize; there is not a groan in my broken spirit that has not an echo in his paternal heart; and that he feels as deeply and as truly interested about me, however obscure, however unknown to the world, however unseen by others, as if I and he were the only twain, and I had none but him to worship, and he had none but me to take care of. Now, this is so very strong a statement that it ought to be borne out by

c

facts. And in order to show that it is real, and to wake up in your hearts, if possible, by the blessing of God, a sense of its reality and an apprehension of its sweetness, I will try to obviate such difficulties as are sometimes suggested against it. For instance, it has been said, How is it possible that God can directly thus take care of me, or can directly listen to my prayer, and meet my want, and arrange for my progress, without interfering with what philosophers call the great laws that govern nature? These philosophers, I may explain, simply as such, on the supposition that they are not Christians, believe that God made the world just as an artist makes a watch ; that he wound it up, and meant it to go for some six thousand years, and then to cease to be ; and having wound it up he has left it to unwind itself in action as long as the machinery will last, or the spring maintain its elasticity. Now this may be a very pretty idea, but it is a very unscriptural one ; and the inference they draw from it is this—as God has made the machine with all its laws, its tendencies, its order, and its fixed action, it is impossible that he can interfere with it, or through it, or in any way disturb it, in order to answer an individual's prayer, or to take care of me. Now whether this be true or not—and we believe the main idea here stated is not true—we assert that God may minister to me, and hear my prayer, and grant me what I need, without disorganizing the machinery of the world, without breaking the laws, as they are called, that govern it ; and that he may interpose special provision, special supply, special answer to individual prayer, without interfering in the least degree with that machinery that he himself has constructed. He may still calm the stormy sea by a look, he may still hush the rude wind by a word; and as Jesus could command disease to leave the sick man when miles intervened between the sick man and the Physician, may not God heal the disease of the solitary sufferer from heaven, without interfering with any one law by which he governs this world? When, for instance, the mother sees the ship tossed upon the ocean and ready to founder, and knows that her only child is in that ship, if she kneels upon the beach, or if the heart kneels, and prays to God that he would deliver that child, a philosopher would step in and say, " How absurd! Is God to hush the winds that are wrecking the ship for you? Is God to lay the storm for you? Is God to work a special miracle for you?" She, not so learned in philosophy, but more instructed in her Bible, would say, "I cannot argue, but I can pray; and therefore I will pray." And it may turn out that the greatest philosopher of the two is the mother praying for deliverance for her child. As long as science had not made sufficient progress— and it is interesting to notice that the more we learn of science, the more we see that God's outer book is in harmony, except so far as sin has marred it, with God's revealed word—before we had learned enough, we thought that there was no possibility of reaching a great end, except by disturbing the intervening means, or media, of reaching that end. But what is now found out? That one can transmit messages, and impulses, and influences, along a wire or a chain hundreds of miles in length; and yet not one link of that chain shall be dissolved, not one atom of that wire shall be disturbed, or disorganized, in transmitting the message that I send hundreds of miles away. Is it not a legitimate inference, that the great Maker of the world may transmit influences through the world to the humblest believer, without disorganizing the laws by which he usually governs the world, or disturbing that wise and beautiful economy which he has constituted in this our present habitation? We see, then, by this analogy, how it is possible in this world, and for men, to transmit influences without disturbing the *media;* and we may very fairly infer it is surely possible for God to transmit deliverances without disturbing what are called the laws that govern the world in which we live. But there is another argument for this, which I think is a very conclusive one; and it is, that everybody in his best and calmest moments believes in a special providence. I say everybody in thinking and calm moments instinctively believes in it; and it is only when he begins to argue as a logician that he ventures to deny it. It has been well argued that the existence of a God is almost proved by the fact that everybody feels it; and that a hereafter is proved by the fact that you find no one who has not a longing after immortality, a fond desire to live hereafter, a horror at falling into nought. And the inference drawn from the soul's instinctive desire to live hereafter is a most just one—that God never could have implanted that instinctive appetite unless he had meant in the end, somewhere, or sometime, to gratify it. So in the same manner we argue that this instinctive appeal to God when we are in peril, is evidence that prayer may be answered, and that God does exercise a special and particular providence. If you have some one near and dear to you on the very verge of death, you will pray that that person may be spared; and you will find people that never prayed before will begin to pray then. If you have some one in the field of battle, or upon the stormy Euxine, exposed to danger, you begin to pray that the God who watches over our world would watch over him. What is this but human nature bursting through the artificial restraints of philosophy, and asserting from its deepest depths that there is a God, and that that God takes care of us? Thus we argue that men's instinctive belief in a special providence, and their instinctive appeal to that special providence in circumstances of peril, becomes a fair argument for inferring that such providence is strictly and literally true. But the truth is, the denial of a special individual providence exercised by God over me, involves logically, and ends legitimately, in the denial of God altogether. I cannot conceive a God such as he is delineated in his blessed book, without inferring that he takes care of the minutest insect, whose ephemeral life is bounded by twelve hours, equally with the greatest archangel that worships continually before him. For what is God? He is defined to be in the Bible, and he is believed to be, even by a sound theist, omnipresent. What is omnipresence? It means he touches every object, every being, in the past, in the present, in the future, at every point, and always. Omnipresence is not an influence that he sends out, it is a being, a personal existence; the idea of an omnipresent God is that all that will evolve in the future he touches, all that is evolved in the past he touches, all that co-exists in the present he touches, with a ceaselessly enveloping presence that never wastes, or wearies, or falters. If so, that omnipresence is as near me as it is to any created intelligence in his universe. And if he be not only omnipresent, but also omniscient, then it is not a dim presence, but it is an active, intelligent omnipresence. In other words, God not only touches me at every point, but he also sees, inspects, intelligently knows; for he is not a material omnipresence, but an active, intelligent, omniscient inspector of every thought, of every affection, of every sympathy, of every feeling. Insect, eagle, elephant, man, angel, soul, body, spirit, thought, motive, aim, hope, God not only touches, but infinitely inspects, sees, comprehends. I cannot therefore conceive of a God who is omnipresent and omniscient, without believing that he sees me as clearly as he sees the highest in the universe. This is the just and fair inference. And therefore I can say, as the poor pilgrim refugee in the wilderness said, not "Thou God seest Abraham;" but "Thou God seest *me.*" I can say as the royal Psalmist said, "If I ascend up into heaven, thou art there : if I make my bed in hell, behold, thou art there. If I take the wings of the morning, and dwell in the uttermost parts of the sea; even there shall thy hand lead me, and thy right hand shall hold me. If I say, Surely the darkness shall cover me ; even the night shall be light about me. Yea, the darkness hideth not from thee." And therefore I can close, as he closes in the same sublime Psalm, "Search *me*, O God, and know *my* thoughts; and see if there be any wicked way in *me*. And thou who leadest the hosts of the skies, lead me in the way everlasting."

But let us look at what philosophers call the laws that govern the world, let us see what these are, and

how far they account for all, and how far God may be
said never to interfere with them. What are these
laws? They instance one, gravitation as it is called,
or that there is a tendency in things to gravitate to a
centre. This earth first revolves on its axis, and next
travels in its orbit round the sun, obedient to its
gravitation toward him, or his attraction. But when
you come to ask a philosopher, What do you mean by
gravitation? What do you mean by attraction? he
says, It is a property of matter. But matter is not
intelligent; a stone cannot put forth active impulses
or active attractions. The fact is, what the philosopher calls the laws by which God governs the world,
a Christian calls the touches and impulses which God
communicates to all created things. We are very apt,
and it is a very serious error, to suppose that God has
given the sun a certain property, and the earth a certain property, and then to infer that this must be so
for ever. But the answer is, that the earth moves
because God wheels it, that the earth bears its relationship to the sun because God so keeps it; that the
heart beats just because God's finger touches it; that
the lungs inspire and respire just because God makes
it so. What the philosopher calls the laws that govern
the world, are only the expressions and evidences of
the omnipresence, omniscience, and omnipotence of
Him in whom we and the world live, and move, and
have our being. If it should be said, however, by way
of answer to this, " Why are these operations so uniform? We find fire always burns; we find that a
certain degree of the absence of heat always leads to
freezing; we find that the sun always attracts the
earth. Why, then, are these so uniform, if they be

God's doing ? " I answer, With God is no caprice ;
he acts with infinite wisdom, infinite knowledge ; and
you are making the very excellence of his action a
ground for denying that he is acting. This uniformity
with which he acts is only evidence of the glory and
the excellence of Him who thus acts. To call, therefore, the laws by which God governs the world, the
causes of the harmony of the world, is absurd. The
laws are not the causes of harmony, but the evidences
of the Great Cause that is behind them, to which all
their harmony must be traced. A law is the mere
will of the lawgiver himself. For instance, civil laws
detached from the power that enforces them are utterly
worthless. A law upon our statute-book never keeps
a thief from stealing, or a murderer from murder.
The thief does not fear the law upon the statute-book,
what he fears is the power behind the law that can
enforce that law, and make it tell upon him when he
ventures to violate it. And so in the same manner
the laws that govern the world are not the sources of
power, the causes of its harmony, but they are the
mere proofs of the active agency of God put forth to
keep the world, and all that is in it, in order and in
harmony. The course of nature is simply a manifestation of the presence of God, not, as some say, a
proof that God constituted it so, and left it to itself.
In the budding leaf, in the germinating blossom, in
the loud wind, and in the fierce tornado, in the gentle
flow of the river, and in the billows of the ocean, and
in the Falls of Niagara, God rules, God is there. All
space is luminous with Deity, all creation bears the
impress of his footprints ; not God was, but God is ;
and not only God is, but God acts and gives impulse

to everything that moves throughout the whole earth. These difficulties, supposed to lie in the way of our reception of this truth, need only to be looked at in order to enable us to see that God does see me, that God is with me; and that each individual, guided and governed by him, will lack no good thing. I might give an analogy to illustrate this of some kind. For instance, God's word is—if I may use comparison—a more perfect thing than God's work. I say, his written word is inspired and is more perfect—though even the Bible is not perfect in one sense, because human language is an imperfect instrument, and it cannot perfectly express magnificent and perfect thoughts—God's word is, in one sense, more perfect than God's work. Yet God has not delegated to his word laws that it shall act without him. And if he has not done it in reference to his written word, we may fairly reason that he has not done so in reference to his created work. For instance, the Bible read does not always convince, the Bible preached does not always convert, the truth proclaimed does not always sanctify; but God making use of the truth convinces and sanctifies. He reserves this sovereign power to himself, while he uses his word as the instrument through which he acts. So in providence, he reserves the sovereign power to himself; and he uses created things as the instruments through which he acts.

But having tried to reason for it from creation, let me appeal to that which, with a Christian mind, carries far greater weight—not "the elder Scripture written by God's own hand," as creation has been called, but the word and the testimony inspired by God's own Holy Spirit. I have quoted the text as a very striking evidence of it; but we have only to open any psalm, or almost any chapter of the Bible that gives one's personal history, to see how much of individualism there is in God's providential dealings. Take the 23rd Psalm: "The Lord is my shepherd, I shall not want. He maketh me to lie down in green pastures: he leadeth me beside the still waters. He restoreth my soul: he leadeth me in the paths of righteousness for his name's sake." Read that psalm, and you would say, if special providence be not true, David must have been the most presumptuous man that ever wrote—to think that God would lead him, and provide for him, and take care of him, when he had so much to do more magnificent in the world besides. But David, taught by God's Spirit, knew better. Again, he prays in another part, " Hold up my goings, that my footsteps slip not; guide me with thy counsel while I live, and afterwards conduct me into glory." And can you wonder at this? The outer world is a very important thing ; but there is, in the silence and the secrecy of my soul, a world ten thousand times more important to me than all the orbs of the sky, or the world in which we now dwell ; and if it could be shown me that God is so absorbed with the outer world that he has no attention to spare, and no time to give to the inner world in myself, I should have little confidence in the present, I should still less hope for the future. That he is concerned with the outer world all Scripture testifies ; but that he is as deeply concerned with the inner world of each individual heart, all Scripture equally testifies. That God rules and governs in the outer world, such psalms, for instance, as the 65th, most strikingly show, when the Psalmist states, " God stilleth the noise of the seas. Thou visitest the earth, and waterest it : thou greatly enrichest it with the river of God, which is full of water; thou waterest the ridges thereof." Now if a mere materialist philosopher who denies God's special providence, and believes that all is governed by laws, were told to write the 65th Psalm, he would write in a very different way. The psalmist says, " Thou stillest the noise of the sea and of the waves ;" the philosopher would say, " The wind ceases, and by the laws of nature the waves are absorbed into the sea again." Again, David says, " Thou visitest the earth, and waterest it; thou enrichest it with the river of God." The philosopher would say, " The sun exhales moisture from the rivers in the shape of steam or vapour; a cold wind passes by, the vapour is condensed, and it falls in the shape of showers." But David says, " It is thou that visitest the earth; thou who waterest it; thou who waterest the rivers thereof, and thou blessest the springing thereof." The philosopher would say, " That is a little carbon, and a little oxygen, and a little of something else; a little water and a few sunbeams; and all mingle together, and the seed germinates and grows up into wheat, and the sun ripens it." But David says, " It is God that blesses the springing of it; it is God that crowns the year with good; it is God that makes the valleys shout for joy and also sing." In other words, the Bible gives evidence throughout its whole structure that God has not left the world to the management of laws, but that he personally rules, directs and governs all. But it will be said by some, Is not this a very degrading idea of God? I answer, it is all the reverse. God is covered with greater grandeur when he gives its throbbing to the least heart of the least living thing that moves, than when he gives his commissions to angels that minister about his throne. God in taking care of the microscopically minute appears a more glorious Being than when he wheels worlds in their orbits, and binds the sisterhood of stars around the central sun. The microscope reveals more of God's greatness than even the telescope. And if that be true in the material world, the analogy is only pursued a little farther, when you say that God in taking care of a poor lowly widow living underground in a cellar, with one trouble, too insignificant for the great world to notice, but not too insignificant for God to minister to, is covered with a greater glory than when he takes care of thrones, and keeps kings and queens sitting upon them. And when I open this blessed book, I find this is asserted by our gracious Lord. Now just mark one text. We lose so much of the Bible by cursorily running over it! Better read every day one text of the Bible and ponder it, than read whole chapters superficially and think nothing of them. Take this one verse. Luke xii. 6: "Are not five sparrows sold for two farthings, and not one of them is forgotten before God?" Now the sparrow is the most worthless bird; it has no sweet song, it has no beautiful plumage, it is the poorest, humblest, most worthless bird—the sparrow on the housetop, so worthless that five may be sold for two farthings, yet "not one of them is forgotten before God;" or as Matthew expresses it, "One of them shall not fall to the ground without your Father." If God takes care of a sparrow on its flight, if it cannot fall wing-wearied to the ground without his cognizance, "how much more will he take care of you, O ye of little faith!"

Let us quote another statement of our blessed Lord, also full of suggestive thought: "But the very hairs of your head are numbered." If I had said so you would reply, "How absurd! to think that God should number the hairs of our head, that are constantly falling and growing—the thing is absurd; it is ridiculous; it is enough to make a person smile." But it is the Lord of glory that has said, "The hairs of your head are numbered." Not a hair can fall that he does not see. And this is not poetry; it is strict, literal, rigid, blessed truth, that God takes care of the minutest interests of the minutest parts of the humblest individual in his created world. What a consolatory truth is this! We are not mere chance creations; we are not leaves tossed by the winds, froth upon the wave, a bubble upon the river; but we are creatures cared for, watched over, ceaselessly taken care of; God takes every day the inventory of the very hairs of our head—so minute, so close, so real, is the inspection, the care, the *surveillance* of our Father who is in heaven.

But in reviewing all these the proofs of his providential care, we may notice some lessons of a very important character that ought to be deduced from them. In the first place, God in his providential care and government of us is extremely discriminating.

We must not think that while he takes care of each and of all specifically, his dispensations towards all are precisely the same. In one sense it is most true his suns and his rains fall upon the just and the unjust; but it is no less true in a higher sense that all things work for good to them that love God and are the called according to his purpose. Therefore we are not to interpret what God does to us by the texts I have quoted, but by the character that we ourselves have. As long as I am not reconciled by the blood of his Son, as long as I am not a believer in the Lord Jesus Christ, as long as I am not washed in his blood, as long as I am not clothed in his righteousness, so long the rains and the sunbeams fall upon me as they fall upon sparrows, upon the oxen, upon the fishes of the deep, or upon the birds of the air; but when I become a Christian, when I am cleansed, and justified, and accepted, and translated from the sonship of Adam into the sonship of God, then all that befalls me is blessing. The pain that feels so acute is a ministry of beneficence. Science denies it, but faith, surer than science, knows it right well. The bitterest cup that is put into my hand to drink has not only a sweetening element, but a remedial work to accomplish for me. And when I see prosperity attend the ungodly, the unrighteous, the unregenerate and the unholy, I view it, if I am sure that this is the character of those that are its subjects, as so much additional calamity; when I see poverty track the footsteps of the Christian and at length come up with him, I view that poverty as an ambassador from God, teaching him a lesson that is needful for his everlasting well-being. God therefore discriminates; all he sends to his own are benedictions; all he sends to the world are either ministries to awaken it to repentance, or like the influences upon Sihon the king of the Amorites, processes of hardening, till judicial blindness supervenes, or it is, " Cut it down, because it cumbereth the ground." And if this be so, let us feel if God is over all, if God thus takes care of all, if God sends his rains on the just and the unjust; but in addition to his rains, his sunshine and his blessing upon them that fear him; then whatever be the state of matters in the world, nothing is really wrong. The optimism as it is called of the old philosopher had an immensity of truth in it. If we are individually right in our relationship to him, everything is beneficent in its action upon us. If we are God's children, storm, and rain, and wind, and tempest, and battle, and plague, and pestilence—all things are yours; Paul, Apollos, Cephas, life, death, things present, things to come—all are yours, because you are Christ's, and Christ is God's; that is, all are ministries helping and assisting you.

Let us learn from all these very practical lessons. First, our Father, speaking as I do to Christians, now presides over all. This truth gives to every Christian heart rich and deep consolation. When we read of nation rising against nation, wars and rumours of wars ; when we read of plague, and pestilence, and famine, and commercial distress, in divers places, we feel all must go right, because God has not forsaken this world. Is it not a most refreshing thought that come what may, gloomy as the day may look, ominous as events may seem, dread prophets of yet dreader evil, as the events taking place upon the earth appear to be, yet what comfort, what consolation to a Christian, that there is nothing going on

that God does not see; that there is nothing permitted
to go an inch beyond its tether; that "Hitherto and
no further," determines what shall be the action, the
end, and the issue of all. I have read the story of a
sailor boy going across the Atlantic to the great
nation beyond it with his father, the master of the
ship, an experienced veteran seaman, and under him
and in obedience to him, though a son. A storm of
unprecedented fury came on; the stoutest heart of
the bravest seaman quailed before it; the ship seemed
in imminent jeopardy; the passengers were in alarm,
some in despair, all anticipating a watery grave.
This boy of fifteen or sixteen years of age was seen
pacing the deck, as if he was master of the wind and
the wave, undisturbed, calm, self-possessed, not the
least alarmed. A person said to him, "My boy, are
you not afraid?" "Afraid, sir!" said the boy.
"Not the least, my father is at the helm." What a
beautiful instance of confidence in the skill of his
father, and in the affection of that father towards him!
We too are on a stormy and tempestuous ocean,
great waves rise, and many a billow sweeps over us;
but when the world asks the Christian, "Are you
not afraid?" the Christian can say, as the gallant
youth said, "No; my Father is at the helm of the
universe; and though many a wind rushes against me,
though many a billow may fall upon me, yet the
destined haven is sure; for infinite wisdom, infinite
power, infinite mercy, are the attributes of Him who
holds the helm, and steers the course of the world in
which we live." Let us have confidence, assurance,
and comfort, in this blessed fact that our Father is
at the helm.

This truth in another respect is fitted to give us not only great comfort, but also great confidence in God. The past reveals what he has done for us ; our own history shows how often he has interfered mercifully to deliver us. And believing that he is at the helm, that he thus governs, restrains, regulates, and overrules, let us not only draw consolation from his government, from his special providence, but let us increase by the blessing and the grace of God our confidence in him; he is just, and merciful, and gracious.

The best ruler in this world may have bad advisers, or he may be infirm, or he may not be wise, and thus he may err; but the great God sees all, can unravel all, knows exactly the true state of all, and therefore all things shall work for good to them that love him. He will be with us in our walk through the desert; he will give us bread and make our water sure. We may exercise unbounded confidence in him as the Governor of the universe, for that Governor is our Father. With this deep conviction we may engage in every duty. Whatever comes before you in the providence of God, if it be duty do not look at the risk of it, but at the commission you have to engage in it. We sow the seed that feeds us in spring ; we trust to God's promise that seed time and harvest shall be ; and harvests have ever come and will come till this dispensation close. We preach the gospel of Christ; God has promised to bless the preaching of that gospel; and we are sure, though we cannot hear them, its echoes will be awakened in the hearts of the remotest inhabitants of the world. God is present everywhere to enforce what he has said anywhere; and we may therefore undertake the most perilous enterprises, go into the most trying circumstances, mingle in the deadly combat or face the terrific storm, perfectly sure that amid the noise of the sea waves when they toss themselves to the sky, and the master's voice cannot be heard amid the shrill whistling of the winds in the shrouds, God nevertheless hears the feeblest prayer. He can hear the faintest beating of the individual heart in battle; amid the noise, the awful noise of conflict, God can hear the petition of the lowest soldier in the ranks. What a magnificent spring of consolation is our God; what a blessed conviction that out of thirty thousand he sees me as if there none else in the battle-field; that in all the crew of that ship he hears me as if there were none else there present; and that he that takes care of a sparrow on its wing, never, never can fail to take care of me, redeemed by his precious blood, and ripening for glory and immortality.

Do you belong to his family? Have you accepted the Son of God as your only Saviour? Have you heard, and seen, and read that this religion, this book, these truths, are meant for your instant acquiescence, heartfelt and personal acceptance? Christianity is not a science amid many. One man may mind politics, another medicine, another law—and he may give himself wholly to his own profession; but religion is for all. It is not a profession amid many, but it is a remedial dispensation for all. If you be the children of God, you can say with all confidence and with unfaltering faith, "The Lord has been with me, the Lord has led and guided me; the Lord knows all my wanderings these forty years, and I have lacked nothing." Has he not blessed you in the past in your work? Have you not much reason for thankfulness in your retrospect? And when things you undertook have not prospered in your sense of prosperity, have you not found that in some way you never expected they did you good? Have you not been often thankful that you did not succeed where your heart was calculating on unbounded success? Where your work has not enriched you, has it not often humbled you? and are you not constrained to say now, after you take an impartial retrospect of thirty, or of forty, or of sixty years, that "The Lord has blessed me in all the works of my hands; and the Lord has been with me, no unconcerned spectator but a minister to me. He has been with my mind teaching me, with my heart sanctifying me; with my conscience regulating it; and I have lacked nothing. I have not got all I wished for. God never promised to give me that, but I have not failed to get what was truly good for me." When we enter into heaven we shall have to thank God more for denying what we have often wished, than for granting what we have often prayed for. We know not what we ask; and if we were to obtain all we wish, we should not have all that we truly want. God's goodness will be seen as fully in withholding what we have asked rashly, as ever it will be seen in granting what we have asked earnestly. Believing these truths let us act upon them. Let us engage in every duty as if all depended upon us; but let us carry into every sphere and province of the fulfilment of that duty, this deep, this blessed, this comforting thought : "God is with me, God knoweth all my walking; God will let me lack nothing." And to his name—Father, Son, and Holy Spirit—be all the glory and the praise. Amen.

CHAPTER III.

THE first fact recorded in this chapter is the
gathering of all the hosts of Og the king of Bashan,
one of the most formidable opponents of the march
of the children of Israel into the long promised land.
It is stated, what has been construed as severe judgment, "We utterly destroyed them, men, women, and
children." But we must recollect that these nations
were specially guilty; and that this was not the revenge of a victorious foe, but the judicial infliction of
a holy and a righteous God.

There is here a statement about the bedstead of
Og that seems at first sight improbable; but we know
that when Alexander the Great wished to frighten
his enemies with an idea of the greatness, and
strength, and irresistible might of his Macedonian
phalanx, he exhibited their beds; and showed what
great men they must be who required so large beds
to lie down on. Probably this bedstead of Og the
king of Bashan was not the measurement of him
that was to occupy it, but a mere demonstration to
frighten those that were opposed to him, by leading

them to believe in his irresistible strength and might. The size of it, we are told, was nine cubits in length, and four cubits in breadth; the cubit, so called in English from the Latin word *cubitus*, means from the elbow to the end of the longest finger, and may properly be put down at eighteen inches; and therefore this bed would be of a very large size indeed.

We read next that Moses asked of God that he might be permitted to enter the promised land; he pleads God's greatness, his goodness, and his mercy, and his past experience of his love; and therefore he says, " Let me go over." But God remembered his own threatening or rather his own sentence, that because Moses had combined with Aaron at the rock in forgetting God's instructions, and in exhibiting pride and display before the children of Israel, that sin was forgiven as a penalty, but it needed to be followed with retribution in the sight of Israel; and therefore Moses was not permitted to enter into the land of promise, though received into that better land of which Canaan was but the faint shadow.

Let us dwell a little on this earnest request of Moses, and on the nature of God's refusal.

Moses was emphatically a man of prayer. From the first moment that he sees God in the burning bush, to the moment that he disappears from the scenes of mortality, on the heights of Pisgah, he seems to have known where blessings were, and how richly they were given ; and that in answer to prayer God would withhold from him no good thing. The petition is one of the most striking proofs of the confidence of Moses in the goodness and the mercy of God. Moses had sinned at Meribah, and God had said on that occasion, "Because ye believed me not to sanctify me in the eyes of the children of Israel, ye shall not bring this congregation into this land." But Moses had seen God so often repent of his threatenings, while he never repented of his promised mercies, that he presumed in great faith that God might forget that awful threatening, revoke that solemn judgment; and in spite of his great demerit admit him, nevertheless, into that good land, and to that glorious mountain which lay in the sunshine of Canaan, not far distant from the spot where he then stood. But God, on this occasion, did not recall his threatening; he refused the prayer of Moses, and told him the doom pronounced at Meribah was irrevocable. This must have been a very bitter stroke; to be on the margin of the long wished for Jordan, and not to be allowed to cross it; to see the sunshine gleaming on the distant snow-clad peaks of Lebanon, and yet not to be allowed to rest under their noble shadow, and to taste of the good things, and the great things, which God had said that land contained for his beloved and believing people. But so it was. Many a husbandman plants a vineyard, and his descendants only are permitted to eat the fruit thereof: many an industrious man toils for bread, accumulates by the blessing of God something over, but he is not spared to the good old age in which he hoped to eat what he had gained: many a soldier has to do duty in the field, falls in the conflict, and so never wears the laurel, or beholds the end of the struggle, and the results for which he toiled and fought. Perhaps it is well. I know not whether, in heaven, we shall have most to thank God for the

blessings that he gave when we asked, or for the
prayers that he refused. Perhaps we shall praise him
for his refusals as much as for his grants. And this
certainly we shall know; that he is—

> " Good when he gives, supremely good,
>   Nor less when he denies;
>   Even crosses from his sovereign hand
>   Are blessings in disguise."

Yet it is interesting to see how God fringes the
dark cloud with a bright and beautiful margin; he
never seems to inflict in absolute and unmitigated
wrath; and therefore he tells Moses, " Though what
is right in the sight of me and of all the earth must be
carried out, and though thou shalt not enter into this
good land; yet that the blow may be softened, that
the judgment may be mitigated by mingled mercy,
I will allow you to ascend Pisgah, as Aaron ascended
mount Hor; that you may see that good land, and
know that all I said about it is true, that the
certainty of your people entering on it never can
be altered; and so before you depart and enter into
the everlasting rest, I will give you a glimpse of the
promised Canaan that shall go with you like an un-
shaded glory into the land of eternal peace and joy.
You shall not enter into it, yet you shall see enough
of it to know before you die that all my promises
are Yea and Amen."

There are two or three lessons here suggested to
us, and these I will try, but briefly, to illustrate.
First, this Canaan was an earthly land employed by
God to be the type of a heavenly. Moses desired to
enter into that earthly Canaan; God's people now in

the language of David often say, or if they do not say,
feel, " Oh that I had wings like a dove, that I might
flee away and be at rest;" or in the language of the
apostle, "I desire to depart and to be with Christ,
which is far better." In other words, there are long-
ings in the heart of every Christian that sometimes
find no expression, that other times find meet expression in the prayers, the inspired prayers, of the
ancient people of God, that are equivalent in their
import to this: "Would that the warfare were over
and the victory won; would that the journey were
ended, and the everlasting home enveloped and en-
compassed us; would that all the separations, trials,
bereavements, afflictions, sorrows, that we feel wer
at an end, and we were where all things are made new,
and there are no more tears, nor crying, nor sorrow."
Let us try to ascertain what leads to this desire, what
lies at the foundation of it. First of all, it is our
thorough consciousness that grows with our years of
the unsatisfying, and, if I may use the word, un-
satisfiable nature of all created things. Everybody
feels his desires outrun the possibilities of their gratification; that he is not only capable of, but that
he craves, a richer satisfaction than anything in this
world can bestow. Creation is too limited to hold
man's heart, and all its springs too small to satisfy
man's thirst; and all its joys, its pleasures, and its
bountiful provisions, too poor to meet the necessities
of a soul that finds its home, where it has its culminating happiness, only in the bosom of its Father
and its God. Dissatisfied with time, instinctively we
long for something beyond it; not that we desire
death, but that we desire the glory, and the excel-

lence, and the joy, that are to be realized on the
other side of that Jordan, in that blessed land, and
under the shadow of that goodly mountain and
Lebanon. We not only feel desires that this world
will not satisfy ; but the more we experience what
we obtain, in answer to our desires in this world,
the more we are convinced that there is nothing in
this world that can give us real and substantial happiness. The brightest scenes fade soonest ; the fairest
joys are the most fleeting. What seemed unmingled
satisfaction in prospect fails to satisfy in possession ;
what appeared to be gold in the distance, when
touched is only the gilding of a toy, from which the
very touch takes off the gilding ; what seemed to us
the table-land, basking in perpetual sunshine, turns
out when we reach it to be only another level on the
mountain side, revealing the great height that still
remains to be climbed. In other words, we learn this
is not our rest; and that neither in prospect nor in
possession has the world anything that can satisfy
the yearnings and desires of an immortal soul. And
when we look around in another point of view, and
see what amount of sorrow there is about us, what
reminiscences of sadness and of loss are on every
side, we must feel yet more that if this world
was meant originally to be the home of man, some
intrusive element has entered, blighted much of its
beauty, marred much of its excellence, and left it
unfit, as it is, to be the lasting home of God's believing people. There is not an acre of it that is not
sown with thorns, or scarred with graves, or bearing
traces of havoc and of ruin ; there is not a bosom on
earth that has not some painful reminiscences, some

nooks in which are stored thoughts the very recollection of which gives pain; in which there are not
images that have no originals on this side the grave,
whose originals are to be found only in that goodly
land, and under the shadow of that mountain which
was the aspiration of Moses and the desire of all the
people of God. This being so, the believer naturally
and instinctively desires, not death, but that which
cannot be reached without crossing the stream that
intervenes between this world and the world that is
to be. The traveller longs for his home, the sailor
for his native shore, the exile for his own beloved
land; the Christian for the true Canaan, the rest that
remaineth for the people of God. But amid all these
things, however much felt, we hold life so dear, and
the continuity of that life so desirable, that we do
not wish to die. This is quite natural. It is no
more natural to desire death than it is to desire pain.
Both are abnormal, unnatural things that were never
meant; and that are only to be accounted for as the
bequests and the legacies of sin. But it is not so
much the evils that we feel that drive us to seek for
heaven, as it is the joys that we know to be there
which attract us to heaven. It is not so much that
we are weary of drinking of the bitter cup which is
sometimes placed in the Christian's hand, but that
we have had a foretaste of the living water, and
long to be where that living water is. A Christian is
not driven from earth, like a coward who cannot
stand its conflicts, to seek shelter in a better place,
but he is attracted to that better place by a foretaste
of its joys; so that seeing it, as Moses saw the land
of promise from afar, he may long to enter and eat of

the bread and drink of its living water. Let us, therefore, view the obverse, and look less at what we feel
here impelling us to look for relief there, and think
more of what we see there attracting us to it, and
making us instinctively long to be the possessor of
so brilliant a prospect. The Christian is quite sure
of an entrance into heaven. He is not one that
doubts of his ultimate safety. Why should he? It
is not his hold of Christ but Christ's hold of him
that gives him safety. " I give unto them eternal
life, and none shall pluck them out of my hand."
" He hath begotten us again to a living hope; to an
inheritance incorruptible and undefiled, and that
fadeth not away." " I know," says the Christian,
" in whom I have believed ; and that he is able to
keep what I have committed to him against that
day." And not only is the Christian sure of heaven,
but he knows the way to it. He has not to ask in
the nineteenth century, as Thomas asked in the
first, " We know not the way ; " the Christian knows
that Christ is the way; that no man cometh unto
the Father but by him; and that "him that cometh
unto me I will," says the Saviour, "in no wise
cast out." We are attracted to this good land and
to this blessed rest by the portraits or the maps
that are given of it in this blessed book — God's
own word. We there read it is " our Father's
house; " beautiful expression is that! It is the
rest that remaineth for the now weary people of
God. It is spoken of as a place where there is no
more sorrow, nor crying, nor grief, nor pain ; but
where all things are made new. Its inhabitants are
before the throne; " they serve him day and night;

they hunger no more, neither thirst any more, neither shall the sun light on them, nor any heat; and the Lamb shall lead them to living waters; and God shall wipe away all tears from their eyes." Ancient paradise has given its name to the new; but the new has a perpetuity that the old had not. The ancient Canaan was the dim type of the heavenly; but the heavenly has a perfection that the ancient Canaan had not. The paradise of Adam and Eve passed away, from the blight of sin entering and tainting all its glory; but the paradise that awaits the people of God has no close; nothing that defileth can enter there; all shall be permanent as it will be pure and happy.

The Christian has, even in this world, and he has very little knowledge of the truth if he has not, some foretaste of what the better world is. There are joys gathered on the Sabbath in the field of the sanctuary, like flowers that are in their tints and in their fragrance, perishable it may be, but real types of the glory and the blessedness of that land, that goodly Canaan, that remaineth for the people of God. In the sanctuary, in the Bible, at a communion table, in his own heart, a Christian does sometimes taste a peace, a joy, an anticipation, a hope, which are in their measure foretastes of the everlasting Sabbath, prelibations of joys that are at God's right hand and pleasures that are for ever and ever. The grapes of Eshcol brought into the desert were to the travellers there a foretaste of the fruitfulness of that good land, just as the twilight of grace is the sure token of the noon of approaching glory. And these foretastes that a Christian has of the peace, the joy, the happiness, the purity, the love of God, are in their measure it may be very small, but still in their measure foretastes of the blessedness of heaven. We do not yet see indeed the holy of holies as it is, but we can see hung up some of the golden lamps that fill it with imperishable splendour, the shining spires, the sparkling minarets, of the New Jerusalem, the capital of that good land, and under the shadow of that mountain Lebanon. And as we see these things, and taste something of the reality of Christianity, which is just a fragment of the reality of heaven, like Moses we wish to see it, and not merely to see it, but to enter and enjoy its blessedness even before the time assigned to us.

That future rest, that Canaan, that good land which the Christian desires, is filled with moral and with spiritual glory; or translated into simple language, it is a pure and a holy place. And a Christian, sympathizing with all that is holy, because regenerated and born again, and hating all that is sinful, longs for that blessed state whose gates shut out all that is sinful, and shut in for ever all that is pure and holy. And when the Christian compares what he sees in this world with what he knows to be the mark and stamp of that better world; when he compares this world, that groans, and longs, and yearns for deliverance; this sky of ours, swept by ceaseless storms, this body burdened constantly, and in which we groan longing to be delivered, this life channelled by courses of tears, and steeped too often in sorrow and in misery; when he sees around him what sin has done and how victoriously it still travels; when he traces to sin all that disfigures, and deforms, and wastes this world, and makes it wretched—is it unnatural to wish that this world may be superseded by a better; that there may burst upon it the sunshine of heaven; that the reign and revel of sin may cease for ever, and that the consecrating footsteps of the Prince of peace may touch the bosom of a world in which peace for centuries has been a stranger, and in which wars, and strifes, and conflicts, the creations of sin, seem endemic, and predominate to so fearful an extent? On that good land, that better rest, the Christian longs to enter, because he knows that there those separations which have occurred here, cannot be. In that land there is no sickness, nor sorrow, nor sighing, nor death. Circles that have been interrupted below will be restored in their perfection above; companionships which we enjoyed here will be there reconstituted in infinitely more than their earliest and their purest loveliness; we come there to mount Zion, to the city of the living God, to the heavenly Jerusalem, to the spirits of just men made perfect. It is the whole family of God, to use the language of an apostle, that is there. And it is a very interesting thought that one day in that blessed rest will make us more acquainted with the past than all the reading of a lifetime here. We shall see Moses, Abraham, Isaac, Jacob, the world's grey sires, patriarchs, prophets, evangelists, martyrs—all that have purely lived, all that have meekly died in Christ, we shall meet and mingle with there: and those that left us too soon will rejoin us there; and those over whom we have mourned we shall rejoice with in praising God there. All that was the cause and spring of bitterness and sorrow upon earth shall have passed away; and more than eye hath seen, or ear hath heard, or heart hath conceived of joy and of peace, will occupy its place. We naturally wish to enter that rest from another consideration—we shall there see unrolled and luminous all the past, and shall understand the precise connection that each event, prosperous or painful, had with our everlasting peace, as we passed through this world on our pilgrimage to glory. One of the greatest joys in heaven will be the economy of time luminous in the light of eternity; events that appear all mystery to us upon earth will then be all clear; problems which perplex us now will be as axioms then; inquiries that we cannot fathom now we shall then know, according to the promise of our Lord, "What I do ye know not now, but ye shall know hereafter." Inquiries that we could not or would not pursue in this world shall then be fully explained, and we shall see that our most painful moments were our most profitable, that our saddest hours were after all the most friendly messengers from God; and that not a link of sorrow or of suffering could have dropped from our experience upon earth without breaking that chain that lifted us from the tears of mortality to the triumphs and the glories of everlasting day. There are no such things as chance incidents and accidents. We have already seen what a special Providence is, and what evidence there is of its reality; and we may rest assured that there is not a pain that feels so severe, not a dispensation we pass through, that has not its meaning, its mission, and its beneficent end; till in fact it was as necessary that I should lose this, or that I should suffer that, as that Christ should die upon the cross for me. Machinery goes wrong not

simply by the absence of the motive power, but by
the loss of a peg, a pinion, or a single link. There is
not a link in our biography that we can spare; there
is nothing that has happened to us that is not the
expression of a perfect optimism. And when we
look back from the margin of the better land upon
all the way that God has led us these many years,
we shall see that nothing was done that was not
necessary, nothing suffered by us that was not useful;
and that the very moments that we thought our worst
and our saddest were working out most powerfully
for us a far more exceeding, even an eternal weight
of glory.

Thus the Christian does sometimes feel, in the
language of Moses, if he does not always pray, "I
pray, let me go over and see that good land that is
beyond Jordan, and that goodly mountain, and Lebanon."

But there is a still more practical question for us :
who are those that may offer up this prayer, and may
indulge the sure expectancy that they will enter into
that land, and be beneath the shadow of that goodly
mountain and Lebanon? Not certainly the mere
worldly man, whose heart is in this world; who, from
Sunday morning till Saturday night, never thinks of
looking beyond the visible diurnal sphere, nor dreams
of anything beyond the horizon of the present; he
does not wish to enter into that good land; he is
neither fit for it nor desirous of entering into it. His
heart is where his money is; his treasure is where his
gains are. A thorough worldly man would never
pray as Moses did; he would rather pray, "Oh let
me remain, that I may add another ten thousand to

E

my capital; that I may add a few more houses, a few
more acres to my estate. I have not gained all that
is yet possible; do not take me away in the mid-time
of my gains! I want to be a little richer, a little
happier, a little more important in the world, a little
weightier in the judgment and estimate of mankind."
The worldly man never expresses a divine wish.
In fact it is a test of what we are that we wish that
the present dispensation were passed away like a
dream, and that the brighter and better had finally
superseded it. It is not the man of pleasure that
ever offers up such a petition as that of Moses.
The man of pleasure lives to eat, to drink, and to be
merry; he lives to enjoy himself thoroughly in this
world, to find out its sunny spots, to drink of its
sweetest streams; and his belief is, partly from ignorance, that there is so much in this world of real enjoyment, that if he could but live in it long enough he
would be able to pick out a great deal more of the
elements of happiness than he or any other ever has
detected in it before. He is utterly mistaken, of
course, but such is his feeling; and, ever seeking a
new pleasure, his greatest desire is to be allowed to
remain just where he is. Those then whose hearts
are in this world, and to whom this world is all, have
no desire to enter into that good land that is beyond
Jordan, into that goodly mountain, that rest that remaineth for the people of God. If not satisfied with
what they find on earth, they hope to be so; if they
have not yet found out what meets their wants, they
expect they will yet be able. These worldly men—
the miser, the man of pleasure, the worldling—are at
this moment busy in digging out cisterns under the

belief, the sincere but mistaken belief, that they will find in some of them a spring of living water. It is in vain we tell them they are mistaken; it is well they should be allowed to exhaust their strength, and learn the lesson at the close, however painful, that there is not in this world a living spring except that which is in connexion with that ocean of living water that flows around the throne of God and of the Lamb. Who are they that can sympathize with the Christian in seeking an entrance into this good land? It is such as David, who can say, " Whom have I in heaven but thee? and there is none upon the earth I desire beside thee." Such as Simeon, who can say, " Lord, now lettest thou thy servant depart in peace; for mine eyes have seen thy salvation." Such as Paul, who can say, " I desire to depart, and to be with Christ, which is far better." Such as Peter, who exclaims, " Whom having not seen we love; in whom, though now we see him not, yet believing we rejoice with joy unspeakable and full of glory." It is all such as have between their hearts on the earth and their hold on the skies a cord created by the Holy Spirit of God, stronger than that which binds the distant exile to his home, the weary traveller to his rest, that knits the soul of a Christian to his Father and his God.

Can we personally say, in something like the language of Moses, " I pray thee, let me go over and see that good land?" I do not ask, can you join in sympathizing with Christians that do so? but can you yourselves really feel so? I do not mean that we should desire to die; but do we desire to see pervading all space, covering the whole earth, the

reign of righteousness, of peace, and of joy? Do
we desire to see sin — the fever that irritates the
earth—put away, and all the progeny of sin that are
now spread over the earth destroyed? Do we desire
to see a day when all shall be just, and true, and holy,
and generous, and good; when no man shall misapprehend his neighbour, when none shall suspect his
brother; when there shall be nothing but the recipro-
city of everlasting esteem, and growing love, and absolute confidence; and the whole earth, at present the
usurped empire of Satan, shall be the very reflection
of heaven, the *facsimile* of the house of God? God
never gives a foretaste of heaven to a heart which he
has not designed and destined for an entrance into it;
God never gives a man sympathy with the true, the
holy, the beautiful, the good, without meaning that
thus sympathizing, he shall one day see the gratification of every sympathy and the fulfilment of every
desire. If this be our hope and expectation, are
we living here under the support of this bright and
blessed expectancy? How little, alas, of the future
is in the heart of the holiest; how much does the
present preponderate over what is to be; how little
of heaven is within the holiest; how much has a
Christian to deplore; how much has a Christian
heart of alloy that needs to be removed; and how
thankful should we be that God does not leave us to
ourselves for a single moment, or let go his hold of us
as the heirs and expectants of glory! But if we are
his people, if we are wishing for what we have tried
to describe; if we do desire really to live on the other
side of that Jordan, and behold that goodly mountain
and Lebanon, or rather in that country of which these

were dim types and foreshadows—we shall in some degree live in this world in a spirit appropriate to such a hope. Do we feel here as strangers? or do we so far forget ourselves as to begin to build as if the inhabitant and the house were to continue for ever? Do we ever so far forget our true destiny and character that we begin to store up in this world, not speaking but entertaining the idea, " This is to last for ever?" The moment you take an interest in anything upon earth absorbing, exclusive, you are trembling between ruin and recovery, between heaven and hell. If you be true Christians, if you be indeed the people of God, you will not be insensible to much that is in this world. To expect that a man should not value money is to expect that he should not be a human being, dependent upon its provision for the perpetuity of his life in the world; to expect that a man should not love what is good, or should not taste what is sweet, or should not enjoy many blessings that are scattered on this world's highway, is to expect that he shall cease to be human; it is to speak neither in the language of Christianity nor of common sense. The gospel does not require you to be stoics, or that you should be petrifactions; but it does demand that you shall so enjoy the good things of this world that you shall trace them to their source, and thank the Giver of them; that you shall never allow any-thing, however good, in this world so to absorb your heart's affections that you shall not think of, and long after, and pray for, a better. It demands not the abnegation of the monk, but the watchfulness of the Christian. It requires that you shall buy, and therefore not be an ascetic;

but buy as though you bought not: that you shall rejoice—and there is no sin in being merry, and there is no virtue in being sad—but at the same time that you shall so watch, during that mirth, that you shall rejoice as though you rejoiced not. It admits that you should weep when you have lost the near and dear; and to say you should not feel and should not weep, when you suffer great loss, is to require that you should not be human beings at all; but it asks you while you weep to watch against despair; and therefore to weep as though you wept not. In short, the Bible, taken as the great law and regulator of human life, bids you weep, rejoice, and marry, and buy, and use the world; it requires no asceticism, no monkery, no abnegation of human nature, in order to attain a transcendental state that is impracticable, impossible, and unscriptural; but it demands that in the midst of all many a thought shall leap from the living heart, and find its repose only beside the Throne; that many a wish shall be expressed from the lips that will find its gratification in a new heaven and a new earth; and that in this world you walk as pilgrims and strangers, in it but not of it, using it but not abusing it; having your hearts where your treasure is—in the presence of God and of the Lamb.

We do not ask you to neglect your business; to be inattentive to your professional obligations. The man that will not work has no title to eat; and the man that will not work, and work hard in this world, will very soon be able to get nothing to eat. All this is proper; only let not that which earns your bread be so absorbing as to take all your

thoughts, your desires, your sympathies. Can you say
when the hand is busiest in this world's duties, that
the heart soars highest to the hopes and level of a
brighter and a better world to come?

CHAPTER IV.

A GREAT portion of this chapter consists of a
most eloquent and affectionate exhortation to the fulfilment of those duties which God had enjoined,
amid circumstances of great solemnity, and the trans-
gression of which the children of Israel had found in
their past experience to be the loss of their liberty,
their happiness, and the protection of their God.
The address in this chapter is pure beyond all comparison, when brought into contrast with the truest
and purest lessons that were ever preached by the
most eminent philosophers of heathen lands; and
well is it worth our while to ask, how it happens that
a people in arts, in science, in literature, so defective
as the Jews were, had yet an apprehension of God,
a sense of duty, a purity of precept, an extent of
morality, that had no parallel, or approach to a
parallel, amid the Greeks, for instance; a people
skilled in all that was elegant—in literature, in
poetry, in painting, in sculpture, and in music. The
reason is just this: man may discover the arts and
sciences, and reach the highest perfection in these;

but it needs God to reveal religion, that man may learn from God the way that leads to heaven, and how God is to be served and worshipped. There is no greater evidence that Israel had a communication from heaven than this fact—that their morality is so pure, their apprehension of God so sublime, their definition of his nature so august, their whole intercourse with heaven so pure, so holy, so different from anything before or around them, that it seems scarcely possible to escape the conclusion that the Greeks were taught by themselves, that the Jews were the pupils of God.

Moses begins, first of all, by exhorting them to hold fast the Scriptures that they had, in all their integrity. " Ye shall not add unto the word which I command you, neither shall ye diminish ought from it, that ye may keep the commandments of the Lord your God which I command you." How remarkable it is that the Bible should begin with a dissuasive from adding to it or subtracting from it, and should end with a similar dissuasive! " If any man shall add unto these things, God shall add unto him the plagues that are written in this book : and if any man shall take away from the words of the book of this prophecy, God shall take away his part out of the book of life." God guards his own worship, and claims it all for himself; he guards his own book, and defends it from every attempt to add to it the traditions of man, or to subtract from it what may not propitiate the taste or minister to the passions of sinners. The Bible in its integrity, from the first chapter of Genesis to the last of Revelation, is the revelation of the mind and the manifestation of the character of God; and adding to it or diminishing from it is to incur the judgments pronounced against those who are thus guilty.

Moses appeals to them that he had taught them statutes and commandments, and that the result of all this was, that they were a great nation. Only, he says, do not let your present greatness lead you to lose a sense of your duty and your responsibility. No past attainments are to make you forget that future prosperity depends upon your constant adherence to the will and word of God. Therefore, he says, "Take heed to thyself, and keep thy soul diligently, lest thou forget the things which thine eyes have seen, and lest they depart from thy heart all the days of thy life." God's goodness in giving them a revelation, their duty in holding fast that revelation, are intimately connected together. We must not make the sovereignty of God a plea for the indolence of man; and we must not make the energy of man a reason for denying the sovereignty and the goodness of God.

He then reminds them, in the 11th and 12th verses, of all that they had seen. He says, "Ye came near and stood under the mountain; and the mountain burned with fire unto the midst of heaven, with darkness, clouds, and thick darkness. And the Lord spake unto you out of the midst of the fire." Now can you conceive that Moses could have made them believe that they saw and heard what he states here, if they had never seen and never heard it? It is impossible to conclude so. The very fact that forty years, nearly forty years, after the scenes to which he alludes, he could tell them that they saw them, and heard them, and were witnesses of them, is the most irresistible evidence that the things actually occurred, and that this book records not the inventions of man, but the communications of God himself.

Then he warns them specially against what was the tendency of human nature then, and what is its tendency now, unless it be carefully guarded against— worshipping God by images. He tells them that they were not to make any image of anything in heaven or in earth, nor of fishes of the sea in the waters under the earth, nor of the moon, nor the sun, or the stars; nor to bow down to any of them, nor to worship them. What explains human nature's craving for a visible likeness of God? Just this: in the depths of the conscience of ancient heathendom there was a strong conviction that God was lost, or that man was torn from his presence, and God dissociated from man; and under this deep feeling it set out in quest of God. Failing to discover him in the height or in the depth, or in any space in creation or in providence, at least so clearly as to comprehend him, nature, in its agony, made what it thought the nearest likeness to God, in order that it might have something external to itself to lean on and trust in for guidance, and for happiness, and for heaven.

This explains the whole of image worship. The truth is, the language of Robespierre, at the close of the scenes of 1793, arose from a sentiment very deep in the heart of man: " The world cannot be worked without God; and rather than try to work it without God, we had better invent a god." Nature feels it cannot get on without the sense of some one greater than itself; and where God had not revealed himself in all his spirituality and his glory, there human nature makes a desperate effort to realize in gold, in silver, and in stone, its own great ideas; and to make the nearest likeness — the nearest supposed likeness— to that God whom it cannot discover in the torn leaves of nature, or in the intricate and perplexing dispensations of providence. But now that God is revealed to us by Christ Jesus, we need no image of him. And I cannot conceive a more condemning mark and brand of apostasy than to set up in the sanctuary now, like the Greek Church, pictures, or like the western Church, images and statues, in order to make God visible to us. The very idea of representing our Redeemer by an image or a statue is monstrously absurd. We know not what he was like; he has left us only one picture of himself; and, strange to say, such is the perversity of human nature, that it prefers its own carved images to the only picture that Christ has left of himself. What is that picture? His own blessed word. If you want to know what Christ was like, read the 53rd chapter of Isaiah. If you want to know what he thought, what he felt, what he said, what he was, trace him through those precious gospels, tread in his footprints, sit at his feet, listen to the accents of him who spake as never man spake; and then you will have a just because a divine conception of the brightness of the Father's glory and the express image of his person. But strange it is that man never ventured to worship what is really a picture of Christ, and the only divine sketch he has bequeathed to us and to all mankind. And the reason is this: as long as man worshipped the image, the image was silent; but if man had attempted to worship this divine portrait of God, even that portrait itself would have given expression to its own deep thoughts, and said, " It is written, Thou shalt worship the Lord thy God; and him only, not even me, shalt thou serve."

We learn in this chapter what are the true elements of national prosperity and greatness. " Righteousness exalteth a nation."

CHAPTER V.

WE have seen in the course of previous explanatory remarks, that a considerable portion of this book is an epitome in brief of much that transpired before, and has been recorded in the Books of Numbers, Exodus, and Leviticus. But in addition to the historic facts as they are recapitulated here, there are instructive lessons of the most precious kind, exhortations, promises, advices, that if Israel had attended to, it would have been well with them and with their children to many generations. In this chapter the children of Israel are reminded again of the covenant made with God in Horeb, when he promised to give them temporal mercies, and they promised in return to obey the statutes and the commandments that he instituted. Moses reminds them of this condescending mercy, that the Lord talked with them face to face, that he came near to them amid the splendours of the pillar of fire by night, and in the burning bush, and on the glorious mount, and spake to them those words

which were not only for his glory, but were calculated
to accomplish their greatest present and everlasting
good. He recapitulates the ten statutes, or commandments, recorded in the 20th chapter of Exodus,
in slightly varying language. This variety, I think, is
very interesting. You will notice in the New Testament that the Lord's Prayer is given in one form by
one evangelist, and in another form by another evangelist; in order to teach us that the excellence is not
in the mere words, but in the meaning, the sense, or
the thoughts, of which the words are the vehicles.
We are prone to worship words, just as we are prone,
like Israel of old, to worship images; and it is very
useful and very important that we should be brought
face to face with the great inner thoughts, and should
be taught to detach the thought from the word, and
to think right thoughts, as well as to speak the right
words in which those thoughts are embodied. So in
the same manner in the Ten Commandments, we
have these great statutes conveyed in one formula in
the 20th chapter of Exodus, which we have selected
as the most common; but we have the very same
thoughts, the same reasons, the same requirements,
embodied in the chapter which we have now read, but
in slightly varying phrases; in order to show us that
it is the obedience of the heart that God requires, and
of the spirit, not merely of the letter; that the language
is but the clothing, and we must pierce the outer robe,
ascertain the inward meaning, and give the heart to
God, and the life to obedience, not merely to his word,
but to the will of which that word is the vehicle. He
begins the recapitulation of the Decalogue here by
the old covenant promise, "I am the Lord thy God;"

and therefore, and upon this basis, I demand the homage which creatures owe to their Creator, which subjects owe to their sovereign, and which redeemed ones owe to Him that redeemed them. And the very first requirement is, "Thou shalt have none other gods before me." That is a most comprehensive one. Not only, Thou shalt not substitute another god for me, which would be very gross, but thou shalt not combine with the worship of me the worship of any other creature, in the heaven above or in the earth beneath. In other words, our worship is to be directed exclusively to God, and to him in the way that he himself has appointed—namely, by a Mediator, without image, or picture, or representation of any sort. Nothing can be more gross, nothing more absurd, than to fancy that the great God can be represented by a picture. An image gives no idea of God, an image gives no idea of the blessed Saviour. Can you prove to me it is his likeness? Can you demonstrate to me that it is a *facsimile* of him? And suppose it were so; suppose the traditional picture which is preserved at this moment on the Continent, and is said to have been painted by Luke—the slight mistake in tradition occurring that Luke was a painter, when Scripture states he was a physician — suppose that picture were the actual representation of our blessed Lord, what would it be to me? It would only be the picture of the outer man, it would not be the picture of the inner Deity, of the inner glory of him that is truly my Lord. It would show me a man upon a cross; but it cannot show me the Saviour bearing my sins and my curse. It might show me his humanity, but it cannot reveal to me his deity. And therefore the attempt is absurd, and wherever it has been made it has proved a failure ; and wherever its consequences have been followed out they have ended in will-worship, idolatry, and superstition. Nothing is more important than this : " Thou shalt not make unto thee any graven image, or any likeness of anything that is in heaven above, or that is in the earth beneath : thou shalt not bow down thyself unto them, nor serve them." I hold that this applies still to churches ; and that there ought to be in churches no pictures of saints, or of angels, or of the Saviour, or the Holy Spirit. I question whether the practice of representing the Holy Spirit by a dove be not positively wicked. It is not implied, as some think, in the gospel that the Holy Spirit took the form of a dove ; but that he descended after the manner of a dove ; and whether or not there was the very similitude of a dove, as σοματικως seems to indicate, he was not incarnate, and it was therefore a transient symbol. But the whole thing is bad. Let our churches be as beautiful and chaste as the genius of the architect can construct them ; but let there be no divine pictures, no images, no figures of saints. This is not puritanism, it is Christianity. And how in the world in the Church of England, where it is most nobly written upon the walls, " Thou shalt not make unto thee the likeness of anything in heaven above or in the earth beneath," any can stick up alongside of that interdict a glass picture that laughs at all perspective, and defies all propriety of form—how they can put up by the side of that divine and solemn prohibition, a palpable and scandalous infraction of it, is to me a most perplexing thing. The Church of England is right ; it's

F

only those that work the machine that have in this matter gone wrong.

We read, in the next place: " Thou shalt not take the name of the Lord thy God in vain." Nothing is more revolting than to hear that great name rashly used. Among the ancient Jews the name of God was called " The unpronounceable name." If they found the name *Yehovah* written upon a piece of paper, that piece of paper was consecrated by the inscription, and laid aside as a holy thing for ever. There may have been superstition in this; but it teaches us this lesson, that you ought not to use the name of God in conversation lightly, as an exclamation, as an oath, as a light appeal. It is now, I am happy to hear on all sides, a most vulgar practice, but it was always a most profane and irreligious one; and if any who indulge in it are not cured by the good usages of social life, they should recollect what is still more conclusive, " Thou shalt not take the name of the Lord thy God in vain."

We have next enjoined the keeping of the Sabbath-day. There is involved a very important idea in that fourth commandment, which many people seem to misunderstand; it is the most decisive prohibition of excessive toil upon the week-day, as well as the demand for the consecration of the Sabbath-day. It is, " Six days shalt thou labour." Here is the protest against avarice; avarice demands six days and six nights' toil; and if the human frame could stand the wear and tear, I dare say that even in this improved age there are masters that will take you for day-work and night-work too, and have the economy to give you only wages equal to six days' work. But this commandment forbids all this. There is a certain amount of labour that is duty, and dignity, and useful, yea, essential; but there is a labour and a toil—whether of the head, or the hand, or the foot—beyond that which is lawful and right. Six days, twelve hours a-day, is the legitimate amount of human toil; whatever goes beyond that is not good for man here, or good for man hereafter. In the Hebrew the definite article *the* is not; it is literally, " But a seventh day is the sabbath of the Lord thy God." When persons object, " How can you say that Sunday is the proper Sabbath ? It is Saturday "—the right way to reply to such objectors is to turn ro d, and say, " Very well; do you observe the Saturda as your Christian Sabbath ? " You find that they do not ; and that their quibble about the change of the day is only a convenient way of putting off from their consciences a sense of their obligation to hallow the Sabbath at all. But the truth is, the day is the ceremonial part; the Sabbath is the divine and lasting part. God did not hallow the seventh day, but he hallowed the Sabbath-day. The Sabbath is a light kindled from heaven ; and all that was done when the day was altered was to transfer the light from the seventh candlestick to the first candlestick. But that was not a repeal of the Sabbath, but a change of the Sabbath from one day tc another day, from one pedestal to another pedestal ; retaining the divine obligation, altering only the day on which it is to be observed. But if it should be said, it is at best a mere ceremony, I answer, this cannot be. Is it likely that a mere ceremony would have been incorporated with nine moral laws, and given in circumstances of such solemnity and grandeur ? And then, in the second place, the Sabbath is stated to be for " the stranger within thy gates." Now ceremonial laws were not for the stranger, they were only for the native-born Israelite. And the very fact, therefore, that this law is enjoined upon " the stranger within thy gates," is evidence that the Sabbath is a moral law, not so much binding as a duty, as an obligatory and precious privilege to all generations. It is matter of wonder that any should speak against the Sabbath-day; you ought rather to be thankful that there is a Sabbath ; you ought to be anxious to retain that blessed day from the intrusion of the exactions of Mammon, and the weary and wasting toil of the week. If the Sabbath were abolished, I believe that human life would very soon be shortened one-half. In France there were two things, in 1793, they discovered they could not do without. When they abolished, as they thought in their impious folly, the existence of a God, and proclaimed " No God," things went on so badly, that Robespierre said, " If there be not a God we must invent one, for society will not hold together without a God." What a striking testimony! And when, in the second place, they had abolished the Sabbath, they found that humanity would wear out, that the machinery would soon be used up, and they invented *decades*, or every tenth day, to be a Sabbath. But human nature, as if it had instincts within it reminding it of its original investi-ture, and rights, and privileges, gave up the *decades*, and returned to the seventh day. And I am rejoiced to hear from various parts of France, that the Sabbath is better observed in that country this year than it has been for many, many years before ; and that there is a growing feeling among that fine people, in proportion as they become enlightened, to hallow the Sabbath-day. Let not Protestant Britain go backward while Roman Catholic France seems to be advancing. We have, next, laws forbidding murder, adultery, theft, false witness against thy neighbour; and then the last law, going to the root of all, and proscribing coveting, or unlawful desire, the source of all the evil; and by prohibiting it, thereby, so far as law can reach, securing the performance of all.

Moses reminds them all of that they had seen and heard; and adds, so beautifully, " O that there were such an heart in them, that they would fear me, and keep all my commandments always, that it might be well with them, and with their children for ever!" This wish reminds me of what is stated in the second commandment, that God visits the iniquity of the fathers upon the children unto the third and fourth generation. Many people have said, " That seems a very severe law. Is it exhausted in Judaism, or does it continue still?" My answer is, It is a true law; and you cannot make it an objection against God's book, unless you shut your eyes to what you see going on around you. It is not true that God condemns to eternal ruin a child for the sin of a parent; that is not the meaning in any sense. But this is true, that if the parent go wrong the children suffer for it. Let a father indulge in drunkenness, what will be the result? He debilitates his own constitution, and his children are debilitated after him. Let a father squander his property in dissipation, or let him be indolent and lazy, and not earn enough for him and his; you find the children suffer. Let a nobleman play the traitor to his Queen, let him be guilty of high treason; —1745, which still lasts, in its effects, will show you that their children have lost their dignity, and are suffering in 1855 for the sin which their fathers committed in 1745. It is a law in the constitution of nature, and in the economy of social life, that the head of the house erring, sinning, doing wrong, sees the shadow of what he has done projected probably into many generations.

But those that quote this law forget the other half of it : "showing mercy unto thousands." It is a pity that in our translation it conveys thousands of individuals, but it is really thousands of generations; and it is meant to show how much more God delights in mercy ; that if he visits the iniquities of the fathers upon the third and fourth generations, he bestows mercies and blessings to thousands of generations ; as if, where wrath exhibited itself in the least, mercy and grace did much more abound.

CHAPTER V.

A NEW HEART. A HEART OF FLESH. A CLEAN HEART. FIXED, CONTRITE. AUTHOR OF THE CHANGE. FRUITS OF. FEAR OF GOD. KEEPING HIS LAW. GOD DESIRES OUR HAPPINESS.

LET us take a special review of these precious words in this chapter :—

" O that there were such an heart in them, that they would fear me, and keep all my commandments always, that it might be well with them, and with their children for ever!"—Verse 29.

SUCH is the wish expressed by God after he had given a recapitulation of the ten commandments in the previous part of this chapter. At the close of this instructive compendium of morality, this expression of a pure and holy law, God says, " O that there were such an heart in them, that they would fear me, and keep all my commandments always, that it might be well with them, and with their children for ever." Let us notice, first, the thing that is required and wished for, in order that they may fear God, keep all his commandments, and keep them always; and that it may be well with them and their children for ever. That pre-requisite essential to such obedience, is a heart within them. Here is the force of all that constitutes character : what the heart is the habits are,

the life is ; the whole tone, colouring, and direction of
the outer life necessarily depend upon the condition
of the inner and the living heart. It is the fountain ;
all we say, think, and do, are the streams, pure or polluted, that continually flow from it. Now, what sort of
a heart is this that is wished for ? It is described in
Scripture first of all as " a new heart." This we need ;
we must be made new creatures, we must be born
again, renewed, regenerate in the spirit of our minds.
And what does this imply ? That the old heart is
wrong ; that it will not do to patch it up, to repair it,
or to mend it by the prescriptions of man. There
must be, not a reformation in it, but a revolution of it ;
the old heart, that is, the moral, spiritual old heart,
taken away, and a new heart substituted in its place.
He speaks, of course, not of the material thing called
the heart, but of that composite, that knot of affections,
sympathies, feelings, desires, appetites, passions, of
which the human heart is constantly said in scripture,
and in our own ordinary language, to be the depository
and the source. Another character of this heart is that
it shall be what is called in scripture, "an heart of flesh."
The promise is, " I will take away the hard and the
stony heart, and will give them an heart of flesh."
What does this imply ? That our heart by nature has
become petrified ; or, translated into simple language,
that our sympathies, appetites, feelings, desires, are
not susceptible to those impressions that God makes,
or alive to those duties, responsibilities, that we owe
to him and to his service. And what we need therefore is, that the heart, which has become petrified,
shall be changed into what is called by the prophet a
heart of flesh ; that is, a heart susceptible of heavenly

impressions, capable of love, of sympathy, of joy, and of hope. It is called by David, in one of the Psalms, " a clean heart;" " Create in me a clean heart;" thereby teaching us that the heart of man by nature has become contaminated ; that instead of being the seat of holy, pure, and heavenly desires, it is the den of many evil appetites and passions ; so many and so overbearing that David cries, under a sense of their presence, " Create in me a clean heart, O Lord, I beseech thee." It is called again, " a heart fixed on God ;" " My heart is fixed ;" a heart resting upon him. And what does this teach us ? That the heart which originally rested upon God, felt its trust, and found its nutriment there, has left God, let go the ground of its trust ; and is now driven like a branch of ivy torn off from the tree of which it was a parasite, seeking for something to rest on ; and unable, blessed be God, to find it till it is regathered by the hand that was pierced for us, and attached again to its proper trust, and trained again for glory, for happiness, and for heaven. It is spoken of in another Psalm, as "a broken and a contrite heart ;" a heart so humble that it sees nothing good in itself, yet never despairing that it can be made all that God would have it to be. Whenever our lowliness of heart ends in despondency or in despair, it is not the lowliness that God inspires. True humility of heart feels its own unworthiness and ruin, but it never despairs, either of its own capability of being made something else, or of God's power to make it all that he could wish or you could desire it to be. The last feature I will notice of this heart, is such a heart as would prompt what is here stated, a prayerful heart. It is not the lips that pray, but the affections of the heart; there may be in the individual heart a congregation full of true and fervent prayer. Prayer is the beat of the heart, the pulse of the new life, the very air we breathe; and thus the heart can express its wants, its wishes, its desires, its feelings, its sorrows, its joys, without the use or the aid of the lips at all. God hears the heart pray and answers petitions conceived there, that are never launched into expression in the outward world. Now, if we had such a heart as that here described, the result of it would be that we should be with God always, that we should keep all his commandments always; and it would be well with us, and well with our children. But, you ask, how can we have such a heart? He that made it, alone can remake it. No sacrament can change the heart by any water of ablution that it can apply; no power of man can exorcise the human heart, and substitute a pure and a holy one. God alone can regenerate; he alone can recreate; and to him we are to apply, and from him we are sure to receive a heart that is broken and contrite, a new heart, a clean heart, a heart of flesh, a heart fixed on God, and praying always.

The result of all this will be, that we shall fear God. What do you mean by that expression, it may be asked, so frequently occurring in the word of God, "fearing God?" Does it mean being afraid of God? Does it mean living in terror every time we recollect his presence, or think of him as near to us, around us, in our lying down and our rising up, our going out and our coming in? Not at all. A slave walks with his master in fear, a maniac with his keeper in terror; but a son goes with a father, a daughter with a mother, a Christian with his God, in the exercise of affection, of confidence, of peace, and filial joy. It cannot therefore mean terror; it means the awe that a creature feels in relation to the Creator, but lighted up with the affection which a son must feel towards a parent. It is a mixture of the service of love, the allegiance of law, of the feeling of obligation that we owe to a Creator, the feeling of gratitude that we cannot but return to One that loved us and gave himself for us.

It is to those that thus fear God that the Sun of Righteousness will arise with healing under his wings. If our feelings to God were only love, it might degenerate into familiarity, or what borders upon it; if our fear were only awe, it would degenerate into terror; but being love and awe, reverence and esteem, gratitude and veneration, it makes up that which we call the fear or reverence of God. Another result of such a heart will be that we shall not only fear God, but "keep all his commandments always." Just note how comprehensive that expression is; "keep all his commandments, and keep them always." Keep them first in our hearts; for unless the law be kept within, it will never be kept without. Take care of the inner feelings, and you need not doubt that the outer life will be all you could desire. Read at your leisure the fifth chapter of St. Matthew's gospel; and you will there find that what is laid down in the Ten Commandments in the shape of outer acts is there forbidden in the shape of inner feeling, and that the sin proscribed in each law is there described to exist, where the feeling out of which that sin emanates is wilfully cherished in the heart. Now there must be,

in order to obey God's commandments, the inner obedience before there can be the outer ; or the inside of
the platter, to use the words of our Lord, must be
made clean, and then the outer will be made clean
also.   We are to keep these commandments also in
words. The tongue is a dangerous member. There is
no man perfect in expression always ; he would be a
perfect man if his speech were always perfect.   But
still, though we are not, and speak not what we
should, yet the effort, the aim, the prayer of a true
Christian, will always be to speak truly what he feels
deeply, as his first prayer will be to feel rightly, so
that he may always speak rightly. Words are the
foliage of affections, the clothing of thoughts, the
audible transference of an idea in one mind into the
mind of another.

The last division that I would notice as important
in keeping these commandments is in the acts.   If
words be the foliage, acts are the fruits of inward affection.   We shall keep these commandments not only
in words, not only in outer acts, but also in our hearts ;
and if the heart were such as is wished for in this
verse, such a heart as I have tried to delineate from
God's word, then we should fear him, and keep in
thought, in word, in deed, his commandments.

Notice, in the next place, the comprehensiveness
of " all my commandments." The pharisees of old
made selections from the Commandments ; they very
often selected one for rigid, exaggerated obedience,
in order that under the shadow of that obedience
they might indulge in the violation of another; and
each pharisee would naturally select the commandment which his own nature did not incline him to

break, for special obedience; and then he thought that this would be an atonement or a compensation for indulging in the breach of that law to which his own nature or disposition inclined him. But we must not select one commandment for preference over another, or for a moment dream that the rigid observance of one can compensate at all for the breach of another; nor must we dilute or subtract from these commandments; we must seek that heart that will enable us to fear the Legislator, and so in thought, and word, and deed, to keep all his commandments. And still more comprehensive is this expression from the word that is added, " always;" keep all his commandments " always." Not zealous obedience to-day, and cold, and calculating, indifferent obedience to-morrow; not to keep commandments in youth which are suitable to old age, or in old age which are suitable to youth; not to obey in prosperity, and disobey in adversity; but to have that heart that will fear God and keep all his commandments, and that always; in youth and in old age, in prosperity and in adversity, in sickness and in health, in our going out and in our coming in.

What is the result of all this? " That it may be well with them." It is not here taught that such obedience is the ground and cause of its being well with us; but on the contrary, that such obedience in the very holiest never can be the price of a single blessing from God. There is not one law of the ten that we can keep perfectly; there is not one law of the ten that we have not in thought, or word, or deed, broken. And to suppose that by any real or hoped-for conformity to that law we could merit anything from God, is to pervert the plainest texts of Scripture. But such a heart, so inclined, is the evidence of previous acceptance; and such conduct, resulting from such a heart, is the evidence of that character which belongs to a Christian, and indicates one whose state has been changed by being found in Christ, and whose character has been elevated by being sanctified by his Holy Spirit. The meaning, therefore, of this passage is, that where there is such a heart developing its feelings in such a course of conduct, the result will be happiness, or being well, to them that have it; in other words, the old law, the way of holiness, is the way of happiness; the reaction of righteousness in the character is happiness in the feelings, and sunshine in the outer life. It is not true, as some think, that Christians, or those that have such a heart, and fear God, and keep his commandments always, are necessarily unhappy men or afflicted men. I believe God's rule is to make his people happy, and to leave his enemies unhappy. It would be strange if God allowed his enemies to be happy, and always made his own people miserable and unhappy. But, you say, do we not find many of God's people suffering and unhappy? I answer, Yes; the law is, that being his people, they shall be happy; but if there be a needs-be, for their own growth, or for promoting his cause, or for illustrating his grace, or in any way contributing to the spread of his kingdom, that they shall suffer, then they suffer. But they suffer, not because they are Christians; but in order that they may glorify God, advance his cause, and do good to others. The general law of God's economy and government, is that a holy people are a happy people; and wherever you see true Christians great sufferers, the reason is, they are suffering, not because they are Christians, but in order that as Christians they may in some way glorify God, appreciate more fully his gospel, and spread it among those that they come into contact with. We see, in the next place, what God really desires; for it is God that uses this earnest expression, "O that there were such an heart in them." God desires the happiness of his people, "that it might be well with them." He cannot reverse his law, and make the unsanctified happy; but he wishes that all may be sanctified, and thus that all may be happy. He desires this happiness not only for immediate believers, but for their children. If he visits the sins of the fathers unto the third and fourth generations, he shows mercy to thousands of generations that love him and that keep his commandments. But you say, and very naturally, or at least one's own feelings naturally suggest, "If God desires the happiness of people, if God says, 'I wish there were such an heart in them that they would do this,' why does he not make all men do it? Why does he not accomplish by omnipotent power what he wishes in this text, in the exercise of infinite mercy?" I answer, God will not treat man contrary to his very nature: if man were a machine God might apply machinery and set it moving; but if man be a responsible being, with will, capable of motive, desire, objects, aims, influenced by reward or punishment, free in his actions, in the sense that nobody fetters him, if God were to force man to heaven, or to move him against his will, or to act upon him without regarding his will, his reason, his intellect, his heart, he would treat him as a brute or as a machine, not as a thinking, reflecting and rational being. You can see, therefore, that God approaches man only through his intellect, his head, and his heart; and if he were to approach him in any other way he would do violence to the very constitution and nature of man. It is because man remains the great creature that he was originally made, though fallen, that God will not force him to heaven, but will persuade him; and if he will not be persuaded, leave him alone. In other words, God says, man can be saved through the knowledge of the truth, and through the knowledge of the truth alone; and hence he has inspired the Scriptures to be written for our learning; he inspired apostles to preach and evangelists to record them; and has called upon his ministers to go and preach the gospel unto every creature. Now if man is to be saved by an act of omnipotence, what is the use of a Bible, a Saviour?— what is the use of Scripture, or of inspiration; finally, what would be the use of preaching the gospel at all? It is evident, therefore, from the fact that God has given this inspired book, and commissioned ministers to preach, that he means that men shall be saved only through the truth, and not in spite of the truth, nor in ignorance and independent of the truth. Hence the prayer, "Sanctify them through thy truth; thy word is truth." God offers men a new heart, he bids them ask it; but if they will not accept it or will not descend to ask it, then they must perish without it. God will draw you to heaven, but he will not drive you to heaven; God invites you to be Christians, but he will not compel you, in spite of your own will and desire. He will treat you as rational beings; if he can persuade you, he will persuade you, and give you a new heart; but he requires that you shall ask that your minds shall be enlightened, taught, and instructed in his word and will; and then if you perish it is your own blame; if you are saved it is by his grace and to his endless glory.

Oh that there were then in us all such an heart! May he give us that heart that will enable us to fear him as children a Father, as subjects a King; and to keep all his commandments, as not grievous, always; that it may be well with us, happy here, happy here after, prosperity attending our footsteps below, and eternal joy receiving our souls above.

May God bless to us these truths; and to his name be praise and glory. Amen.

CHAPTER VI.

You will perceive that in the opening part of the
chapter Moses lays down only the statutes and commandments which he had received from the Lord his
God; and these alone, not his own opinions, or the
traditions of the elders, he proclaims to be binding
upon the whole host of Israel, that they should obey
them in the land whither they were going to possess
it. He tells them that the great scope and end of all
this revelation of God's will, this recapitulation of
God's statutes, was that they might fear the Lord;
that is, feel the mixture of the awe that a creature
feels to the Creator, and the affection that a child feels
to a parent; "to keep all his statutes and his commandments, which I command thee." Moses therefore
again warns them, " Hear, O Israel, and observe to do
it;" and he says the result of all will be, "that it
may be well with thee;" well with thee in time, and
well with thee in eternity. " Seek first the kingdom
of God and his righteousness; and all other things
will be added unto you."

Then, in the fourth verse, he announces the celebrated maxim of Israel—a maxim they have on their phylacteries, on their fringes, continually in their lips, that has become, I fear, a form rather than a reality, but which in itself is a precious truth, peculiar to Israel, and unknown to the Gentile nations round about them. It is what they repeat at the end of the Psalms : " Hear, O Israel, the Lord our God is one God." Now just recollect that all the nations round about Israel, not only then, but in long after ages, bowed down to idols of wood, and gold, and stone, the workmanship of men's hands ; and that this nation of Israel, with none of the philosophy that the Gentiles had, with none of their arts, their sciences, their literature, their poetry, their painting, yet retained this great truth, acted upon it, were the living exponents of it ; so that it was the peculiarity of their nation— a distinguishing and glorious peculiarity—that they recognized the one living and true God, and him only they served. Now, if the highest literature, science, and attainments in secular knowledge, did not enable the Gentiles to reach this truth, we may be sure that the ignorance of the Jews could not possibly attain it ; and, therefore, that God must have revealed it to them expressly from heaven.

He then gives the epitome of the first half of the Decalogue, in these words, " Thou shalt love the Lord thy God with all thine heart." Let us mark how reasonable this is : " Thou shalt love the Lord thy God," not more than you are able, nor beyond what you are capable of, but " with all thine heart,"—with nothing less and with nothing more. The commandment is therefore reasonable ; and there can be no excuse for not obeying the law, and loving the Lord our God with all our heart. And one can see how justly the whole Decalogue is comprehended in these two prescriptions, " Thou shalt love the Lord thy God with all thy heart, and thy neighbour as thyself." What is love ? The root of all obedience. Love to a person is the secret of devotedness, and service, and sacrifice for his sake. In the absence of love there may be the outward form, originated by the prospect of profit, or by expediency, or in hypocrisy ; but only when a service is inspired by love is it real and acceptable to God. And so, if you love your neighbour as yourself, you will not violate those laws that relate to him, because his safety, his happiness, his comfort, will be desired by you in the same way in which you desire to secure your own. These two brief epitomes of the Decalogue, the more they are analyzed, the more they indicate a divine origin ; and if retained and cherished in the hearts of Christians, they will lead to the highest allegiance to God, and to the deepest sympathy with all our brethren of mankind.

He then instructs them to teach these things to themselves and to their children ; and specially does he warn them against forgetting God, in language extremely beautiful. " When the Lord thy God shall have brought thee into the land which he sware unto thy fathers, to Abraham, to Isaac, and to Jacob, to give thee great and goodly cities, which thou buildest not, and houses full of all good things, which thou filledst not, and wells digged, which thou diggedst not, vineyards and olive trees, which thou plantedst not ; when thou shalt have eaten and be full, then beware lest thou forget the Lord." In poverty man is disposed to despond, or to despair, or to blaspheme; in riches and abundance man is disposed to forget the Lord his God, and to think that his own hands digged the well, and planted the vineyards, and filled the house with all good things.

We then read, " Ye shall not go after other gods " —that is, the idols or images of the heathen—" of the gods of the people which are round about you." And in the 16th verse, " Ye shall not tempt the Lord your God, as ye tempted him in Massah." Now it is a very remarkable proof of the deity of our blessed Lord, that Paul, referring to the temptation at Massah, says, "Neither let us tempt Christ, as some of them tempted him ;" indicating thereby that the divine and glorious Being who shone in the burning bush, and glowed in the fiery pillar by night, which marched in the desert, the pioneer of the hosts of Israel, was none else than the Second Person in the blessed Trinity, afterwards who became man, and died for us and for our salvation. It is one of those indirect testimonies to the deity of Christ which are extremely precious, and thoroughly conclusive. There is another very interesting lesson brought out here, that the religion of the Bible is a religion that will bear inquiry ; and wherever there is an inquirer for information there ought to be some one ready to answer, and to give a reason for the faith that is in him. And therefore, " When thy son asketh thee in time to come, saying, What mean the testimonies, and the statutes, and the judgments, which the Lord our God hath commanded you ? " are you to say, " You must not exercise private judgment in such deep matters? " Are you to say, " Think of politics, literature, science; but religion is too high, too sacred, too solemn, for you to inquire into?" No; in those days they were told that when the children shall ask the parents, What mean ye by these things? the parents shall instantly enter into an explanation, and instruct them what these things mean, and point them to the goodness of God, to the safety of his people, to the promises of his blessed Word, to the hopes of his kingdom and glory as the results of loving him and serving him all the days of their life. The parent, therefore, that cannot explain such things to his children, or that cannot answer the inquiry, What mean ye by these things? ought himself to go to school and learn the elements of the gospel of Christ, not for his own sake only, but for the sake of those that are around him.

One more remark upon the 20th verse. You will notice that the expression, *mean*—" What mean the testimonies"—is in italics. Now in the original there is no word for *mean;* it might be as strictly translated, " What are the testimonies and statutes ?" So again, in that other question, " What *mean* ye by this service ? " in the original it is, " What *is* this service ? " Now do not such expressions show that *is* and *are*, in the Hebrew language, are employed in the same sense in which we employ the words *signify* and *mean ?* It is in the original, not " What *mean* ye by this service ?" but " What *is* this service ? " It is here not, " What *mean* the testimonies and the statutes ? " but, " What *are* the testimonies and the statutes ? " And if this be the invariable usage in the Old Testament Hebrew, may we not justly infer that the words, " This *is* my body," are used precisely in the same sense, and after the same model; and that they mean strictly, " This *signifies*, or *means*, my body?" If one be guided by the analogy of Scripture as well as by common sense, that must be the conclusion.

CHAPTER VI.

IN this chapter words occur worthy of special study : they are these :—

" And these words, which I command thee this day, shall be in thine heart : and thou shalt teach them diligently unto thy children, and shalt talk of them when thou sittest in thine house, and when thou walkest by the way, and when thou liest down, and when thou risest up. And thou shalt bind them for a sign upon thine hand, and they shall be as frontlets between thine eyes. And thou shalt write them upon the posts of thy house, and on thy gates."—Ver. 6—9.

The very first thought that occurs here is, that the words which Moses echoed from God, and which he conveyed to the children of Israel, were to be first of all in their hearts : " The words which I command thee this day shall be in thine heart ; " the heart, the seat of affection,—the heart with which we love God with all our heart, and soul, and strength. Truths embraced by the intellect may be clear, but they are cold as the frost ; truths received into the heart, and especially when blessed and owned by the Holy Spirit, become the prolific seeds of whatsoever things are pure, and just, and lovely, and of good report. Unsanctified truth in the intellect leads often to scepticism; unsanctified truth in the heart leads often to superstition: but truth received by the mind, deposited in the heart, warmed and blessed by the Holy Spirit, bursts forth into all the green foliage and the fragrant fruits of living and of true Christianity. Now, as the command here is specially that "these words shall be in thine heart," let me notice what must necessarily precede. First, the truths must be understood by the intellect before they can be deposited in the heart. The intellect first discriminates what is truth before the heart consents to accept it as a precious and important deposit. We may love the unseen, but we cannot love the unknown. We must therefore see clearly with our intellect that this is truth, before we can embrace fully in our hearts that truth in all the love and in all the power of it. Now God's word is a very intelligible book; it is a book rich in good sense; it is a book whose thoughts are couched in the simplest terms, the shortest words, the plainest language. Metaphysicians may be perplexed by it, but wayfaring men, who read it only to find the way to heaven, never yet failed in discovering that truth. But, in the second place, before these truths can be deposited in the heart they must not only be understood by the intellect, but they must also be appreciated by the heart. We do not embrace with the affections of the heart that which is worthless or of no value. The human heart refuses to extend the current of its sympathies, its attachments, and its love, to anything that is inferior to itself or of no real and substantial value. Worthless things are tolerated, they are not loved; they are endured, they are not cherished;

they are accepted and borne with as a necessity, they are not loved and cherished as of real value. We must therefore be able to value and appreciate, as well as to understand these truths, in order that we may truly love them with our hearts. Now we notice in the Bible how truly its contents are loved by those that have best understood them. Jesus referred the inquirer to the law and to the testimony ; the apostles bade their audience search the Scriptures whether these things were so ; one said, " All scripture is given by inspiration of God, and is profitable ; " and if there be one lesson more prominent upon the surface of the Bible than another, it is that all true Christians have loved it as gold, felt it sweeter than the honey and the honeycomb ; and have regarded it as a lamp to their feet and a light to their path ; and because they have first understood it, secondly valued it, they have thirdly, and naturally, loved it, and cherished it in their hearts. This therefore leads me to the next idea, which is that God's word, or, as Moses calls it here, " All these words," " shall be in thine heart." The heart is the seat of love, of sympathy, of earnest, inexhaustible affection. After the intellect has discriminated, after the judgment has appreciated, then the heart holds fast the deposit as a loved, and precious, and important thing. It is not enough to understand the Bible, it is not enough to value the Bible ; we must go a step further, and love the Bible. There are some things you thoroughly understand, but which you do not like ; there are some men you admire, whom you can never love ; but this is a book that may be understood, that should be valued, and that must be by every true Christian loved and cherished in the inmost depths of his heart. You notice, in the next place, that wherever this word is thus cherished, thus loved, thus deposited, as Moses says, in the heart, the whole life is toned, and shaped, and sustained and regulated by it. Our blessed Lord says, " Out of the heart proceed evil thoughts; " that is, out of the natural heart proceed evil thoughts. But out of the regenerated heart proceed thoughts of whatsoever things are pure, and lovely, and of good report. And this shows the wisdom of this blessed book, that in order to make man what man is meant to be, this divine Physician, this pure and holy reformer of what is wrong, begins at the seat and source of all plastic influence and power. When man wants to reform man, he lops off a branch here, lops off another branch there, alters his circumstances, changes the patient's bed, gives him money, or wealth, or property, or power; but there is no real change for the better. But when God deals with man, he touches the heart, the fountain of all, to a finer issue ; he casts into its polluted springs the sweetening and the sanctifying branch. Man changes the patient's bed that the patient may feel at ease ; God heals the patient's sickness, that he may be well. Man gives to the sufferer something that he has not, which he thinks will make him well; God makes the sufferer that which he is not, a new creature in Christ Jesus. Therefore he says here so justly and so beautifully, and, if I may use the word, so philosophically, " These words which I command thee this day may be on thy gates, on thy phylacteries, on thy lips, in thy intellect; but primarily and emphatically in thine heart ; " the seat, the source, the centre, of all those forces that mould, and shape, and elevate to communion with heaven the fallen affections of mankind. Now this is the truth deposited in the heart I have spoken of as a great source of new character. But I do not mean to convey, and you will not understand me as conveying, that even God's truth alone is all that is needed in the human heart to make it what it should be. I think it is one of the most humbling thoughts, that it needs not only the inspiration of God's truth in the outer page, but the same Inspirer of that truth to plant it, and nurse it, and foster it in the human heart. Just as we should never think of going to heaven depending upon our own righteousness, and expecting glory as the recompense ; so we should never think of savingly understanding this blessed book except by the Author of it himself sanctifying us. It is as great sin to read the Bible without thinking of the Author of the Bible, as if our reading it was all that was requisite, as it is to engage in acts of mercy and of goodness, and to trust in these instead of in the righteousness of Him who is our only right and title to heaven and to eternal joy. Never therefore forget whilst you read this blessed book, that it needs the Holy Spirit that inspired it as a perfect lesson upon the outer page, to re-inspire it as a practical life in the inner heart. You may understand the Bible theoretically, but you cannot understand the Bible savingly without God's Holy Spirit. And therefore we read, " We are born again of the incorruptible seed ; " and again, " Sanctify them "—speaking to God the Spirit, " Sanctify them through thy truth ; thy word is truth." There is no book so plain, no book so precious, no book so rich in poetry, in eloquence, in instructive history, as the Bible : but you may read it as a scholar, and not as a Christian. To read it as a scholar you may treat it as you treat other books ; but to read it as a sinner expecting to be saved, you must look above the Bible, not because the Bible is imperfect, but because you are blind, that the Author of the Bible may open your eyes and impress upon your hearts its blessed and its sanctifying truths. All the tradition of man is midnight ; reason applied to the Bible is moonlight ; the Holy Spirit shining on the heart of the reader of the Bible is lasting and glorious sunlight. And, lastly, upon this head, let me again remind you, if I have reminded you before, that the presence of the heart in the reading of the Bible, next to the Spirit teaching that heart, is the most essential thought you can carry with you to that joyous and solemn exercise. In all the praises that you pour forth, in all the prayers that you give expression to, in all the lessons that you learn, in all the services you render, if the heart be not there, there is but the tinkling cymbal, the sounding brass, the grand altar without a fire or a sacrifice, a form without life, a body without power. What therefore is essential, as this text teaches us, and, indeed, as the whole chapter teaches us, is the heart. And if men felt more profoundly that heart-worship is the main thing, they would quarrel much less about forms and ceremonies, and ecclesiastical etiquette, and all the subordinate questions which have perplexed and puzzled mankind. The great demand of God in every act of worship is, " My son, give me thy heart ; " and if the heart be not there, there is no real religion. You may give the allegiance of reason, but the religion of reason alone is cold and freezing scepticism. You may give the homage of the religion of imagination, but the religion of imagination is picturesque forms, beautiful architecture, fine painting, music, and poetry; or you may give the religion of conscience, but the religion of conscience alone is sepulchral, terrible, repulsive. The religion that is true is the religion of the Bible incorporated into the heart, and on that heart written by the finger of Him that wrote the Decalogue on the tables of stone, indelible for ever and ever. Such is the thought embodied in the important text, "These words which I command thee this day shall be," first of all, " in thine heart." Unless they be there the rest of the prescriptions will be altogether impracticable. No man will teach truly what he does not love in his heart. The secret of a good teacher, whether in science, mathematics, Greek, Latin, religion, or whatever it be—the secret of his excellence, his force, and his success, lies in this, that the thing is near his heart, that he values it, that he loves it, and therefore he goes forth to teach it.

The next prescription here is, that after these things have been embodied in thine heart, " thou shalt teach them diligently unto thy children."— Then children need to be taught; children are ignorant, and need to be instructed; they are wayward, and they need to be trained. It is one of the greatest follies in the world to assume that a child left to itself, untouched by the surrounding atmosphere of a fallen world, will instinctively and intuitively develop itself into a Christian saint, or, if needs be, an illustrious martyr. It is true of every infant that is born, that it is fallen, lost, dead in trespasses and in sins, and before it can enter into the kingdom of heaven it must be born again. The very first things that you are to teach your children, are the lessons of the gospel of Christ. By all means teach them the wisdom of Solomon, but never forget to teach them the wisdom of a higher than Solomon, who is here—the wisdom of Christ. The secular knowledge that is now so much admired—and it cannot be too much admired in its place—makes men talented, clever, and illumines the intellect, stores the memory, multiplies the resources; but it does not teach the heart. Now we need not only light to show us the way, but an impulse to go in the right way. We need not only to know what is right, which the remains of conscience will often tell us, but we need to have implanted within us a sympathy with the right and a determination to pursue it. Mere secular knowledge, which is taught, and ought to be taught, and properly taught, begins in time and it ends in time. But if your children are left destitute of the living gospel of Christ, then, when earthly knowledge has exhausted itself, and time is finished, they have no bread for the journey that goes beyond, that leads to God, to heaven, and to happiness. The knowledge of time, like the rainbow, starts from the earth, vaults into the sky, seems to enter into heaven, but it returns to the earth again. But the knowledge of Christ, and of him crucified, is like that beautiful bow inverted; it begins in the heaven, it sweeps past and transforms while it touches our globe, and it returns and melts into the heaven again. The one is of the earth, earthly; the other is of God, and leads to God.

The father and the mother are here assumed to be the teachers of the children committed to their charge. " These words shall be in thine heart; and thou shalt teach them diligently unto thy children." It is strange that this book, despised by many of the wise as an obsolete document, useless for modern life, is the only book that seems in its earliest stages, so early as the days of Moses, to have appreciated and insisted on the vast importance of Christian early education. The accomplished Greeks cared so little about the education of the young, and had so low and wretched a conception of it, that they left their slaves to be the tutors of their sons; and the ancient Romans, the lords of the world of their day, had so poor an idea of the excellence of education, that the Greek and Spartan serfs were employed by them also to be the tutors of the sons of the patricians of Rome. But here, Moses, that often despised and undervalued servant, lays down rules for the instruction of the young, and for the selection of the lesson-books to be employed; and as to where the responsibility of their instruction rests, that men are only beginning to appreciate in the nineteenth century, as if to show that the Bible is never behind the age, but the age invariably a thousand years behind the Bible. It is here insisted that parents instructed in the truths of the gospel are to teach them to their children. It is Christianity alone that has constituted what is called home. The word "family," so beautiful and so precious a word now, meant in ancient Rome the collection of slaves that might be destroyed by the master. And what has transformed a collection of slaves into a home? Just the teaching of this blessed book, this precious gospel. Here then we have the duty of the parents to teach to their children these truths. And do you think by teaching your children the truths of religion, that you will make those children miserable, melancholy, as some people, even in the more enlightened classes of society, think? All the very reverse. Infidelity may make children gay,—superstition will make them melancholy; but true religion will give them the solemnity, and the joy, and the happiness of Christians. Teach children to live without religion, and they have all the unrestrained gaiety of the world; teach them a corrupt religion, Tractarianism or Popery, and they will become gloomy, melancholy, ascetic, monkish, and sepulchral; but teach them the warm, glowing, inspiring, cheerful lessons of the New Testament, and your children will be happy as well as solemn. But you say, very naturally, "Are the parents only to be the teachers of children; and is it their duty to attend to it exclusively, and not to commit their children to the teaching of any other?" There has been a great deal said on this subject on both sides, verging to extremes. Some say the parent in every case is to be absolutely the teacher of his children, and none else may perform that duty. Others say the parent's attention is of immaterial consequence, provided only he takes the children and places them in the hands and under the care of a good and efficient teacher. There are mistakes in both views. I think the parent is to be responsible

H

for the selection of the right teacher, and of the right lesson; and, being responsible, he may teach himself if he can, which is a very rare accomplishment; or he may teach by another if he can afford it, which is not so rare nor so difficult. It would be the greatest calamity in the world if you were to insist upon every parent personally teaching his own children; for are you aware that teaching is now a profession—a very difficult one? I have met with very few people that are first-rate teachers. It is easier to be an eloquent preacher in the pulpit than to be an effective teacher in a Sabbath-school. Men may undervalue the teacher's office; but it is a most important, a most difficult, and a most responsible one; and it is not so frequently well done as some think. At all events, the world does not seem to have yet appreciated the excellence of a first-rate teacher, for too often high families in the land will give thirty pounds, forty pounds a-year to a cook, and offer fifteen pounds or twenty pounds to an educated lady, who is an able, an enlightened, and Christian teacher. Never will your children be efficiently taught till you see that your nursery is far more important than the kitchen, and far more interesting than the drawing-room. Stint your expenditure in your drawing-room, but be lavish in your expenditure on the instruction of your children. The parents need not personally teach their children. It requires tact, long study, experience, preparation, to teach the young efficiently. And therefore the parent, I humbly conceive, retaining the responsibility of the teaching of his family, a responsibility of which he may not and must not disrobe himself, may yet substitute for himself a Christian person, trained, and taught, and acquainted by experience and practice with all the resources of that most difficult, but most important profession, the education of the young. One does rejoice to see progress, however. There are now normal schools for teaching teachers, that teachers themselves may be efficient. In former days, even within my recollection, if a man failed in his business, if he was obliged from his indolence and want of business habits to cease to keep a shop, he was thought good enough to start a school. But that idea is almost abolished now; and the world itself is more and more rising to an apprehension of the great truth, that the teaching of the young is a most important duty, as it is a most difficult one; and that when you have given the largest sum and expended the greatest trouble in securing the ablest teacher for your children, you have only done what was dutiful to them and right in the sight of God. Thus shall we teach our children these laws, commandments and lessons, which are first of all to be implanted in our own hearts.

You are to "talk of them when thou sittest down and when thou risest up." We have seen, first of all, the holy of holies, the inner sanctuary of truth, the heart; we have seen, secondly, the next important place for Christian lessons, namely, the school; let us now cross the threshold of another sanctuary, only second to either of those I have specified, namely, the home; and see what ought to be the topics and the subjects of our converse there. If I take the divine prescription, it is, "Thou shalt speak of these truths when thou risest up and when thou liest down." What is the reason that so many people thoroughly understand political parties, but so little seem to understand the doctrines of the gospel? I believe the reason is this, that they often take home the one, and that they rarely take home the other. You are perhaps not aware that the way to teach yourself most efficiently is to try to teach or tell others. A teacher in a school becomes a better scholar just by teaching; a Christian in a family becomes more acquainted with the gospel just by conversing. "As iron sharpeneth iron, so does man's face his fellow." Conversation enables you to think more, to try to apprehend more clearly what you attempt to express distinctly and plainly; and the very fact that you are obliged in any circumstances to converse about religion, will necessitate a clearer, sharper, and warmer apprehension of what the truths of religion are. If you want to comprehend a truth thoroughly, sit down with pen and paper, and write out your thoughts upon it. If next to that you want to comprehend it, and to make others comprehend it, begin and discuss it day by day, and you will be struck with the progress that you make in comprehending a truth, just by the efforts that you make to explain that truth to others. I never understood the gospel so well till I began to preach it; and the more I write on it and speak on it, the more clearly and fully I comprehend it, and the more fully and beautifully it dawns upon my mind. But it is not only for your own sakes that you are to speak of these things when you sit down and when you rise up, it is for the sake of your family and your children. Many parents who are surrounded by very young children carry on conversations that are not fit for children to hear; and they fancy, "Oh, they are too young to

retain one recollection of what we say, or to turn
into practical life a single thought to which we have
been pleased to give expression." You do not give
children credit enough for susceptibility of heart, for
quickness and brilliancy of apprehension. You may
rest assured that they understand far more than you
give them credit for ; and they can comprehend things
and thoughts that you think are too high for them ;
and you will find in the nursery and in the school-
room that the incidental expressions you have dropped,
hoping or expecting they would not hear them, are
there translated into bad tempers, or into excuses for
them to those that have their superintendence and
instruction. It is wrong to attempt to deceive a
child ; it is more, it is very difficult to deceive a child ;
and many a conversation, most incidental, in itself
unexceptional, has left upon infant minds a tone that
has shaped a character for twenty years to come ; and
conversations held around the hearth are passing
into those quick and active minds, to project shadow
or sunshine into long-enduring ages. Let us, therefore, when we sit down and when we rise up, that is,
in domestic intercourse, speak these truths ; certainly
forbear to speak what is not for edification, still more
what may possibly pervert and injure the hearts of
them that listen to them.

"Thou shalt speak of these things when thou
walkest by the way." We have seen the inner school,
the heart ; we have seen the outer school, the teacher
and his pupils ; we have seen the domestic school, or the
parents and their families ; we next see the traveller
by the wayside : "when thou walkest by the way thou
shalt also speak of them." Now just let us take home

this lesson practically to ourselves. Two Christians are placed in the same railway carriage, in the same steamboat cabin, in the same inn by the roadside. In such circumstances they must not be ostentatious of their religion, but they may not conceal or quench beneath a bushel the religion that they have. It requires much good sense, much delicacy of feeling, to avoid upon the one hand that parade of one's religion, which next to hypocrisy is the most offensive display, and yet to avoid, upon the other hand, that shrinking from duty, that failure to seize an opportunity of usefulness, which may be productive of lasting and of blessed consequences. There is a time in the conversation of the stranger when a word in season, behold how good it is. It will rest with good sense, with common sense, sustained by true piety, to select when that season is. To force your religious convictions in the midst of your transactions in business, in the market, to bring out your Bible and read a text when you ought to be giving receipts to your bills, to mix up ostentatiously the forms of religion with the duties and necessities of business, is hypocrisy, or it is the absence of ordinary good sense. But to watch in the counting-house, in the warehouse, in the shop, in the street, by the wayside, to edge in a thought less expressed in scriptural language and more suggestive of trains of thought, that is the true idea. When persons, as you may have sometimes heard, have recourse to profane language, or recklessly imprecate God's vengeance upon them, just say to them, " Well, what do you mean by that ? Suppose what you say were actually done to you ; what would be the result of it ? " And if you can start a train of thought in the person's mind using such language, he will himself see the utter wickedness and folly of it ; and if instead of quoting a commandment you will edge in a suggestive thought, you may bring him at last to the commandment, in a far more speedy and successful way. By the wayside, then, you are to talk of these things as well as when you sit down. If Christians are in the railway carriage they cannot but be missionaries, because if lights they cannot but be luminous; if salt they cannot but touch and infect all that are around them. The Ethiopian eunuch, travelling in his carriage, was reading Isaiah the prophet. Philip was not guilty of discourtesy, or rudeness, or ill-mannered interruption of a prime minister, when he said to him, in quiet, but very plain terms, " Understandest thou what thou readest ? " and immediately it led to his conviction and conversion to God. Two disciples were one day journeying to Emmaus ; they began talking about the things that had happened, and instead of such talk being disowned of God, Jesus appeared in the midst of them, and taught them more fully. Paul was taken a prisoner in a ship to Rome ; the ship was in great danger in a storm ; he told them simple truths, and so mixed with good sense that these truths commended themselves, and the crew was given him, and given through him to Christ his Lord and Master. Paul showed them, first, the truths of religion, or the providential presence of God amid the roaring waves and the howling winds ; but he taught also the necessity of human means, when he said, " Unless these keep in the ship they cannot be saved." And that mixture of good sense meeting the emergency in which he was involved, and that application of seasonable truth, was blessed and owned by the Spirit of God.

There is a church in the school, a church in the family, a church in the railway, a church in the cabin on the ocean's bosom, a church in the prime minister's chariot, a church everywhere and anywhere, as true, as pure, as precious, as ever met in large chapel, or in lofty cathedral.

We thus see how God's people are, first, to cherish these truths in their hearts; next, to teach them to their children; next, to talk of them in their homes; next, to speak of them when they walk by the way; and, lastly, to speak of them when they lie down and when they rise up. And is there not reason for doing so? There may be a church in the bedchamber, in the dressing-room, as well as in the cathedral. When the sun shuts down upon another day, and reminds you as he sinks beneath the horizon of having left undone much you ought to have done, and done much that you ought not to have done, is not that suggestive of prayer for pardon? When the sun rises again upon another day, and gilds the east with his glorious beams, is not that suggestive of prayer for strength for the day's trials, of a blessing upon your going out and upon your coming in? When the day closes God requires praise for his goodness; when the day begins we require strength from God for the day's journey. There is no place discrowned of its sacredness; there is no ground that is unholy. In all places, when thou liest down and when thou risest up, when thou goest out, and when thou comest in, speak, and because you speak, think of the things that relate to the kingdom of God.

Some I have read of have in their bedrooms crosses, crucifixes, pictures and images; and I was asked once by a person, Was it not most proper to have a crucifix at the head of one's bed? When I asked the reason of it, this lady said, " To remind me of the Saviour's death, sacrifice, and suffering." I put the question, " But how do you know that is like Christ? It may be like the thief upon the cross; it is as like him as it is the Saviour; there is no more reason for believing it is the one than the other. And besides, there is a clear commandment, Thou shalt not make unto thee the likeness of anything in heaven above, or in the earth beneath." And there is no likeness of our blessed Lord; the only likeness he has left us is his own word; and they that speak together about Christ, the gospel, duty, privilege, responsibility, consecrate their bedchambers and their dressing-rooms truly; when they that hang up pictures, images, and crucifixes, only desecrate them with a revolting superstition. It is the truth of the gospel that is the nearest likeness, because it is the inspiration of the Son of God. It is the heart that adores, it is the heart that worships, it is the heart that feels, and out of the abundance of the heart the mouth speaketh.

" It shall be also," it is added in the last place, " a sign and frontlets between thine eyes." In ancient days the Scriptures occupied a large quantity of parchment; perhaps two or three persons would have been required to carry a copy of the complete Bible. Printing is one of the great providential mercies for which we ought to praise and thank God most heartily. But the Jews in those days, when one single book in the Bible occupied an enormous roll of parchment, were in the habit, and scripturally so, of selecting choice texts, expressive and eloquent passages, and having these bits of parchment fastened upon their heads, their foreheads, the foreheads of their caps, upon their dresses or their long robes, and they usually called them, superstitiously I admit, phylacteries, from the Greek verb, " to guard," or " to take care of ;" as if these texts upon their garments were charms, or guards, or defences. This superstitious custom had its origin in what was good—namely, in keeping constantly before them directive and precious texts. And far better carry into your counting-house, into the world, one single text inscribed upon your memory, pondered in your heart, prayed over in your spirit, than read superficially a whole chapter without attaching to it, or deriving from it, any precious or instructive meaning. Now, you are not to attach charms to your caps, phylacteries to your robes, but you are to take texts as lights to your feet and lamps to your path, and lessons ever to be remembered. What a precious book must this Bible be, that it is to be carried into every place ! It is to enter into the cabinet of monarchs, into the congress of the republic, into the divan of the Moslem himself ; it is to shape all things, all plans, all inspirations, by its celestial presence. It is to be present at our daily meals as truly as at the sacramental table. It is to be dominant on the desk in the counting-house as truly as in the pulpit of the sanctuary. It ought to inspire and give fragrance to the atmosphere of the home, the nursery, the school, the academy, the university, everywhere. It is to nerve us everywhere to act ; it is to compose us anywhere to suffer ; it is to steep the wounds of the heart in the oil and wine of its own cordial; it is to light up the eyes of the dying with the glorious hopes of glory, and to enable them to fall asleep in Jesus, departing in peace, having seen the Lord's Christ. It is a book for every age, for every country, for every department of social life; and that department of social life which will not bear the light of a present Bible, will not bear to be reflected on amidst the light of the judgment-seat of Christ. You are in the path of holy duty wherever you can take the Bible with you as a light to your feet and a lamp to your path; but wherever you feel in your own conscience that any book would be suitable here except the Bible, there God never led you in his providence, and there you have no right to expect that God will preserve you by his grace. Let us carry this blessed book, then, into every place, let us cherish and defend it in our schools. I know no calamity or catastrophe more terrible than that which would take God's word from our schools, or proscribe the teaching of its lessons to the young, or mark it as a book only fit for certain hours; and for those whose hearts' enmity to God by nature would naturally dispose them to pay no attention to it at all.

The Bible is meant for the laity; it is for the fathers and mothers of Israel. We have evidence that it was useful in their hands, when we read that Timothy had all his best and holiest lessons from his mother and grandmother, Lois and Eunice. What we have learned ourselves to appreciate, to love, to value, it is our duty, our privilege, and our very instinct, to communicate to others also. No man is made a Christian for himself; no man has a Bible only for himself. This blessed book is not to be the monopoly of a few; it is to be the privilege and the possession of all mankind. Let us learn this important lesson, that it is as dutiful to teach as it is to preach. The school is the best porch of the sanctuary; whatever dims the light of the school will diminish the efficiency of the house of God. And, lastly, the most precious legacy you can leave your children is a thoroughly sound Christian education. If you are rich and leave them your wealth, it may take away stimulus to effort, it may destroy the spring of enterprise, it may generate habits of indolence, of idleness, and of dissipation. But if you give them a thoroughly sound scriptural education, you give them that which they may forget, but which they can never abuse, and which, when early taught, will never be finally and for ever forgotten; for in the worst and most distant aberration from God, some early light, struck out in the susceptive years of infancy and child-hood, will leap like a live spark from the memory; as was the case with John Newton, when a prodigal at the helm in a tempestuous sea,—the text forgotten for twenty years, but taught him by his mother in the nursery, was the pivot on which turned his everlasting and his happy destiny.

CHAPTER VII.

In the very opening part of the chapter we have
read, God assumes the absolute certainty of the
triumph of the children of Israel over the countless
tribes of Canaanites, and Perizzites, and Jebusites,
seven great nations that should be opposed to them;
and as no less a certainty that " the Lord will deliver
them before thee." And then, upon the strength
and certainty of what shall be in God's providential
government, he inculcates the duties that devolve
upon them, namely, to smite them, and utterly destroy them, and make no covenant with them. We
have noticed before the objection urged against this
command, that it seems to savour of cruelty and pre-
scriptive vengeance. But it really does not so. The
Canaanites were a people intensely depraved, fearfully
guilty in the face of conscience, conviction, judgments; a most guilty, debased, and degraded race;
and when God commanded the Israelites to extirpate
them, he merely inflicted upon them those judicial
retributions which great criminals are still visited
with in society, and in the providential government of
God. If the Israelites, out of spite, revenge, ani-

mosity, excitement, had put the Canaanites to the sword, they would have done wrong; but when they simply acted as the executioners of Him who is just and wise, and who alone was able to weigh the demerits of the race they were called upon to extirpate, I cannot see how there can be any valid objection against God's word, or against God's dealing in this matter.

After that he warns them against entering into associations with them : " Neither shalt thou make marriages with them." You will notice here an assertion, or rather a prediction, which almost invariably turns out to be true : " Thou shalt not make marriages with the Canaanites." Why ? " For they will turn away thy son from following me." You hear persons still say, if one, a Protestant and a true Christian, has married an intensely bigoted Roman Catholic, the Protestant hopes—his preferences, I fear, dictating his prophecies—that he will be the instrument of converting the Roman Catholic. But the Roman Catholic knows better, and knows what is far surer to occur ; for the almost universal result is not that the Roman Catholic becomes a Protestant, but that the Protestant becomes a Roman Catholic. And you see it asserted here, " Thou shalt not marry them." The Israelite might have said, " If I choose to marry a Canaanite woman, I have confidence in my creed that I shall convert her to the true religion." But God regards it, you observe, as a certainty that this would not be the result, but the very opposite. And now, why so ? Because the Canaanite that marries the Israelite does so in ignorance ; but the Israelite that marries the Canaanite does so in the face of God's word, his own conscience, and the light that he has superior to the light of the companion to whom he is married. So that you may lay it down as a great law that the one that has light especially sins; and, therefore, is left to taste the retributions that result from a practice wrong in principle, and never ending, almost never ending, in any other way than in disaster. How full of wisdom is this blessed book; how worthy of study, even for the most enlightened in modern times!

They were not only not to marry with them, but also they were to " destroy their altars, and break down their images, and cut down their groves, and burn their graven images with fire." All that was the highest wisdom. It is astonishing how powerful is the least trace of sin; and, with the human heart inflammable, a single spark left smouldering behind may kindle a conflagration that we may never live to see the issue of. So God here says, in order to be sure to be kept right, remove from you all temptation to do wrong. I have made the remark, I think, before, in commenting on a previous chapter, that it was upon some such ground as this that John Knox acted when he swept away, not the cathedrals, for that he never wished to do, and never did, but the nunneries and convents. He thought it was better to break them all up, and practical results have testified to the wisdom of that great and good man; for idolatry and superstition have found no footing in the land that he so thoroughly cleansed.

We read next of God's great distinguishing love to the children of Israel; that " the Lord did not set his love upon you, nor choose you, because ye were more in

number than any people;" teaching them to notice
that it was from sovereignty that God had done them
good; and instead of being any ground for boasting,
there was only ground for humility, for thanksgiving,
and for praise.   God selected them in spite of their
demerits; his love lighted upon them notwithstanding
their sins; and he ma῾ them his people, not because
they were a prosperou῾, ᾿ mighty, or a powerful
people—but because he loved them.   That expression
is in all respects worthy of ῾῾᾿ ῾ chose them in
spite of their being the fewest of people; "He did
not set his love upon you, nor choose you, because ye
were more in number than any people; but because
he loved you."   "He loved you."   Now that very
remark is one of the striking traits of Deity.   When
man loves, he loves because of something loveable in
the object loved ; when God loves, he loves in spite of
the absence of everything loveable.   Man loves the
creature because the creature has in it something
loveable; God loves the creature notwithstanding its
unloveableness, in order to make it loveable.   The
one love is that of a creature, dependent upon an excitement without; the other is the love of Deity,—
sovereign, making the creature what the creature
should be ; and loving that creature in spite of sins
that deform and deface it.   So the whole economy of
the gospel is explained: "God so loved the world,
that he gave his only begotten Son, that whosoever
believeth in him might not perish, but have eternal
life."

We then read, that if the Israelites would hearken
to these judgments that God had laid down, he would
love them still, and bless them, and multiply them,

and give them all kinds of temporal blessings. The Israelites did not do so; as a nation they apostatized from God; their last sin was the rejection of the Saviour; that weighty sin, under the pressure of which every Jew upon our streets is bowed down and broken this day. You have only to read what is stated in Deuteronomy, and in subsequent chapters of this book, to see the land of Palestine, at this moment, uttering a voice from beneath every blighted acre, from beneath every rock and hill, " Thy word, O God, is truth." There is no more striking or impressive evidence of the inspiration of the prophecies of this book than to take the book of Deuteronomy, and the chapters that succeed that which I have now read, and to compare them with the Jew in any land, and especially with the Jew in what once was his own land, and is his in destiny or in reversion still, though not now in possession.

Then he encourages them by saying, " If thou shalt say in thine heart, These nations are more than I, how can I dispossess them?" God says, " Thou shalt not be afraid;" but remember the past, and remember what God is, and know that you shall succeed. Now we are taught by this—and this is a very important lesson—that in war we are not to look so much at the greatness of the host that is opposed to us, as to the goodness of the cause in which we are embarked. A few, with a right cause behind them, and a right object before them, will be more than masters over the greatest multitude that have a bad cause, and an evil and a wicked design. If we could only in all our national and social duties, and in the solemn crisis in which we now are, when event

I

thunders upon event, startling the wide world, and making the most atheistic feel there is a God, and a God acting, governing, arranging, disposing, from the palace to the hut, if we felt more assured that right is might, that God with us is more than ten thousand times ten thousand against us, we should go into the path of duty with unswerving hearts, unfainting spirits; and the expectation of success, apart from anything else, is success. Not that this should lead us to neglect duty: nothing can be more absurd than the notion that some men have, "If we are only sure that we are right, and that the cause is right; and if we only pray, we may leave all the rest." Pray to God for his blessing as the first thing; but do not neglect your commissariat as the second thing: pray to God that he would prosper the cause that is right; but do not leave all in confusion as the next thing; but combine that confidence in God which becomes the Christian, with that practical and personal exertion which acts and toils as if all depended upon it. The apparent contradictory, but really harmonious feeling of a Christian is, "I will look up to God for his blessing as if I were absolutely paralyzed; and, secondly, I will go out and work as if all depended upon my exertions, and yet my heart looking above them." Thus praying, thus working, God, our own God, will bless us.

CHAPTER VIII.

A FATHER'S APPEAL. THE FOOD AND RAIMENT OF ISRAEL.
OUR LIFE STILL MIRACULOUS. WARNINGS AGAINST UN-
THANKFULNESS. CONTENTMENT.

How full of instructive counsels and paternal affection is the interesting, I might say the eloquent
chapter now read! It is a Father speaking to his
family, the Fountain of all mercies addressing the
recipients of them, and appealing to what is deepest,
tenderest, and fullest in the human heart, in order to
ensure obedience to his law, and progress in conformity with his holy and his blessed will. He tells
them that all the commandments that he gave he
wished them to do; and on their doing so was con-
tingent their possession of that land in all its fertility
and riches which he had long promised to their
fathers. He gives them the moral history of their
progress through the wilderness : " He humbled thee,
and suffered thee to hunger." But for what purpose?
That you might be fed with celestial manna; he suffered you to meet with affliction, in order that you
might taste the riches of inexhaustible comfort; and
that he might assure you, and make you feel that man
lives not by bread which the earth yields, but by
God's blessing on it; and by every word that proceedeth out of his mouth.

Then he reminds them of their past experience :

"Thy raiment waxed not old upon thee." It seems the opinion of most that their raiment was preserved by a ceaseless and miraculous presence. It is quite plain that in marching through a desert—about 600,000 armed men,—with their wives and their children, making a mass of human beings amounting nearly to two millions, it is quite impossible that during the lapse of forty years the raiment with which they left Egypt, or such stores as they could place in their wardrobes and were able to carry with them, could have endured for a fourth of that long period. It is

quite plain that as there was no means of supply in the desert, no possibility of a commissariat with them equal to their wants, they must have been sustained by a ceaseless miracle with food, and clothed by the ceaseless and immediate beneficence of Him whose people, and care, and flock they were. And therefore he appeals to them, that by a ceaseless miracle they were fed, by a ceaseless miracle they were clothed; and therefore, seeing that they owed so much to God, the least they could do as the expression of their gratitude to Him, was to keep the commandments of the Lord their God. Now it is true that they were thus fed and thus clothed by a miracle; but it is no less true that we are clothed and fed still, not in a way equally impressive to the senses, but in a way equally supernatural. Why does the seed, cast into the soil, germinate and grow up into a golden

harvest? It is by God. Why, at this moment, are we clothed as we are? It is by antecedent processes that we call natural; but which are just as much the inspiration and action of God as when he suffered not their raiment to wax old upon them. Only in the one case he clothed them in a way contrary to what are called the laws of nature; in the latter case he acts with a uniformity that we come to place in the room of the actor, and so sinfully we give glory to the laws of nature, instead of glory to the God of nature.

He then tells them that when he bringeth them into a good land, a land of brooks and water; a land of wheat, and barley, and vines, and pomegranates; a land of oil olive, and honey; a land wherein they shall eat bread without scarceness; whose very stones are iron, and out of whose hills they might dig copper; then he says, "When you are brought into this land, a land of all good things, take care of a reaction in the opposite way. When you were without these things you repined; when you shall have them you will be ungrateful." What a strange phenomenon is man! When he wants, he murmurs that he has not obtained what he deserves; when he is full, he gives praise to himself, his own genius, or his good fortune. And thus prosperity and adversity equally serve in the case of the unrenewed heart to draw it away from God. God therefore warns them, "When thou hast eaten and art full—surrounded with all the blessings of the earth below, and with all the blessings of the heaven above—then beware of the tendency that develops itself in such circumstances: beware that thou forget not the Lord thy God." "Lest when thou hast eaten and art full, and hast built goodly houses, and dwelt therein; and when thy herds and thy flocks multiply, and thy silver and thy gold is multiplied, and all that thou hast is multiplied; that thine heart be lifted up." The Being that wrote this knew the human heart; he was acquainted with its history, he thoroughly appreciated all its tendencies; and therefore he makes provision for them all. "Beware, lest thine heart be lifted up, and thou forget the Lord thy God, which brought thee forth out of the land of Egypt, from the house of bondage; who led thee through that great and terrible wilderness; who brought thee forth water out of the rock of flint; who fed thee in the wilderness with manna, which thy fathers knew not. And beware of the monstrous wickedness of saying, after this experience of a ceaseless miracle, My power and the might of mine hand hath gotten me this wealth." They did so; they repined against God when pilgrims and strangers in the desert; they idolized and glorified themselves when they obtained the good land; they degenerated into a dark and overshadowing apostasy; and their sins expelled them from that land into which their own merits did not bring them, and have left them till this day wanderers over all the face of the earth; a people without a country, a family without a home; bearing the deep and indelible marks of their past history, and showing how evil a thing it is to rebel against God, and to depart from the ways in which he has commanded them to walk.

Let us learn from the whole of this interesting review, in adversity to trust, in prosperity to pray; never to murmur if we have not what we think we should have, because we may depend upon it its absence is best for us; never to be proud when we have what God has given us, but to hold it as his; and to give him the praise, the thanksgiving, and the glory.

I do not know a more touching recapitulation of distinguishing providential mercies showered down from heaven upon earth than what is contained in this chapter. God, by his servant Moses, recapitulates in it all that God had done, the design that he had in view, and also the effects, the inadequate effects that so great mercies produced upon so highly favoured and so privileged a people. He says, " Thou shalt remember all the way which the Lord thy God led thee these forty years in the wilderness "—a very long period; and the end of it, " to humble thee "—what we all need,—" and to prove thee;" that we may know whether our Christianity be a name or a reality; "and that thou mightest know what was in thine heart." And then he tells them that their raiment waxed not old. In their case it was miraculously ever kept new; in our case the old is laid aside, and new is supplied; and the providential goodness in giving us raiment to wear, air to breathe, and bread to eat in the nineteenth century, though we connect it with visible causes and visible means, is not less real and not less precious than the special providential power that kept their raiment from waxing old, their feet from swelling, and their shoes from wearing out. It is just as much a miracle in God to give us bread from making a stalk germinate from a seed, grow into the ripe ear, be ground, and baked into useful household bread, as it was in raining manna from heaven, and in striking the flinty rock that they might be refreshed thereby. There is no more connexion really, except in God's will, between a seed cast into the soil and the feeding of millions, than there was between a cloud passing over the sky and depositing manna upon the fields, or upon the desert. It is God's fiat that makes the connexion; only we

are so accustomed to the one process, that we call it
natural, that is, we try to account for it without God;
and we are so unaccustomed to the other process, that
we call it supernatural; or we feel driven to admit the
presence and the power of God. But God is just as
mighty, as present, and as really so, when he works
with means, as when he works without means. No
good and beneficent result can happen to us except
by his immediate power; and whether he is pleased
to give that result in spite of means, or without
means, or through means, it is equally sovereign
power, unmerited goodness, divine beneficence. He
tells them, therefore, that it was the Lord that was
bringing them into a good land. And then, at the
close of the chapter, and in that passage which I have
just read to you, he bids them beware, lest they forget
God; he bids them beware, lest as they despaired
when they had not, they should become proud when
they had; lest as they murmured and repined against
God when they were hungry, they should begin to
congratulate themselves, and take to themselves all
the credit, when they were full and increased in goods.
And therefore he says, "When thy herds and thy
flocks multiply, and thy silver and thy gold is multiplied, and all that thou hast is multiplied; take care
lest thine heart be lifted up." How sad that our
want of what we need should make us fret against
God; that our possession of what we need should
make us forget God! What a strange thing that the
very largeness of the gift should intercept our apprehension and sight of the blessed Giver! How sad is
it, and how strikingly demonstrative of the great
eclipse that has passed upon us all, that the more the

creature has, not the more thankful he feels, but the more forgetful he is of the God that blessed him! I know not whether we have most need of prayer when we have not, or when we have. When we have not, we may pray that we may have; but when we have, we should pray that we may never forget, or our hearts be lifted up, or tempted to give expression to the feeling, "Mine own hand and mine own power hath gotten me this."

Now, you will notice in the part of the chapter I have read that he recapitulates to them the distinguishing blessings that they had received; and bids them take care lest they should forget Him who had thus blessed them. The very first that he mentions is, that God delivered them out of the land of Egypt and from the house of bondage. Now we should have thought that slaves snatched from the brick-kilns of Egypt never could have forgotten that they were there, and that by God's outstretched hand, and in spite of Pharaoh's power, they were delivered and emancipated from them. One would almost think it was an insult to humanity to say, "Do not forget that you were once slaves, and that God has graciously and mercifully delivered you." And yet God estimated man aright. God saw that the slave, made a freeman by distinguishing goodness, would forget, and in some cases deny that he ever was a slave at all; for no man is so forgetful of his past as he who has been delivered from the deepest depression, and elevated to the greatest privilege. God therefore says to them, "Take care, lest you forget that you were once bondmen." The Israelites did forget; their hearts were lifted up; they maintained with falsehood, that only equalled their folly, " We were always free, and never were slaves to any man." But we learn a lesson from this. Have we been delivered? Were we once the slaves, the unreluctant slaves of Satan, and of sin, and of the world? Did we once live, obeying the world's wish, actuated by the world's motives, looking forward only to the world's profits ? Were we once as completely under the jurisdiction of this world as if there were no future; as entirely the slaves of sense, and sin, and passion, and prejudice, as if there was no freedom either promised or possible to us ? And have we been delivered? Are we now actuated by new motives, drawn onward by bright hopes ? Do we now feel, " Thou, God, seest me ? " Are we translated into the freedom of God's sons, into the dignity of God's servants ? If we are, are we ever tempted to forget who it is that has delivered us; who it is that has snatched us from the brick-kilns, not of Pharaoh, but from the bondage and corruption of the wicked one ? Are we ever prone to thank our good luck, our talent, our genius; the sermon we heard, the minister that preached, the privileges we enjoyed, instead of looking above them and beyond them, and giving all the praise to Him who alone in his sovereign mercy has kept our eyes from tears, our feet from falling, and delivered our souls from death ?

But he goes on to say, not only that God delivered them out of the house of bondage, but "led thee through the great and terrible wilderness, wherein were fiery serpents, and scorpions, and drought." Now one would suppose that it was almost supererogation in Moses to warn the children of Israel never to forget that they had been led through the great and terrible wilderness. Why, how could they forget? We know quite well how little disposed we are to forget circumstances of great danger, or of extraordinary difficulty, through which we have been led. The Israelites, for instance, had seen the Red Sea open its waves, make itself into a pathway for them to march through dryshod; they had stood upon the opposite bank and seen all the hosts, and the cavalry, and the chariots of Pharaoh engulfed in the midst of it. One would have thought it would be very difficult to forget that fact. Another thing they had seen was, in the dark night, when there was not a taper upon earth, or a star twinkling in the firmament, a flame, at least a mile in height, its base thirty, forty, fifty feet in breadth, touching the earth, and its top soaring a mile towards the firmament, all blazing splendour, brighter than noon-day, marched before them; where it halted they halted; when it moved they moved; and it always guided them, not in the way they wanted, but in the way that was best. One would think they could scarcely ever forget that. And, in the daytime again, when the sultry sun sent down his intense and all but intolerable splendour upon their naked heads, this same pillar of fire turned itself into a massive pillar of cloud, that shaded them from the sultry heat, and still guided them through the intricacies of the perplexing desert, and always in the right way. Now, one would think it would be impossible for flesh and blood to forget such extraordinary phenomena as these; one would infer it must be supererogation to bid a people recollect this. Yet that very people forgot it; conveniently forgot it; expunged it from their memories, because they did not wish to feel in their hearts indebted to God as their guide and leader through the desert by the fiery pillar by night, and by the cloudy pillar by day. Now let us feel, however, that we, too, may forget God's goodness to us just as really, and far more sinfully, than they forgot his goodness in guiding them. We, too, are in a desert; not a physical one, which could be easily trodden; but a moral one, which is very difficult, and hard, and desolate indeed. We have wants that the world cannot fill; a hunger that its bread cannot supply, a nakedness that its raiment cannot cover. We are pilgrims and strangers, ever wanting to be happy, never absolutely happy by anything that the world can give. We find God giving us bread from heaven; satisfying our hearts, not by something visible that we can taste, and handle, and eat; but by an inspiration that is real, actual, and true—keeping us from falling, defending us from ourselves; and when we are on the verge of going wrong, mysteriously but truly putting us right—guiding us at this moment as really, through this world's desert, as he ever guided Israel. Are you not conscious, that many a time, if you had turned an inch to the right, you had been destroyed; and that some impulse that you could not account for made you move to the left, and made you thus happy? Are you not conscious that it depended upon this little incident, upon that accidental encounter, upon this incidental circumstance, that you were saved from great peril, delivered from great sin, preserved amid great mercies? And what is this but the cloud by day, and the fiery pillar by night; or, rather, the God that was in both, guiding his people through the desert, keeping them as the apple of his eye, and saving them from what would be their everlasting ruin? He gives us all the goodness, he exacts only all the glory. Beware, lest you forget who it is that guides and keeps you in the great and terrible wilderness!

It is added, too, very beautifully, that he not only guided them through the desert; but also, " he brought water out of the rock of flint; and fed thee in the wilderness with manna, which thy fathers knew not." Now, one would suppose that here, too, it would be impossible for the children of Israel ever to forget this. They must have recollected that all the food they took out of Egypt was soon exhausted; that all the water they carried on their camels was soon spent; that the desert grew no corn; that if they sowed it they would not be in the same place to reap it, even if the soil would produce it. They must, therefore, have recollected that if God had not given them manna, which their fathers knew not, spiritual bread from heaven that they never had before, that they must have perished in the desert of very hunger. They must have recollected that the springs in the desert were few and far between; that there were no rivers; that the salt sea could not satisfy their thirst. They must have recollected, surely, that Moses smote the rock with his rod, at the bidding of God, and that water gushed from the rock of flint. How could they forget this? How was it possible that such phenomena could have failed to make a deep and lasting impression on their memories, even if they did not on their hearts?

✳ Yet the truth is, and you will find it in the Psalms,✳ that they forgot it all, and not only forgot it all, but their children denied it all; they assumed the credit of feeding themselves; they took all the glory of their own commissariat; they forgot God their Saviour; and, therefore, it was with prophetic knowledge that Moses said, "Take care, lest ye forget that he fed you with manna, that your fathers knew not; and opened the flinty rock that he might refresh you with water that they had never tasted."

✳ But let us take the lesson to ourselves. We have been fed all our life long; the worst of us have had more than we ever deserved; some of us have had more than we ever expected. We have had not only temporal, but spiritual mercies. God has given us his truth; he has told us that "man doth not live by bread alone, but by every word that proceedeth from the mouth of God." He has given us, therefore, living bread; he has fed us with spiritual nutriment. We do know what thousands do not know; we do feel what thousands do not feel; we have motives, we have hopes, we have a happiness, we have a peace, through the knowledge of the contents of this blessed book, and from Him who is the Author of them, that millions of our race know nothing of. It is a matter that we cannot doubt, that we are made to differ; it is palpable, visible, unmistakable, that we who are Christians have something, feel something, taste something, know something; live, act, hope, rejoice, in a way that they who are not Christians do not. Who has made you to differ? Beware, lest you forget Him who has fed you with manna, that the world knows not of; who has opened the flinty rock and refreshed you with streams that the world appreciates not. If the Israelites were guilty, in expunging from their memories so great and hallowed recollections, how much more guilty shall we be if we expel from our hearts the gratitude that is due for so rich and so distinguishing goodness? It is a pity that the very commonness of our mercies makes us insensible to them. We are never so ungrateful as when God is most beneficent. It is very odd; one can scarcely understand it, though one may explain it; when we have not we think, "Oh, how thankful should we be if we only had this which we desire!" We not only get what we desire, but tenfold more, and the very magnitude of the gift makes us forget, as it hides from us the Giver.

Such, then, is the warning to Israel, such the recapitulation of their mercies. Let us apply it still more to ourselves; let us learn here a lesson for us as a nation. We are, with all our faults as a nation,— and we have many faults in rulers, in subjects, on all sides, and in all respects; but take this great nation altogether, and, since the nation of Israel, there never has been a nation so near to God. We have the privilege of an open Bible; we can read it without any man daring to ask us why, or to interpose his shadow between the eye of the reader and the page that he reads. We have the preaching of the gospel, and can go to any church or chapel that we like; and no man has a right to stand between us, and say, "Why go there?" or, "How dare you go here?" We have just laws, we have wise and righteous judges and magistrates; we have had forty years of peace; we have never seen a hostile sail upon our shores; we have never heard the tramp of a hostile foot upon our land; we are a people that have been

signally and singularly blessed and favoured and
exalted, amid the nations of the earth. Take heed
lest you forget to whom the glory and the thanksgiving are due; for the moment that a nation says,
"It is our Saxon blood; it is our insular situation;
it is the heroism of our troops, or the intrepidity
of our sailors, that have made us so," its right hand
will part with its strength; and we shall learn,
as our boasting has led us to learn, that it is not by
might, nor by power, but by God's blessing that we
can prosper and prevail. In the next place, let us
learn here a lesson for all Christians. Are we forgiven? Whose is the glory? Are we regenerated?
To whom do we owe the praise? Are we walking in
the light, while surrounding churches are involved in
apostasy? Are we worshipping Jesus only, whilst
millions in Europe are worshipping practically the
Virgin Mary? Have we the privilege of an open
Bible, while they have none? Are we, as Christians,
blessed, and exalted, and privileged, and favoured?
Beware, lest you forget who it is that opens the
heavens to give us manna, and the flinty rock to give
us water, and to whom is due the thanksgiving, and
the praise, and the honour, and the glory. The greater
our privileges, the richer our mercies, the greater is
our guilt in undervaluing the one or forgetting the
other. "Take heed, lest there be in any of you an
evil heart of unbelief, in departing from the living
God." But let us, by humble prayer, seek blessings
from God; and when we have obtained them, let us,
by heartfelt praise, acknowledge, "Not unto us, not
unto us, but unto thy name, O Lord, be the glory."
Amen and Amen.

CHAPTER VIII.

THE following practical lesson is worthy of our
deepest study :—

> "And thou shalt remember all the way which the Lord thy
> God led thee these forty years in the wilderness, to
> humble thee, and to prove thee, to know what was in
> thine heart, whether thou wouldest keep his command-
> ments, or no."—DEUT. viii. 2.

BY the very constitution of things under which
we live youth is prospective, always stretching into
futurity. Old age is retrospective, always searching
the transactions of the past, and drawing from them
either hopes or joys for the future. The prospective
future is delineated in the page of prophecy; and
from it we may imbibe joys and comforts for the
present: the retrospect of the past is contained in
our own biography. The most level and ordinary life
has incidents, and accidents, and mercies, and miracles as real, if not as resplendent, as the Israelites
in the desert. Our present exercise is retrospective.
"Thou shalt remember all the way." It is the func-

K

tion of memory that is here alluded to. It is a review,
a clear and impartial review, of all the scenes through
which we have passed, during, in some cases, twenty,—
in some forty, in some sixty,—and in some, it may be,
seventy years. That we may derive from the retrospect
that humility which becomes sinners, that trust which
is the privilege of Christians, that hope that may cheer
us as we descend into the valley of life, and cherish
the prospect of an upward and endless ascent, the
Holy Spirit is promised to improve memory. We often
think that the Holy Spirit changes the heart only ;
but there is a special promise, that " he will bring all
things to your remembrance, whatsoever I have said
unto you." Regeneration touches to a finer issue
every faculty of the soul ; impresses the heart with
deeper susceptibility of truth ; improves the memory,
so that it recollects those things to which the heart
is instinctive enmity ; and thus the whole man, with
all his affections, faculties, powers, hopes, and recollections, is regenerated, sanctified, improved. I have
said the Holy Spirit improves the memory. We
might see this from the fact that this faculty is so
often referred to in Scripture : " Remember thy
Creator in the days of thy youth," indicating our
proneness to forget him. " Remember the Sabbath
day to keep it holy ; " an ancient institution that we
need to recollect, not a new constitution that we need
for the first time to accept. " Do this in remembrance
of me," is the last command of our Blessed Lord.
What a wondrous faculty is memory ! If hope has its
pleasures, as one poet has beautifully sung, memory
has its treasures, as another poet has no less sweetly
sung. And when one thinks what memory is ; that

every incident that happens in life hangs up its shadow in that mysterious picture gallery of the past; that on every page of its countless tablets there is impressed, by every incident and accident, however minute, a memorial that never can be altogether washed away; when we think of its wondrous and its countless cells, in which every incident has been most carefully folded and deposited; and that a scene, an accident, an incident, a sermon, a conversation, will bring forth from their sleeping places phantoms we thought evanished for ever, and make real and actual in the present all the scenes and transactions of the past, we must be struck with the wondrous power of that faculty we are called upon here to exercise, and pray that a gift of so great power may be richly renewed and sanctified by the Holy Spirit of God. If memory be so important, let me suggest, as I pass, how useful it is to store it in early days with precious and instructive truths. The memory of the young is intensely susceptible. What is given to it it holds with a grasp, which is rarely, if ever, relaxed. I appeal to the old, is it not your experience that the events of last week you very easily forget, but the events of your earliest days come up at your bidding with a freshness, a force, and a beauty, that translate the past into the present, and make your heart feel green and young again? If thoughts impressed in our earlier years are so deeply engraven upon the heart; if memory, in the declining days of life, brings up so freshly the scenes, the lessons, the thoughts of our earlier years; then you cannot too richly store the susceptible memory of the young with instructive, useful, and guiding truths, drawn from the fountain of truth, God's holy and blessed word.

In this call to take a retrospect of the past, you will notice it is not a retrospect for any sentimental or abstract purpose ; it is for a personal and practical improvement. " Thou shalt remember all the way that the Lord thy God led thee, to humble thee and to prove thee." It is not a sentimental review ; it is not recollections put in exercise in order to draw up a journal, or to replenish a diary ; but it is memory made subservient to the sanctification of the heart, to the humbling of pride, to the testing of character, to the glory of God. It is that you may descend into the depths of your memory, and come forth, like the man that descended into the grave of Elisha, reinvigorated, revived, sanctified, refreshed. It is memory here that you are asked to make subservient to your heart, a minister to the growth of your soul, an aid in preparing for happiness and for heaven. Let us, then, pray that the Spirit of God, who alone can sanctify the memory as well as the heart, may sanctify ours. Let us try to review all the way in the wilderness which the Lord our God has led us these forty years. Let us notice the nature and the scene of the journey. It is all the way in the wilderness. Now, in the case of Israel it was physically a desert ; there was no flower or fruit ; no springs, except what God's mercy struck from the rock ; no green fields, and bread only in the shape of manna from heaven ; so that the scene of their journey was literally a desert. Is ours in any sense so ? Can it be said, for instance, that the man who has lands, and houses, and wealth, and dignities, and influence, and power, is in any respect a pilgrim; or that the scene of his progress is aught but a triumphant and a beautiful march? They that know their own hearts best, know that this world, even in its sunniest and its greenest spots, is, after all, an unsatisfactory desert. They may be clad in purple and fine linen every day; they may feed upon the finest of the wheat; they may fare sumptuously; yet these feel capacities within them that all the springs of time cannot fill; wants, and aches, and chasms in the depths of their soul, that all the riches of the world never can supply. They feel that in this world, on its loftiest pinnacles, in its most favoured, loved, and envied spots, there is no more rest for the soul, than there is for the sailor, tossed upon the stormy ocean; or for the pilgrim of ancient Israel, when he marched through the desert, with his back on Egypt, and his face towards Canaan. It is not the mere fanatic, or ascetic, but the truest and the most advanced Christian, who feels in greatest force, "This is not my rest. I find my soul bigger than this world; I feel my heart yearning for a joy which this world cannot give. I ever am to be blessed; I never am actually blessed." Common sense looking round would conclude that this world cannot be our Paradise; it cannot be in its present estate our heaven. Once it was the garden of the Lord; but all its fragrance and its beauty have perished like a dream. Man sinned, and man's abode instantly was shattered. To learn what it is, count its graves, its battle-fields, its autumns, its winters, its wrecks. The ruins of our world exceed in number its restorations; its dead sleeping in its bosom outnumber vastly the living that are treading on its streets. How any one can suppose that God made this world as it is, or meant it, as it now is, to be a home, I cannot easily conceive. In its best estate it is a desert; in its best condition we feel it cannot meet the wants of our nature. Do you, therefore, regard it as a journey? Do you pass through it with the speed and the disinterestedness of a pilgrim and a stranger? Or are you trying to build up your happiness upon earth, or to find a rest here? If so, you are spending money for that which is not bread, and your labour for that which will not satisfy; for when you have done all, you will find it is not your rest; that its springs are cisterns, and those broken and unable to hold water.

If such, then, be the world through which we are passing, let me look, in the second place, to the way on its face along which we are led:—"Thou shalt remember all the way in the wilderness which the Lord thy God led thee." To an Israelite this must have been, indeed, a thrilling and splendid recollection. First, they would recollect their triumphant march from Egypt, with the pursuing hosts of Pharaoh; next, the Red Sea cleaving in twain to form a march for the chosen of God, and to collapse upon the pursuing hosts of Pharaoh. They would next recollect that water came from the flint, rather than that they should be exhausted and perish; that the very clouds of heaven rained down bread lest they should feel hungry; and that a pillar of supernatural fire marched through the desert by night to lead them, and a pillar of supernatural cloud overshadowed

them with its cool and refreshing presence amid the
sultriness of noon-day. They would recollect that
though their course was often zig-zag, occasionally re-
trograde, it was always right, best for them, and most
for the honour of God. They would recollect mercies
that were fresh every morning, and sins that were
forgiven every night; judgments mitigated or sus-
pended, or altogether withdrawn, though by them
they were terribly provoked. As they remembered
all the way, so radiant with startling incidents, so
lighted up with mercies, and beneficence, and goodness, and miracles, they would surely, O surely, give
the praise, and glory, and honour to Him, whose presence had been a ceaseless miracle, whose hand had
been ever open, in whom they had literally lived, and
moved, and had their being.

But if the Israelites had so splendid and so startling
a march as that which I have tried to delineate, is
there nothing in our way—for we, too, are in the way,
as it is called in the Acts of the Apostles—as supernatural, though not so splendidly and visibly so, which
we are called upon to recollect, and to give honour,
and praise, and thanksgiving to God for? Let me
appeal to the last twenty years, the last thirty, or the
last forty years, and let me ask you first to think of
your sins. It is painful to think of them; it is profitable, nevertheless. Are there no sins whose shadows
on your memory are at this moment deep, dark,
sharply defined? Is there no one sin that at this
moment projects a shadow from the past, lying cold
and chill upon the conscience? Are there not sins
in your past, — thanks be to God, forgiven by his
mercy, but that can never be expunged from your

memory, or permanently forgotten? Let me ask you to review, if not prominent sins, resolves nipped in the bud, vows formed by the bed of sickness and of suffering, that you never carried into action. Though such a retrospect may be a very painful one to the sensitive conscience of the Christian, it is a very profitable one; for its result will be what the review of Israel was intended to be, to humble you and to prove you, and to know what is in your heart. But I should be sorry if your retrospect of your journey referred only to the dark days in the past. Our journey has been, like the April day, clouds and sunshine, tears and smiles. If we have thought of the dark clouds, let us not shut our eyes to the bright mercies that have leaped from their bosoms. Therefore, I ask you to review your mercies. Does not an impartial retrospect reveal mercies in your past, shining like the dew-drops upon the blades of the morning, and as countless also? Has not daily bread been supplied when its failure seemed inevitable? Has not health been restored when you thought it was gone for ever? Have you not had all the reality of Israel's miracles without the lightning splendour of them and the thunder at their heels? Have you not been equally fed by a divine presence, and have you not often found spiritual blessings burst from the cloud, careering, dark and threatening, on your horizon, when you were expecting it would burst in desolating and in overwhelming judgments? Does not your memory contain many an Ebenezer, " Hitherto the Lord hath helped me," that eternity will not overturn? Are you not at this moment conscious that there are mercies in the past undeserved, unexpected, and often unsought in prayer, whose lineaments are so deeply engraven upon your hearts that the wear and tear of this world will never be able utterly to expunge them ?

If you recollect your sins, they should humble you; do not forget, in the midst of those sins, in spite of those sins,—and what is more mysterious still, to which those sins were overruled,—great, unmerited and rich mercies. But in taking a retrospect of all the way that the Lord has led you, let me ask you also to review and take a retrospect of your greatest mercies, commonly known by the name of afflictions. Let me ask you to review them. These were bitter whilst they were tasted, grievous whilst you endured them; but they have been, as you can testify and feel, sanctified and profitable in their action. Trace the issue of the bitterest moment that you ever passed through; and I venture to assert that without an exception, you will find it has been a blessed dispensation to your soul. Trace the result of the sorest blow, of the most painful and pining trial, of the most severe and almost insupportable ordeal; and you will be constrained to say, that, at least, it weaned you from the excessive love of a world that was becoming your idol; it lifted your heart to seek, and grope, and search for something nobler, better, more enduring than the world can supply. It dimmed the sheen and the glare of things seen and temporal; and if it covered the earth with its densest pall, it was only like the night, that covers up the splendours of the earth below to reveal the lustre of ten thousand suns in the firmament above you. I ask of the most afflicted, the most oppressed in the past, have you not found that your saddest days have been your most sanctifying, and your most sorrowful hours your sweetest? and that the afflictions that saturated your heart as the dew does the soil, softened it and subdued it also? Have not poignant losses been to you great gains? And when your near, your dear, your most cherished passed away like airy shadows from the dial of time, was it not to draw your hearts into closer, more intimate, more tender contact with the glories and the lights of eternity? As the earthly home became darkened, did not the heavenly one seem brighter? As your father's house grew desolate on earth, did not the many mansions seem more beautiful in heaven? And are you not constrained— is it not your experience—I appeal not to facts, I appeal to that which is deepest and truest in the human heart—is it not your experience that your light affliction, which was but for a moment, wrought out for you a far more exceeding, even an eternal weight of glory? and though no tribulation for the present seemeth joyous, yet afterwards it worketh out the peaceable fruits of righteousness to them that are exercised thereby? Take, then, a review of the sins that have stained you, that you may be humbled in the very dust; take a retrospect of the mercies that have glistened in your way, and tracked your footsteps, that you may be thankful as you never were before. Take a retrospect of the disguised mercies, clothed in the mournful garbs of affliction, and you will be constrained to say that these were the choicest, the dearest, and the highest ministries that God ever vouchsafed to your soul in all the way in the wilderness in which he has led you.

In all this retrospect God reminds them that it was he, the Lord their God, that led them,—" the Lord thy God hath led thee." Now I have no doubt it often seemed to the Israelites as if God was too busy with great things to condescend to notice the minute things of their march; or that they were too insignificant to command the sympathies and the presence of the great God of Israel. But that is not so. How often have I said, what every day becomes only clearer, —there are no accidents in providential history any more than there are interpolations in God's written Scripture. For every accident in providential history that you can prove to me God had nothing to do with, I will show you, what I know is impossible, an interpolation in the chapters of the Bible which God's Holy Spirit never inspired. But the one is just as impossible as the other. God is as much in the tiniest text in the Bible as he is in the Old and New Testament together; and he is as much in the minutest incident, that the world calls an accident, in history, as he is in the fall of the avalanche, in the death of the Czar, in the destruction of a dynasty, in the overturning of a throne. Nay, minute things are often, in their issues, more stupendous than the things that we call great, and that, in our estimate, really and truly are so. If God be thus in all things, I must see and feel that God led me all the way through the desert. Amid miracles and mercies God has led me. And to show the very minuteness of his attention to the Israelites, let me read that exquisitely beautiful text, in this same Book of Deuteronomy: " God found Israel in a desert land, and in the waste howling wilderness; he led him about, he instructed him, he kept him "—what an exquisite thought!—" as the apple of his eye." Just think of that thought. Whenever, by a strange and exquisite arrangement in our organization, a mote, however minute, approaches the eye, without our having the least thought or taking the least precaution, the eyelid closes instinctively upon it, and shelters it. Well, a believer is to God—beautiful thought!—as the apple of his eye. When that believer is exposed to what is real peril— not seeming, but real peril—God's omnipotence, like an eyelid, closes over the humblest believer, and he is safe as if he were in the everlasting arms, in the very presence of the third heaven itself. " He kept him as the apple of his eye." " As an eagle stirreth up her nest, fluttereth over her young, spreadeth abroad her wings, taketh them, beareth them on her wings: so the Lord did lead him." In the northern mountains of Scotland, if you watch the eagle at its eyrie, when training its young, you will see in its history what is here stated. The parent bird first takes a flight a few feet above the level of the nest, that the young eaglets, just fledged, and preparing to fly, may imitate her example. She will then take a loftier sweep, more majestic and of longer diameter, that they may make a bolder experiment. And when she has provoked the eaglet to ascend too high, or beyond its physical infant strength; just as the eaglet finds its tender muscles give way, and begins to fall like a stone, the parent eagle will dash down with the speed of a thunder-bolt beneath it, intercept its descent, catch the eaglet upon its back, between its wings, and bear it to the nest again. " So did the Lord thy God carry thee." How true, how tender, how watchful, the care of Him who has led us all the way through the wilderness! Can you doubt that this is more or less your experience also? I will put it in this way:—Has not often an unexpected incident that you neither dreamed of nor anticipated at the moment, shot up, whence you knew not, and how you could not say, and so intercepted the course you were pursuing, that, in after life, you were constrained to say, "If that incident had not shot up at that very moment, if it had been a minute earlier or a minute later, I had gone where I had, humanly speaking, perished for ever"? Are you not constrained, as you take the retrospect, to say, "If that incidental conversation had not taken place at some one's dinner table, or in some one's drawing-room, or in the cabin of a ship, or in a railway carriage, I had never thought of going to that place of worship, where I heard the sermon that was the turning point in my everlasting destiny"? Have you not been constrained to feel that it was the turning of a corner—nay, I will take a more proverbial, but not the less significant expression,—that it was the turning of a straw that has made you the wife of that husband, or the husband of that wife; the son of that father,—the father of that son? Grant me that there are any incidents in the chapter of human life so minute as to have nothing to do with God's immediate action, and I will go logically and consistently to the conclusion that there is no God at all; and that we are an orphan world, and a fatherless family, without a hope and without a home.

I appeal to you again. In taking a retrospect of all the way, has not an unseen hand often protected you from yourselves, and made you what you now are? Has not often a mysterious thread appeared in the intricacies of the labyrinth, in which all was dark and puzzled and perplexed, and guided you through; and when you knew not which was the way—the blind walking in a way they knew not—has not a voice with all the softness of the tones of a Father's whispered in the chambers of your soul unmistakeable and clear, " This is the way ; walk ye in it ? " If you have not had the literal pillar of fire as Israel had, do you think you have been without guidance? If you have not had the clouds as your commissariat, have you been without provision in your journey through the way in the battle of life? Nay, Red Seas have cloven in twain for you to go through; pillars of fire have blazed in the desert to guide you ; rocks have burst to refresh you, and clouds have rained down manna to feed you; and when you walked through the flame it did not kindle upon you, and through the waters they did not overflow you. But God with me is as great and magnificent a reality as it was 1800 years before Christ, the Light to lighten the Gentiles, and the glory of his people Israel. I do believe it is a grievous error, into which thousands plunge, that God was before the Flood, at Sinai, and in the desert; but that God has now, having done so much for the world, left it alone to make the best of its way to its everlasting rest. My dear friends, he is the Alpha and the Omega; he is as near, as close to me—to you—to the sailor in the Euxine—to the soldier in the Crimea, as he ever was to Abraham, to Isaac, to Jacob, to Moses, or to Isaiah ; and he takes as deep an interest in the obscurest Christian in the realms of

our Queen as he ever took in Joshua, the leader of
the hosts of Israel. Do not entertain the idea, God
was; do not be satisfied with the definition, God is;
but glory in the blessed thought that He not only is,
but acts, and is near to every one of us; and that in
him we literally live, and move, and have our being.
This thought, that God is thus taking care of me,
watching over me, remembering me, when I forget
him and forget myself together, is one of the most
consolatory thoughts. It makes heroes out of
cowards; it makes martyrs out of timid believers;
it gives the heart a pulse, and the soul a hope, and
the whole Christian life an energy, a direction, and a
shape that brings heaven to earth, and covers the
lowliest floor of this world with as great a grandeur
and a consecration as the sacred floor of the temple of
Jerusalem itself.

Having seen, by an appeal to everyone's own experience, the *desert* in which we are, the *way* in which
we have been led, and the marks in that way, and the
leader in it, let me call your attention, in the next
place, to the object of it. I stated in the commencement of my remarks, that the great design of God in
thus leading his people, whether in ancient days or
now, was not a sentimental one, or a mere exercise of
the memory, but that it had a great personal and
practical object; namely, first of all to humble them;
first of all, I say, to humble them. What! the Israelites perishing for want of bread, and water, and
clothing, in the desert, needing to be humbled? One
would have thought that such beggars, such starve-
lings, needed nothing from heaven in order to make
them humble. I may say of ourselves, What! man

dependent for his heart beating another day upon the grains that grow upon the field and ripen in autumn ; compassed with infirmities, a thousand diseases seeking access to his body at every pore, in order to bring it down to the very dust; proud, conceited? Man, who knows that though his present house may be a noble or a royal hall, yet his last one must be six feet long, the worm his sister, corruption his mother—this being proud! The startling inconsistency in that strange thing, man, is that he is proud even of his sins, which ought to be his shame ; that he is proud of his mercies, as if they were his own merits ; and those things which are his shame, and which he ought to shrink from and to hate, he glories in, as some of his highest ornaments, his noblest decorations. Therefore he needs to be humbled : humility is essential in one sense, I admit in a secondary sense, but in one sense to salvation. Unless we are humbled in the dust, under a deep sense that we can never save ourselves, we shall never be induced to apply to Him who alone is able and willing to do so. Man must be emptied of everything in which he boasts, before he can be filled with grace and glory. As long as man can get one single thing to lean upon that is his own, or that he thinks his own, so long he refuses to be obliged to God for any help to heaven. And, therefore, one of God's great purposes in dealing with man is to humble him in the dust, that no flesh should glory in his sight; to lay him low upon the very earth, that he may feel that he is poor, and blind, and naked, and destitute of all things. And when we think of it, what is there in which we should be proud? What is there in our history that should not humble us? Our sins should humble us, for they are exclusively our own; our virtues and our graces should humble us, for they are none of them in any sense or shape our own. Therefore, what is our own should humble us; and what is not our own should humble us. And when God brings these before us as they are, and enables us to see that we are debtors for the least excellence, and deserve nothing, then we are humbled and laid low. About the broken ruins of an ancient castle abbey or cathedral, the green moss and incidental flowerets break out from the rifts and rents, as if they would beautify the ruin. So it is amid the wrecks of a broken heart that the sweet flowerets of humility, and lowliness, and love, and peace, begin to germinate and grow, refreshed by God's sun and watered by his dews, and adorning the character that his grace has created, and making it the admiration of others, and acceptable to himself. " What doth the Lord require of thee, but to do justly, and to love mercy, and to walk humbly with thy God?" Let us ask ourselves, are we humble? Humility is not assumption; it is not pretension; it is not speaking in a certain strain, and looking with a certain shape and definite look of countenance,—that is not humility; that may be the essence of pride. It is not wearing a monk's robe, or a Quaker's garb; that may be the covering of a prouder heart than throbs under imperial robes. But true humility is gentle: it may be playful; it is without pretension; it is without assumption. It is said the greatest genius is often the most humble; the truest humility is often the least pretentious; and to the vulgar, that cannot discriminate, that will be set down as pride which is true lowliness; but to the Christian there will be seen, under the outer aspect of eating, walking, drinking, living like other men, the true and inner elements of genuine humility in the sight of God.

But God had another design besides humbling them, namely to prove them. Not to prove them for his satisfaction, for their own comfort, and progress, and growth in grace. God puts us in darkness—now, can we walk in darkness, when we have no light, and, in the language of the prophet, trust in the Lord, and stay ourselves upon our God? That is to say, when we cannot see the end of a thing; when we are perplexed by its present influence; when we are inclined to be depressed, cast down, foreboding, gloomy, apprehensive; can we, in such circumstances—God is proving us if we can—trust in the Lord, and stay ourselves upon our God? Can we believe a promise as really, and act upon it just as we can lean upon a staff, and walk by it? Can we treat a promise in the Bible as being a no less substantial reality than a possession in the world? Can a Christian take what God has promised, and say, "This is my trust"? And can he take what God has commanded, and say, "This is my duty"; and have no hesitation, or equivocation, or doubt, upon the subject? God is testing our faith, our trust, and our confidence; he is leaving us often feeble, that we may find in him strength; he is often letting us stumble, that we may see where alone we can be supported; he sometimes leads us, so that we may feel in this dependence how true it is that we need his grace, not

only at the commencement of our career, but to keep
us every day from falling, and to present us faultless
before his presence with exceeding joy. And, then,
in his providence, he is trying us by a thousand
things. Afflictions try us. If afflictions that come
upon us be not sanctified, they are like the winter
storms that leave wreck and ruin and desolation
behind; but if afflictions be really sanctified and
sweetened to us, they are like the April showers of
spring, that usher in the bright and the everlasting
summer. Blessings also try us. When blessings
come to us do we grasp them tenaciously, as if they
were ours by right; or do we accept them meekly,
and give God the praise and the glory? Temptations
try us, in our homes, in the market, in the sanctuary,
in the world—everywhere. Opportunities of doing
good try us. Every opportunity of doing good, every
occasion when we are asked to give what will benefit
another, is testing us: it is putting our character to
the test. Religious privileges try us; our Sabbaths
try us. What use do you make of them? Our
Bibles try us; what good do you get from them?
Our sacraments try us, our sermons try us; what
good do you get from them? All these things are
meant to humble us, to test us, to develop what we
are, to bring out otherwise hidden and obscure elements, in order that we may be humble, retrace what
is wrong, recall what is bad, and trust henceforth more
implicitly in Him in whom alone we can be strong.

The whole Church of Christ is thus handled, that
God may test it, and prove it, and humble it. What
is the character of the age in which we live? De-

velopment of character; everybody's character is coming out, and being thrown up with greater clearness. If men are inclining to Romanism, their character is developed more fully. If men are loving the truth, vital and essential truth, their character is brought out more fully. The whole church of Christ, at this moment, is in the crucible; the alloy and the gold are being daily more and more separated. You remember the last stage of this dispensation is the manifestation of God's people; that is, in all their completeness in number, completeness in character; a glorious church, without spot or blemish. Now, towards that the whole church is moving; and its alloy is dropping off. There are more true Christians at the present moment, with all our faults, and wickedness, and sins, than there have been in this country for two hundred years before. Day by day the true Christian is becoming more distinct, less bigoted, less the child of form, less the creature of system, more clearly the creation of the Holy Spirit of God. And so the Romanist, the Tractarian, in all their grades, and in all their branches and shades, are becoming more and more defined, distinct, unmistakeable. A great separation is taking place every day. Every mind is finding its polarity; each going to his own place. And, by-and-by, there will be but two churches upon earth; the church of Antichrist, clustering round him, the great Apostasy; the Church of Christ, clinging to Him, the manifestation of the sons of God.

Our country, at this moment, is no less in the crucible. Can any man doubt that this great nation is passing through, at this moment, a climacteric of

awful and portentous importance? And, surely,
instead of people deriding the call, or the command,
of our Queen to have a day for humiliation, they
ought to rejoice in such an appointment as that.
Wherever the fault may be, on whom it lies—it lies,
I fear, upon all—it lies beyond all; it is God's providential dealing with us. Surely, oh! surely, there is
a call, at least for this, that we should pray that we
may have forgiveness—our rulers, and our ministers,
and our people, all ranks, and grades, and classes—
that we may have forgiveness for the past, and
grace to help us in time to come. Surely it is dutiful to do that. Surely the very position of our
country, never, if in jeopardy at all, so much in
jeopardy as now, in the crucible, tested, tried, proved
and humbled, is surely a call, a solemn call, for
prayer. And let us, as individuals, ask ourselves at
this moment, have we been humbled by the retrospect? Are we humbled as individuals? It is so
easy for eloquent men to lay the blame on others; it
is so unpleasant to take the guilt to our own consciences. Had we prayed as we should have done;
had we lived as we should have done; had
churches been less camps than they have been, all
the camps of Europe had been more like churches
than they now are. May it not be that the fault
begins, where the judgment always begins, at the
house of God? And if judgment begin there, what
shall be the end of them that believe not the gospel
of Christ? Let us search ourselves, and weigh ourselves, and see where our faults are; and pray, in the
retrospect, "Search me, O God, and try me, and
know my thoughts; and see if there be any wicked

way "—not in our Cabinet, not in our House of Commons, not in our House of Lords—it is very clever and it is very pleasant to find out faults there; but, "if there be any wicked way *in me*, and lead me in the way everlasting." Amen, and amen.

CHAPTER IX.

THE address contained in the chapter we have read
was made to the children of Israel upon the eve
of their entrance into that long-promised land which
was the burden of their best, their brightest and
their most sustaining hopes. And just as they are
about to obtain the long-sought triumph, and to cross
the Jordan, and to set their foot on the promised
soil, Moses is commanded to address them, and to
tell them that when they should gain the victory and
possess the land, it would not be because of their
moral superiority and excellence in the sight of God,
but rather because God had driven out the people
that were in it because of their abounding wickedness and crimes in his sight. This was a very important lesson to teach the Israelites. They were so
prone to plunge into despair with the very least reverse,
and so prone, on the other hand, to be elated to the very
skies with the least success; and in their reverses to
blame God, and in their prosperity to take the credit to
themselves, that they needed the lessons here so humb-

ling to be urged, and impressed and inculcated upon them. God very frequently gives a people a possession, not because they are worthy of it, but because others have justly and righteously forfeited it. He tells the Israelites at the same time exactly what the spies told them; that the people you are going to fight are the children of the Anakim, tall and powerful; that they dwell in cities great and fenced up to the very heavens. But you will see the two different meanings, and ends, and objects in the same description. When the spies gave this account to the Israelites it was to discourage them, and to make them turn back to Egypt; when Moses gave this account of the formidable obstructions they would meet with, it was that they might understand that "the Lord their God is he that goeth before them;" and that the credit will not be due to your valour, but to the undeserved goodness, mercy, and compassion of God. How very important it is that we should all feel that in our enterprises, success is not given to might, but given in sovereignty, according to God's good pleasure; that whilst he honours the industry that toils, he reserves to himself the sovereignty of giving or withholding the blessing that maketh rich and that addeth no sorrow. Of all things, however, we must have noticed frequently in this book that pride, self-righteousness and vain-glory are most detestable in the sight of God; and wherever they burst forth, either in the national heart or in the individual bosom, there he is sure to punish them. And I have often thought that the recent reverses that we have met with, if they can be called reverses,—certainly sufferings, are to be traced to the vain-glory, pride, and elated pro-

spects with which, alas! too many engaged in
this enterprise. God honours them that trust in
him and do their duty; he chastens even his own
when they give way to pride, vain-glory and self-
righteousness. That lesson is taught in every chapter of the Pentateuch; it is emphatically taught in
that which we are now reading ; and when we gain the
victory in such circumstances, it will be in such a way
as will show the sovereignty of God, the weakness
and the worthlessness of the mightiest, and inculcate
deeper than ever the lesson we are so prone to forget,
that in individual life, in social life, in national life, in
the arts, in science, in literature, in politics, in war, it
is "not by might, nor by power, but by my spirit, saith
the Lord of hosts."

After God had thus warned them, he reminds them
what they are, a stiff-necked and a rebellious people ;
and he calls before them their past sins, that they
might see how little they had to glory in. Their sins
were their own, and they should humble them ; their
excellences were from God, and they must humble
them ; and in neither had they anything of which
they should be proud. Moses reminds them of his
going up into the mount, and also of abiding there
forty days and forty nights, when he did neither eat
bread nor drink water. That was plainly a miraculous sustenance. Moses could not have said so to
people that did not know it to be a fact. You can see,
in constant allusive references here to past facts, that
Moses was speaking to a people that saw and witnessed those facts ; and so far there is contained in this
an indirect proof of the authenticity, the genuineness,
and the inspiration of the document. He says that he

did neither eat bread nor drink water. Our Blessed Lord was the same time in the desert, and he there too fasted in the same way. But it is a great mistake, into which some people fall, to think that fasting means simply abstinence from food and drink. I have searched the Scriptures with the utmost care; I may be mistaken, it may have escaped my notice; but I cannot find in the Bible a single command addressed to any one to abstain from food and drink as a thing acceptable to God. That there are instances of persons having done so is perfectly true; but that there is a command from God to do so is, I think, not true. And those who say that they ought to fast in the sense of abstinence from food ought not to stop there; because, if they are to observe a fast with all the ceremonial of the ancient Levitical rubrics, they ought, first to abstain from food, secondly to cast ashes on their heads, and thirdly to wrap themselves up in sackcloth. The three things, mind you, were always together; and if you will insist upon the rubrical ceremonial observance of a fast as the Jews observed it of old, you must not be satisfied with abstaining from food; that is but a third part of it; you must also take the other accompaniments. If that be not the meaning of fasting, what is the meaning of fasting? The meaning of fasting is not abstaining from food; that is very easily done. It is withdrawing the mind, the heart, the thoughts, the anxieties, the hopes, the sympathies from the profits, the pleasures, the enjoyments, the works of the world; and turning all those affections, sympathies, hopes, to the things that relate to the kingdom of God.

The fasting is an inner thing, not an outer thing; it is the heart that fasts, it is not the flesh that fasts; only it is so easy to abstain from food, and fancy that the sensation of hunger is a sort of expiation for the misdemeanors of a lifetime, that one does not wonder that it becomes extremely popular; but on the other hand, it is very difficult to fast in the loftier sense of abstaining from worldly employment, worldly engagements, worldly duties; and devoting the whole time to thoughts that relate to God, to the soul, to heaven, to eternity, to our state as a nation, to our prospects as a people. In speaking of the fast recently appointed by our gracious Sovereign the Queen, the light in which I look upon it is not as a day for fasting from food, but as a day for solemn and united prayer, that becomes a nation that feels its responsibility, to God; that he would be pleased to forgive the sins that have provoked what seem to us his judgments, or at least his chastisements; and that he would be pleased, in a cause which in our consciences we believe to be a just and a righteous one, to bestow that blessing, without which the bravest soldier will lose his courage when it is most needed, and the most skilful counsels be blasted when they are most demanded. And if we meet together on that day, each flock within the walls of its own sanctuary, and join together, according to a special promise, that where two or three are agreed as touching one thing God will be in the midst of them and grant it, I think we have reason, we have precedent, we have authority from Scripture to believe that the blessing will indeed descend upon us. I know quite well what many worldly men feel, and what I think Christian men should regard; it is a great hardship upon many a poor man to lose his day's wages. I have not a doubt it is; and I feel all the difficulty of it; and I can understand that the very scoffs and satires of those newspapers that seem to have an infidel spirit have a certain foundation in fact. It is hard that the poor man should lose his day's wages; it is, you will say, also hard that the master should be constrained to pay for work not done. But I think, if a master can afford it, it will be far better fasting to give a poor journeyman his three and sixpence, or his five shillings for that day, than to abstain from food all day. The true fasting is to "undo the heavy burdens, and to let the oppressed go free; to deal thy bread to the fatherless, and that thou withhold not thyself from thine own flesh." I would recommend, therefore, if you will have an outward fast, that every employer and master continue their wages to those that are subject to him, just as if they had worked all the day; and you will find it will not be such a loss in the end. God honours them that honour him; and you know quite well, if our united prayers shall be the means of bringing down a blessing on our country, and hastening the dawn of lasting European peace, that will be a greater contribution to our substantial prosperity, than all that you may lose, or all you might otherwise gain, upon that day.

Moses then reminds them of all the scenes in their past history; and draws from them the great lesson, that they were not to be proud or exalted. And then he concludes the chapter by praying to God that he would remember the promises he had made to Abraham, and Isaac, and Jacob; that he would not cast off the land that he had blessed with sunshine, but would visit it, and bring his inheritance into the enjoyment of the promises he had made, for his own great name's sake.

CHAPTER X.

IN the last chapter we had a recapitulation of the reasons, the sovereign and distinguishing reasons, why God selected that people, and made them so great a people, and the subjects of so brilliant and enduring promises. He told them, in order to humble them, that he selected them, not from intrinsic moral, or spiritual, or material excellence in them, but solely in his own sovereign love to make them what they should be, not because they were what they ought to have been. In this present chapter he calls upon them to show to him great and peculiar gratitude, expressed not in lip service, but in life conduct, for his own great goodness to them after he chose them, and made them, by a special covenant, his adopted, and his believing, and his worshipping people. He begins the chapter, therefore, with recapitulating the first of God's great mercies ; in that when he revealed the Law to them, and when their misconduct roused to an excessive pitch the temper of Moses, and the sacred stones were broken as they fell from his hands, God might have refused another transcript; he did not do so; but he forgave the indiscretion of his servant, the misconduct of his people, and gave a second edition of that law, of which he was not even compelled to give a first. When we refer to God's holy law, let us never forget that the law of the Ten Commandments was not created on Mount Sinai; it was only then expressed on Mount Sinai. It was eternally true—it remains eternally true; and when God revealed it, he condescended in great mercy to let his subjects know what were the laws that he once engraved upon their hearts, that he now wished them to remember, and to acquiesce in, and accept for the future. Let us also recollect, when people argue, for instance, against the fourth commandment, and say it is a mere ceremony. Is it not strange, if it be so, that it should have been embodied in the law given amid the splendours of the mount, in circumstances so solemn; amid ten commandments, nine of which are confessedly moral? It would be strange, it would seem inconsistent, that, in the midst of the ten, nine being moral, there should be one of a transient nature, meant to pass away with the economy in which it had its birth. It does seem to me that the rest of the laws of Israel given in other circumstances may be ceremonial; but that the Ten Commandments, given in so remarkable, so impressive, and memorable circumstances, must, every one of them, have been essentially moral, obligatory on all, and lasting through all ages. God wrote them, it is said, upon the stone—how or why we know not; that it was so is expressly recorded; and these stones were laid up in the ark of the testimony. But this law he writes now upon the hearts of his people; and God's will, engraved upon the sensitive and susceptible heart of a Christian, will outlast the pyramids of Egypt, outlive the stones that came down from the Mount Sinai in the hand of Moses, and endure for ever and for ever. It is a nobler thing to write the law upon human hearts, and more miraculous, than to write it with his own finger upon the dead and perishing stone.

We then read of the appointment of the Levites, which Moses also recapitulates, who were to aid the priests in the administration of the sanctuary, and who had no section of the land as their peculiar inheritance, but lived literally and strictly by the altar, —evidently with this design, that they might have no mercantile or worldly interests to attend to, or sympathies to absorb their feelings or withdraw their affections and attention from the service of God. At the same time I ought to state that Levi here is used as embracing in the name both priests and Levites strictly so called; it was the whole ministry of the temple of the children of Israel.

Then God says to them again, to humble them or to make them thankful, that "the heaven of heavens is the Lord's;" that is, all that you see in the starry firmament above, all that you behold in the productive and fertile earth below, all is the Lord's. Then, if he wanted something for himself, he had no need to select you. Yet says Moses, "The Lord had a delight in thy fathers to love them, and he chose their children after them, even you above all people, as it is this day." The very sovereignty of his choice must have made them grateful. He that is throned upon the riches of the universe, who might create countless orbs, more beautiful and far more loyal than this, condescended to regard this with especial favour, and to make this earth of ours the theatre of scenes and the lesson-book of truths unparalleled in the present and unprecedented in the past. And this was owing, not to anything intrinsically excellent in us, but to his own sovereign, and gracious, and undeserved love.

He reminds them, " The Lord your God is God of gods, and Lord of lords, a great God." And then he states a noble lesson : " He regardeth not persons, nor taketh reward; " that is, in God's dealings with man his eye penetrates the circumstantial robe, and fastens on the inner and the secret heart. It is not lawn, or purple, or ermine, or any other symbols of outward pomp, and dignity, and rank, that have the least influence with God. A rich man is no more acceptable in his sight than the poorest beggar. Man estimates man as he looks; God judges man as he is. Man's estimate is often purely outward, based upon varying and evanescent traits, and necessarily imperfect ; but God's judgment is always true. He regards all the distinctions of life, useful in their place, as of no weight at the judgment-seat. The person of prince or peasant is not regarded by him. Nor does he take any reward ; he judges righteous judgment. What a comforting thought it is to the misrepresented, the maligned, the calumniated among mankind, that there is One that judgeth righteous judgment! Of all men he must be the most miserable who is opposed by the world, misrepresented by its bad ones, mistaken by its good ones, and has nothing to fall back upon ; while he never can despair, or be very desolate, or very

M

deeply cast down, who sees the whole world arrayed against him, but has the inner and sustaining consciousness that God acquits, approves, and applauds him.

Then says Moses, as the result of all this, " He doth execute the judgment of the fatherless and widow, and loveth the stranger." And what a beautiful thought is here : " Love ye therefore the stranger." Why ? " For ye were strangers in the land of Egypt." So it is recommended in the New Testament ; " given to hospitality ; for some have entertained angels unawares." Not to cast out the stranger because he is so ; but rather to respect him because he is so. When you notice all these traits in this book, how, I ask, does it come to pass that writings which appeared in other lands almost cotemporaneous with these, or at least soon after, are characterized by a low, base, miserable standard of morality ; and that these writings, so characterized by a defective morality, should appear amid a people celebrated for their arts, their sciences, their sculpture, their poetry, their painting, their æsthetic accomplishments ; while in the midst of a people barbarous in reference to art, to science, to painting, to sculpture, to poetry, there should spring up a morality which ages that have attained to the loftiest pitch of social and moral excellence, are obliged to look back and recognize in them a morality they have never reached, and prescriptions they feel they would do well still to adopt ? The answer is, the cultivated Greek was without God ; the barbarous Jew, as the Greek would have called him, was taught and instructed by the very finger of God.

Here, finally, is the winding up of all that is contained in this chapter:

> "And now, Israel, what doth the Lord thy God require of thee, but to fear the Lord thy God, to walk in all his ways, and to love him, and to serve the Lord thy God with all thy heart and with all thy soul, to keep the commandments of the Lord, and his statutes, which I command thee this day for thy good."—Vers. 12, 13.

We have seen an illustration of the sovereignty of God in the selection of a people to reflect his glory and to obey his will. We have read in the lesson this day an illustration, a bright string rather, of the precious blessings that God bestowed upon that people, in order that, if humbled by his sovereign election, as recorded in the previous chapter, they might be thankful for his special blessings, as these are strung together in the chapter which we have now read. "Not for thy righteousness, or for the uprightness of thine heart, did God choose thee or send thee to possess this land:" "Not by works of righteousness which we have done, but according to his mercy he saved us, by the washing of regeneration, and renewing of the Holy Ghost; which he shed on us abundantly through Jesus Christ our Saviour; that being justified by his grace, we should be made heirs according to the hope of eternal life." "What doth the Lord thy God, O Israel, require of thee, but to fear him, and to love him, and to serve him with all thy heart." "This is a faithful saying, and these things I will that thou affirm constantly, that they which have believed in God," as the sovereign disposer of blessings, as the beneficent bestower of those bless-

ings, "might be careful to maintain good works."
Or, as it is expressed here, "To fear God, to walk in
his ways, to love him with all their heart, and that for
their good." We thus see that the religion that sets
forth the sovereignty of God in the choice of a people
for himself—and along with that the great and blessed
truth that we are justified, and accepted, and transformed, not from anything done by us, nor from anything wrought in us, but wholly and solely, without
limitation, or exception, or distinction of any sort, by
the righteousness of Him who was made sin for us
that we might be made the righteousness of God by
him—requires of us to lead a life that will express
the intensity of our gratitude, and bring forth all
those fragrant fruits which show that our religion is
according to godliness; and that they calumniate and
misrepresent our faith who say that our doctrines
make void the law of God. We are admitted into
heaven, not by anything we have done, nor anything
we can do; but solely by what Christ has done for
us; we are delivered from eternal ruin, not from anything we suffer, nor anything we pay, nor anything
we sacrifice, but by what Christ has suffered for us.
Christ suffered for us all that we deserved as sinners,
and Christ paid for us all that we owed as creatures;
therefore, some may say, "Let us live as we like; let
us plunge into every folly, dissipation, frivolity, and
sin; for all is settled independent of us, external to
us; and therefore it matters not how we live." You
are utterly mistaken; for the same grace that gives
us a change of state, and leaves us justified instead of
condemned, follows up the transference with a change
of heart, which makes us holy when we were unholy

before; and never, never is any one so bound to bring forth all the fruits of Christian character, as when he feels he owes nothing of his everlasting inheritance to anything he has done, or anything he can do. The reason on which we base this is obvious. Because Christ alone is our right and title to heaven, we are not, therefore, absolved from obedience to the law of God. Because good works are not in our title to heaven, they are not therefore not in our qualification for heaven. We lift obedience from the place of justification, where it is not only useless, but noxious; and we hold it fast in the place of sanctification, where it is essential, ornamental, acceptable to God and beautiful before man. In other words, those who hold what are called evangelical views, which are those of the Spirit of God, do not extinguish the necessity of good works; they only transfer the necessity from the *state*, in which they are of no use, to the *character*, where they are essential evidences and marks of a true Christian. Holiness of character is no part of our right to heaven, but it is an essential element in our qualification for heaven. If I enter a place where there is a musical performance, my ticket entitles me to cross the threshold; but if I have no musical ear I shall have no enjoyment. In the same manner, if you have a right in something done for you that will warrant and enable you to cross the threshold of heaven, yet if you have no heart prepared for the exercises and the joys of heaven, it can be no happiness to you. But the supposition is impossible; the two are never separated. The man that is justified by a righteousness without him, is always the subject of a sanctifying process within him; and he that asserts

his safety at a judgment-seat, but lives in known violation of the law of God, deceives himself, and deceives
those to whom he makes the assertion also. In short,
the argument we use is perfectly plain; because good
works, holiness, or holy life, is not the right, it does
not follow that it may not and should not be the fruit.
We argue that where there is a good tree there will be
good fruit; where a fire burns there will be warmth;
where the sun shines there will be light; and where a
man is united to Christ by living faith in him as his
only Saviour, it will be as impossible for him to fail to
bring forth the fruits of the Holy Spirit, as for the
sun to shine without light, or the fire to burn without heat, or a good tree not to bring forth good and
fragrant fruit. It is therefore altogether mistaken
reasoning in those who say we absolve from practical
duties by preaching the righteousness of Christ as
the ground of our title to heaven; and if you put
the experiment to the test, you will find that the
very men who speak of Christ as all and in all as
the ground of their acceptance, are most characterized
by whatsoever things are pure, and just, and honest,
and lovely, and of good report. I do not say that
many a natural man does not bring forth moral fruits.
Men that do not profess Christianity on the Royal
Exchange, are characterized by an honour, a sensitive
attachment to what is right, that Christians might do
well to imitate. Other men, again, are temperate,
sober, just, upright, in the estimate of every discriminating mind. But because they are so, that does not
show that Christians are absolved from being so. On
the contrary, we ought to be all that the children
of nature are, and something nobler, and greater, and

better still; so that the loftiest moralist on the low level of this world, looking up to you upon the loftier level of Christian profession, may be able to say, "I see that Christianity is not an Antinomian heresy nor a barren creed; it makes its people, as sons of God, far holier, far wiser, far better, far happier than others. I will go and drink from the same fountain, and taste of the same living bread; and see if it cannot transform me, also, into a son and an heir of God." We thus see how unfair is the argument that those who seek to be justified through the righteousness of Christ will necessarily live an inconsistent and an unholy life.

On another ground I base this requirement. We observed a day of national prayer, supplication, and even thanksgiving. We met together in our respective sanctuaries, and we implored forgiveness for the errors, the indiscretions, the blunders, the sins of the past; and we sought strength, and grace, and wisdom for our rulers, and our senators, and our magistrates, and our judges, and our soldiers, and our sailors, in the arrangement and in all the duties and obligations of the future. Now, O England, O Scotland, what doth the Lord require of thee now, after you have made this solemn supplication? To sit still and say, "We have made an atonement for the past, and we now may disregard the obligations of the future?" Is it now to say, "We have fasted, and now we may feast and enjoy ourselves just as much as we like?" Will you call this a fast? It is mocking God. If our nation has prayed right, its rulers, its senators, its judges, its magistrates, its families, will practise as they never did before; and men of common

sense will estimate the value of the fast appointed by
our gracious Sovereign by the weight, and fragrance,
and preciousness of the fruits that grow from it.
Therefore, if you regard the fast-day exactly as the
Roman Catholic does the absolution of his priest, as
a complete cancel of the past score, and a warrant
to begin a new one, calculating upon another absolution, it would have been better if no such fast-day
had been appointed. But I trust that is not the impression. I trust you will never forget, O England,
O our nation, what doth the Lord thy God require
of thee now, after you have fasted and prayed, but
to fear the Lord thy God, to walk in all his ways, to
love him and to serve him with all your hearts and
all your souls; and it is for your good. If you wish
to know the obligations of a fast, hear the magnificent
description of one by an inspired penman: "Is it
such a fast that I have chosen? saith the Lord; a day
for a man to afflict his soul? is it to bow down his
head as a bulrush, and to spread sackcloth and ashes
under him? wilt thou call this a fast, and an acceptable
day to the Lord? Is not this the fast that I have
chosen? to loose the bands of wickedness, to undo the
heavy burdens, and to let the oppressed go free, and
that ye break every yoke? Is it not to deal thy bread
to the hungry, and that thou bring the poor that are
cast out to thy house? when thou seest the naked,
that thou cover him; and that thou hide not thyself
from thine own flesh? Then shall thy light break
forth as the morning, and thine health shall spring
forth speedily: and thy righteousness shall go before
thee; the glory of the Lord shall be thy rereward."
Now if these be the fruits of your fast you have fasted

rightly. And instead of abstaining from food in Lent that after it is done you may feast the more ; instead of making a fast-day a purgatory for the flesh, if you would only make it a spring of new strength and energy of soul and heart, you would fast in the way that the Lord has appointed. ₁True fasting, true repentance,

> " Is not to cry, Have mercy, or to sit
> And droop, or to confess that thou hast fail'd ;
> But to bewail the sins thou didst commit,
> And not commit the sins thou hast bewail'd."

This is the repentance, this the fast that the Lord requires. To pray like a saint, and practise like the greatest sinner ; to fast like a monk, and plunge into all the excesses of the world, like the worldly man— all this is only a sort of consecrated mockery, a splendid hypocrisy, an abomination in the sight of God.

Let us study the clauses of this requirement. "What doth the Lord require of thee, but to fear him?" God's exactions, if we be Christians, are our own free-will offerings. What God demands in this verse, is what thankful hearts should gladly give. Did God ask of us some costly victim, did he demand some precious sacrifice, did he even exact some painful and tormenting penance ; did he bid us do something that would inflict upon us pain, or loss, or injury of any sort, then, indeed, we might hesitate to do what the Lord requires of us ; yet, strange enough, we would not hesitate ; for it is a singular fact that a man will wrap himself forty days in sackcloth, live on bread and water, walk upon pebbles or sharp

flints barefooted, or crawl up mountains, in order
to expiate sin, or at the bidding of his priest, or
endure any torment rather than do justly, love mercy,
walk humbly with God. It is so easy to mortify the
flesh; it is so unpalatable to mortify the lusts of the
flesh. It is so much easier to do penance, however
painful or agonizing it may be, if it will purchase
indulgence for the future, than it is to repent in the
sight and hearing of a holy God. It is so much more
easy to confess to a sympathizing father, and get
absolution for a trifle and start afresh in your indulg-
ences, than it is to confess before the holy, heart-
searching God, and seek forgiveness for the past and
grace for the future. It is the old story: " Where-
withal shall I come before the Lord, and bow myself
before the most high God?" And what is the
answer? " Shall I come before him with," what I am
quite ready to bring, " burnt offerings, or with calves
of a year old? Or will the Lord be pleased with
thousands of rams?"—I will willingly give that—" or
with ten thousand rivers of oil?"—I will even pour
out that—" or shall I give my firstborn for the sin of
my soul?" Human nature is willing to do all that.
But the answer is, " He hath showed thee, O man,
what is good; and what doth the Lord require of
thee but to do justly, and to love mercy, and to walk
humbly with thy God?" This is more painful to the
natural man than all the sacrifices he proposes; but it
is the requirement of thee, O Israel, by the Lord thy
God, to fear him, and to walk in his ways, and to love
him with all thy heart.

All is founded upon God's covenant relationship
to us: "What doth the Lord *thy* God require of

thee?" Mark the basis of our conduct, the spring of our obedience—it is that the Lord is *thy* God. What a magnificent relationship is this—the Lord is my God! What do I mean by saying a thing is mine? If I say, "That house is mine," it means that it is for my convenience; if I say, "That physician is mine," it means that I can draw upon him for all the resources of his skill; if I say, "That friend is mine," it means that in the day of calamity and trouble I will appeal to him, and I can calculate upon his help; and if I say, "The Lord God is mine," what does that imply? His omniscience is my sentinel to watch me; his omnipotence my guard to encompass me; his love the spring of the mercies that enrich me; his peace the power that continually keeps me; all the attributes of my God, like the mountains around Jerusalem, are encamped around me, the humblest, the weakest of his family, but his own, to keep mine eyes from tears, my feet from falling, my soul from death. Is this a truth, or is it a mere poetic fancy? It is a truth so often repeated, so often dwelt on in every page of the Sacred Volume, that one is surprised that any one could miss it. All the attributes of God are encamped around the humblest Christian soldier at Balaklava, or at Sebastopol, as they are around the angels of the sky, or the cherubim beside his throne. No arrow, no bullet, no ball, can touch a hair of the head of him round whom God is, and where he has not given permission to death to come. There is no chance in death; before the humblest Christian can fall, God's consent must be obtained; each one of us, if believers, is immortal till his work is done. The day, the hour, the how, the where, the when, of each of our deaths is appointed. But that does not make me presume, but only confident and happy in the thought that I am not a fatherless orphan, that this world is not a forsaken orb; but that God's eye is on me in the shadow and in the sunshine, on the height and in the depth, in my going out and in my coming in; that there is not a thought in my heart that he does not see, not a word on my lips that he does not hear, nor a peril that approaches me that he does not preserve and protect me in. Blessed thought! go forth wherever duty bids you, and fear not while you can realize this thought—all the attributes of God are around you; the Lord is our God. But whilst he is thus my God, does he ask of me anything by way of recognition of this? Yes, unquestionably; he requires of you, if you will enjoy the immunity of being his, the allegiance and the love that are naturally dictated by it. If God gives you so much, the least you can give is the return that he here requires. First of all he asks you to fear him: "What doth the Lord thy God require of thee but to fear him?" What is meant by this expression, "to fear?" Does it mean to be terrified at God? That is the natural man's religion. It is singular that every natural man, and every child, before that child is taught and instructed better, looks upon the idea of God with terror and alarm. Many a person in the counting-house could say, "Let anybody come in here, but do not let God." Many a heart can say, "I would not mind who were to investigate or to inspect—only not God." The feeling of the natural man is terror and alarm at the very thought of God. Hence his idea is that the

Christian religion is a sepulchral and gloomy thing, fit enough for sick and dying people, and for funerals, and for everything that is distressing; so that the minister of the gospel is very much classified with the under-taker, and the sanctuary with the grave, and gloom and darkness regarded as its appropriate consecrating air. To a Christian it is all the reverse. He has no doubt, no alarm; he walks with God, he courts his presence, he carries a sense of it into every sphere in which he moves, and feels in that presence not an element of alarm, but an inspiration of hope, of joy, of happiness and of peace. We fear the hostile, we sus-pect the unknown; but can a child fear his father? Can a sinner saved fear the Saviour that redeemed him with his blood? Can a friend dread a friend, if he be the Lord our God? How can we entertain an emotion of terror towards him? The meaning of fear here is reverence, worship, adoration, a sense of his presence; in short, what is expressed in the prayer, " Hallowed be thy name," is fearing God. And not only are we called upon to fear him, but also "to walk in his ways." All the ways of God proceed from one source, and they all terminate in the same source again. There are many varieties of expression, but there is but one religion. There is the way of righteousness, the way of truth, the way of peace, the way of safety, the way of happiness, the way of pleasantness. All these are different paths that God has prescribed for his people; and they that are his people are found walking in them. Suppose there be two ways pre-sented for our acceptance; one is smooth, illuminated with all the colours of the rainbow, trodden by count-less and apparently happy feet—but not recognized by

God. Another way is rugged, crooked, amid thorns and flints, with deep streams below, and hills above, and very few walking in it—but it is unequivocally the way recommended by God; if you be one of his people you will take the crooked, the rough, the thorny, the flinty road, and you will turn your back upon the bright, and sunny, and popular one. In other words, you will take your way, not from the seeming lights of expediency, but from the sure testimony of God's holy and blessed word. It will not be the multitudes that beat it; nor the flowers that adorn it; nor the lights that sparkle on it; but the name and the superscription of God, that will determine the way in which you are to walk. It is required of God's people that they should walk in his ways. That expression, again, is very remarkable—walk in his ways. Even in his ways we may sometimes be disposed to be very partial. If there be two ways that are equally God's, and if we choose we might say, "We should prefer this;" but if he clearly says, "This is the way; walk ye in it;" you are to say, "Not my will, but thy will be done." Of two of God's ways, both equally right, you are to take the one that you prefer if there is left a discretion; but if not, you must take the way that God himself points out. In these ways you are to walk. You are not to stand still; but to walk and to advance in them. Many people think they can stand still in the path that leads to God; they never do so really. They think they are standing still; in truth and in fact they are retrograding and going rapidly backwards. Every true Christian, who is really so, is walking, growing, advancing, increasing, either in distrust of himself, in humbleness of mind, or in conformity to God, in obedience to his law, in superiority over all the temptations that try and beset him. But never forget this—no Christian stands still: in some shape there is development, expansion, progress; and the best advice I can give, is not to calculate the distance, or to estimate the progress, but to look still at the Great Example, to pray more to the Holy Spirit; and while you are seeking the spring of progress, your progress will be only the more rapid.

But not only are you to walk in his ways, but as he requires, you are to love him. Were the fear enjoined in the first clause terror, then it would be impossible that we could love him. The very fact that we love him, shows that the fear is reverence and worship, not terror or alarm. Now, "love God," is just the fulfilment of the law. Love is the germ in the heart that blossoms and bursts into all the fragrant fruits that are demanded by God's holy law. Love originates the fruits that the law demands. The law, like the imperious taskmaster, says, "Give me fruit," and you cannot; but love in the heart softly, gently, but progressively, originates and develops all the fruits of the Spirit. Love is law in the heart; the law is love exhibited in the life. Wherever there is love infused into the heart you may be sure there will be obedience developed in the life. And, therefore, the very first thing to secure the highest conformity to law is to have God's love implanted in the heart—that vital element that permeates every branch, breaks forth into the green leaf that never withers; and ultimately into the fragrant blossom and the precious fruit that is for food. Love in the heart makes all life a joyful festival, sacrifice a willing privilege; and even martyrdom it has glorified with unearthly attractions. This love to God will overflow in love to all our brethren of mankind; creating a sense of brotherhood wherever there is a Christian, as it is itself the sense of fatherhood in our relationship to God himself. And, lastly, this love will culminate in heaven; faith issuing in hope, hope dissolving in possession; of these three, faith, hope, and love, love will continue for ever. This love to God is not an accidental embellishment of Christian character, that may be or may not be—it is a vital force, an essential element. The absence of love to God is, in plain terms, the absence of Christianity altogether. This love to God we lost at the Fall, we regained at the Cross. This love implanted in the heart is the result of our seeing and tasting God's love to us. What is the way to make a man love me? It is to show him how much I have loved him, by teaching him how much I have done for him. God's great plan for recovering the world to himself, is by showing them disinterested, infinite, inexhaustible love. God said upon Mount Sinai, "Thou shalt love;" yet man did not love. God promised rewards to him that would love; but man did not love. God threatened penalties upon them that would not love. But we all know that love towards another can neither be bribed into the heart, nor threatened into the heart, nor commanded into the heart. How then can it be produced? Love in one heart is produced by the exhibition of love in another. And hence the language of Scripture, "We love him because he first loved us." And hence the grand effect of the gospel, wherever it is thoroughly understood, is the creation in the individual heart of that love to God that counts his yoke easy, his burden light, and rejoices and is refreshed in obeying all his commandments, walking in his ways, fearing him, and serving him all the days of our life. This love shall have for the measure and extent of it all your hearts; God requires you to love him with all your hearts and all your souls. I have often thought of the equity of that law—" Thou shalt love the Lord thy God with all thy heart." Persons say, " What is the use of God requiring us to do what we cannot ? " God does not require you to love him with more than human strength, or with intenser than earthly fervour; he only asks you to love him just as much as you rightly ought —" with all thy heart, with all thy soul; " not with more than the heart can feel, nor less than the soul can offer. But this shows the greatness of that requirement of God; this requirement of Sinai, this inspiration of Pentecost—" with all thy soul and with all thy heart." Not a cold and calculating preference, but a warm, cordial attachment; not a blind and an unintelligible attachment, but with all thy soul; not the cold and freezing recognition that is at zero, not the scorching fanaticism that exhibits itself in a volcano, but intelligently, with all the soul, cordially, with all the heart, always and at all times. No one can say, " I have done so." You know that you have not loved him with every pulse of the heart; you know that you have not always given him the preference where the controversy was whether God or Mammon should have the precedence. We all know, every one, if he looks into his own heart, knows that he has not loved God with all his heart and with all his soul; and, therefore, " If thou, O Lord, shouldest mark iniquity, who could stand?" and, therefore, "Enter not into judgment with thy servant, O Lord; for in thy sight no man living can be justified." One suspension in the human heart of perfect love to God is a breach of his holy law; one cessation of supreme love to him is sin. It is by seeing the greatness, the clearness, the reasonableness of his exactions, that you are enabled to see the depth and count the number of your transgressions against him. But not only are you to love him with all the heart, but also to serve him. The word *service* here is used in the sense of worship. For instance, the word liturgy means strictly service; and here, when it is said, "Ye shall serve him with all the heart," it is adore, praise, pray to him; worship outwardly, publicly and privately, with all the heart and soul. We see in this what is the essence of all truly acceptable and pure worship in the sight of God. It is not the material glory or the ritual splendour of a service that makes it acceptable in the sight of God; but the depth of sincerity, the intensity of love, the supremacy of God in the heart, that gives religious service its acceptance in his sight through Christ, and is so in the estimate and judgment of every rational man. The simpler and severer the service of God is the purer. Wherever there are gorgeous ceremonies, the attention of the worshipper is lost in the splendour of the rite, and drawn from the object and subject of it, the Lord. No music, however rich and beautiful, is accepted instead of the music of the affections within; clean hands lifted up to God are far preferable to priestly robes; and the bodies of Christians, those living temples, are nobler in the sight of God than all the cathedrals of mediæval

Europe; and that service which most transparently and most clearly expresses the wants of the worshippers, is most suitable in the sight of a holy God. It is essential to every act of praise, to every act of prayer: "My son, give me thy heart." The heart may be the lonely worshipper, while the lips are closed, and God will accept it; but the most eloquent expression of the lip, without the heart inspiring it with its celestial warmth, is altogether unacceptable, if not an abomination in the sight of God. How very instructive, as well as expressive, are the words of our Lord to the woman, "Woman, the hour cometh when neither on this mountain nor at Jerusalem shall ye worship the Father;" in other words, there shall no more be consecrated places with peculiar prerogatives; but wherever the heart beats right, wherever the affections cluster round God, wherever there is earnest prayer, however short, wherever there is sincere praise, however plain—be it on the sea, be it in the midst of conflict, be it in the home, be it on the streets, be it on the stones of the Exchange—wherever there is a heart that beats prayer, there is a God that hears, and answers, and accepts it. What a blessed thought! "Believe me, the hour cometh and now is, when the true worshippers shall worship the Father in spirit and in truth; for the Father seeketh such to worship him."

And now, what is the end of all this? First, God asks this of his children, not for his benefit, but for their good. He says, "God requires you to honour him, to walk in his ways, and to serve him, and to obey all the commandments I command thee this day for thy good." Is there no refreshment

in unloading the thankful heart in praise? Is there
no peace, and calm, and serenity that follows the expression of one's deep wants in prayer? Is there no
benefit or enjoyment from mingling together in the
house of God, where all are peers, and God the Maker
of us all? Is there no real good enjoyed when you
ask God to give you those things that you most deeply
stand in need of? and when you praise God for those
things that he has most richly bestowed on you, do
you not find that while you glorify God he benefits
and blesses you? In other words, it is no obsolete
maxim, but a living prescription, realized by every
Christian: "Seek first the kingdom of God and his
righteousness, and all other things will be added unto
you." "Them that honour me I will honour." Why
has our nation been prospered and blessed in the
past? Because as a nation it professes to serve him
only. Why is it true still that Christians are the
happiest portion of the human family? Just because
they are his people. It would be a strange thing if
God made his enemies happy, but left his own sons
and servants miserable. But it is all the reverse.
When you give the greatest glory, worship, adoration,
homage to God, the reaction of it is showers of blessings, and mercies, and privileges on yourselves. God
requires all this. He requires it in his word, which
we read, and study, and pray over. He requires it in
the season of affliction, when God takes away those
you love, in order that the vacuity may be filled
by himself. Often in seasons of prosperity he requires
it, when he asks you to recognize in the gift the
Giver; and he requires it, too, that the holy effects
of the gospel may be seen, and men feel that the

religion that absolves, and justifies, and forgives, is the religion that sanctifies and purifies. And it is for the good of the world; the Lots in Sodom preserve it; the salt of the earth saves it; and that day is hastened on, as numbers increase in serving, honouring, and loving God, when the whole earth shall be filled with his glory. The sons of God are his best and his most devoted servants. They that are justified by his righteousness, freely serve, fear, love, reverence him, and walk in all his ways. We are thus satisfied that the best evidence that you are Christians is what you feel, think, suffer, sacrifice, do; not as servants obeying God for reward, but as sons serving God out of affection. And if that grace do not teach us to live soberly, righteously, and godly; to do justly, to love mercy, to walk humbly with God, to fear him, to love him, to walk in his ways, and serve him with all our hearts—it is the mimickry of a magnificent original, it is not the grace of God implanted in our hearts.

CHAPTER XI.

You will at once see from the perusal of the previous chapter, and that which we have now read together, that the first verse of the 11th chapter ought to have been the last of the 10th, and not to have commenced another and distinct section of Christian story. It ends with "therefore." Why, on what account? Because of all the privileges and blessings God had enumerated in the previous chapter— " therefore thou shalt love the Lord thy God." Great privileges always entail great responsibilities; to whom much has been given of them much will be required. And it is certainly a little thing that God asks of us in return for his great mercies to us, to do that which is our own highest honour, contributes to our own greatest good, and makes us, as a nation, a people, and as individuals, great, and lasting, and powerful.

He appeals to them, in the 2nd verse, in words which are so strongly corroborative of the truth and reality of all that is recorded in this book. He says: " I speak not with your children which have not known; but I speak unto you, who have seen the chastisement of the Lord your God, his miracles and acts in the midst of Egypt and before Pharaoh; the Red Sea overflowing the hosts of Egypt, and all the miracles that were done. And then the destruction of Dathan and Abiram, the sons of Eliab. Your eyes have seen all the great acts of the Lord which he did." Now this was evidence at once of the truth and authenticity of every statement in the previous part. Could Moses—on the supposition made by sceptics that Moses imposed upon the people, told them a romance, and made them fancy that all these things were facts—could he have addressed the very parties, and said, " Your eyes saw these things, and your ears heard them ? " Their answer would have been unquestionably, " We never saw them; we never heard them; " and the second generation, having heard this denial of all that Moses declared had been done before them, would never have given Moses the authority of a great legislator, or his statements the place of God's inspired word. I think there is, therefore, upon the face of the narrative, its own irresistible credential. I need but to read the five books of Moses with honesty and impartiality to come to the conclusion that this is not a beautiful romance, nor an elegant myth; but that it is what it professes to be, the record of facts on earth, and the inspiration of God from heaven.

He proceeds to tell them what shall be the result. He first says, " These great mercies which God has bestowed upon you, ought to make you love him; " and he goes on to tell them what will be the result of their obedience to his commandments. He says,

"The result will be, that if you will keep all the commandments of your Lord, you shall be strong, and go in to possess the land; and you shall prolong your days in the land which the Lord sware unto your fathers." This teaches us the great lesson that we are very slow to learn, and that all Scripture is constantly inculcating, that there is an inseparable connection between moral character and material progress, blessings and success. In the case of nations it is always so. Nations have no judgment-seat hereafter; the judgment goes on in the case of nations now. As nations they cease to exist in futurity; as nations they are responsible now; and God has written, what no sophistry can possibly overthrow, "Righteousness exalteth a nation; and sin is the ruin of any people." Perhaps some object, and say, But the Jews lived under a theocracy. But we naturally ask, in reply, What is a theocracy? It is the visible government of God; God acting visibly in rewards and punishments upon the earth. But because God is not now visibly acting, he is not therefore the less acting. The whole difference between the ancient economy and ours is, that the curtain, in their case, was drawn aside, and we saw God issuing rewards and punishments; but, in our case, we walk not by sense and sight of what God is, but by a faith which is as real, a faith founded upon his own assertions. And we, too, live under a theocracy, though a theocracy adapted to the peculiarities of a dispensation in which we walk not by sense and sight, but by faith, the substance of things hoped for, the evidence of things not seen. And what is the result? Read the history of nations. Next to the word of God I know nothing more instructive than authentic history. And what does it tell you? That no nation ever fell before an external foe: nations die suicides; they are never slain. A nation strong in the truth, in the love, in the fear and the blessing of God, will endure for ever: a nation weak in its moral character, but mighty in its physical resources, will be found like Samson shorn of his hair. It will go forth, as of old, to fight its great battles; but it will feel, to its bitter mortification, that its strength departed from it when it lost that which is a nation's strength, the fear of God, the love of God, and the service of God, and righteousness and justice and truth in the midst of it. Hence God says now, that if they will be what they ought to be, that land will be theirs. And he contrasts it with the land from which they came out, in the 10th verse. He says: "For the land, whither thou goest in to possess it, is not as the land of Egypt, from whence ye came out, where thou sowedst thy seed, and wateredst it with thy foot, as a garden of herbs." This is, if I may use the expression, a gentle insinuation that would awake in the heart of the Jew the remembrance of what he had often said in his folly: "Better we had served in Egypt and died in Egypt." God says, Egypt after all is not such a lovely spot: even were it morally so, physically it is not so. And he alludes here to a feature which shows again that Moses describes realities. In Egypt there is either little or no rain, it is dependent for the fertility of its soil upon the periodical inundation or overflowing of the Nile. And whenever the Nile overflowed there were little currents created by the overflowing of the water; the Egyptian directed the larger currents into smaller rivulets; and he did so by collecting the earth with his foot, forming a sort of embankment, that the little rivulets spreading over all the land might so saturate the soil as well as cover it with a fertilizing deposit, that it should be productive of an abundant harvest. Now this, which we know to be the case at the present day, Moses refers to as the fact in the age in which he lived; another of those incidental references to physical facts that show he was describing, not a distant country, but the characteristics of a land in which they had lived. But, he says, the land of Canaan will have its early and its latter rain. How very beautiful is that language : " The land that you go in to possess drinks in the water of the heavens; a land that the Lord thy God careth for; the eyes of the Lord thy God are always upon it. And I will give you the rain of your land in its due season; the first rain and the latter rain; that thou mayest gather in thy corn, and thy wine, and thine oil." We often think that the seasons are more in our own control than they are; but we generally find in the long run that it is God that gives the rain; that all the excellency of legislation, all the influence of imperial power, cannot command a single shower, or create a single sunbeam. It is one of the humbling facts that we ought more to feel, that with all the resources of science, and all our progress in agricultural knowledge, we must still look up and wait; we cannot command the clouds, we cannot create the sunbeams; we must defer to a higher power—a power that acts in sovereignty, and is not tied to fixed laws; in other words, to Him who gives the rain to our land in due season, the early and the latter rain.

And after he has told them all this, he adds, "Take heed to yourselves, that your heart be not deceived, and ye turn aside, and serve other gods." Some one will say, Well, that was very applicable to the Jews, but there is no chance that we English, Scotch, and Irish will bow down and serve Jupiter, and Mars, and Saturn, or images of gold and silver. I answer, I think your good taste will keep you from vulgar idolatry ; but the human heart is as inclined to idolatry as it ever was. It may be a more æsthetic idolatry, a more tasteful polytheism; but he who ascribes all that occurs to what he calls the laws of nature, has a pantheon as truly as the ancient Roman or Greek. He that ascribes to certain fixed laws, which after all are not fixed laws, but merely evidence of a Being that never changes, and the manifestation of a power that acts not by fits and starts, but regularly—the rains and sunshine, and all the other effects of God's great goodness, really worships the gods of the heathen as truly as ever Egyptian, Roman, Greek did. True, we have refined the idolatry, but we have not destroyed it ; and therefore it is as applicable to you in this nineteenth century as it was to them many thousand years ago, "Take heed that your heart be not deceived, and that ye do not turn aside and serve other gods." "For then the Lord's wrath will be kindled against you." He is speaking here of a nation, and showing that if a nation serve other gods ; if a nation's heart, its rulers, its princes, its senators, its judges, all its representatives, turn aside and serve other gods, then the judgment will light upon them. "But so far from doing this," he says to them, "you shall rather teach these truths to your children." The first schoolmaster is the parent, and the best schoolmaster also ; and the necessity of another schoolmaster is not shifting the responsibility, but keeping the responsibility, and supplementing powers and abilities that may not be there. Some think the Sunday-school interferes with parental control. I ask how are we to do in those cases where there is no parental control, and where the parents have no sympathy with the well-being of their child? And I think it would be good for the parents of children in the very highest class of life, if they were to send their children to the Sunday-school; because the Sunday-school master is a pious man, trained in the ways of inculcating divine truth ; and many an excellent parent, scholar, and Christian, has not the gift of teaching as a Sunday-school teacher has ; and I do not see, therefore, why a Christian parent should not avail himself or herself of the higher powers possessed by a Sunday-school teacher, who possesses that knowledge which leads to the enjoyment of everlasting life.

"Thou shalt write them upon the door-posts of thine house, and upon thy gates." It was a common practice among the Egyptians, as some of the inscriptions on their monuments show, to write their names and favourite texts upon the door-post. And he tells them that the consequence of all this will be, "That your days shall be multiplied, and the days of your children in the land." Now what do we find in the present day ? I do not believe that the great superiority of our own beloved land lies in the amount of its population, or the superiority of its soil. What is it that keeps India subject to us? The *prestige* of England's greatness. But what is the *prestige* of her greatness? The creation of her moral and her Christian convictions. And take away that which is the secret of our power, and all our mighty empire will crumble into ruin. Let the nations of the earth feel what the vast population of India and of the colonies all feel, that we do justly, that we love mercy, that we walk humbly with God; that we are a people in our policy not actuated by selfish, mean, grasping motives, but a people that live and let live, and treat our colonies as a parent would treat her children, and try to do that which is just between man and man, and the fear and the dread of our native land will be upon all the nations of the earth ; and they will say, as they look at us, " This is a great, and a wise, and an understanding people; and a people whom the Lord has blessed."

CHAPTER XI.

THE following momentous words are justly entitled
to our particular and prayerful attention :—

" Behold, I set before you this day a blessing and a curse ; a
blessing, if ye obey the commandments of the Lord your
God, which I command you this day : and a curse, if ye
will not obey them."—Verses 26—28.

These words are the two extremes of that eternity
into either of which all are constantly rushing, and
must soon enter ; a blessing, the lofty extreme of
heaven ; a curse, the awful extreme and calamity of
the lost. What is that blessing, let me ask, which
is here set before us ; secondly, what is that curse ;
and, thirdly, are there any reasons that can be
reasonably pleaded why we should be doomed to
the curse, or why we should not be inheritors of
the blessing ? Let us ascertain, first of all, what is
that blessing which is here placed before us ? It is
the blessing of him whose sins are forgiven, whose
iniquities are blotted out ; it is the blessing of the
poor in spirit, the blessing of the pure in heart, the
blessing of the peacemakers, the blessing of them that

die in the Lord, who rest from their labours and their works do follow them; a blessing composed of joys that are at God's right hand, an inheritance incorruptible and full of glory, eternal mansions, a weight of glory. These are the elements, however briefly stated, of the blessing as it is tasted upon earth, and of the richer manifestation of that blessing as it is enjoyed in heaven. What is the way to possess this blessing? We lost the blessing in Paradise; and we know not naturally, what is no less great a calamity, the way to regain it. No wealth that we can bring into the market can purchase it; no power that we can put forth can retrieve it; no access that ingenuity can strike out can carry us to it. We are without strength, we are without righteousness; we are pilgrims and strangers, having left Paradise with all its beauty, like a distant and unapproachable vision; and we are wanderers now in a waste howling wilderness, by nature without God and without hope in the world. But if we have lost these blessings, so rich, and if we have lost the way to them, so precious, let us ask, has God revealed to us what we have not in ourselves, a way to regain the blessing? He has revealed it in such memorable words as these, words that fall upon the listening heart like music from the skies: " God so loved those men that had lost the blessing by their crimes, that had lost the way to it in their ignorance, that he gave his only begotten Son, that whosoever believeth on him might not perish." " Lord, we know not the way; show us the way." " I am the way, the truth, and the life; no man cometh to the Father," in order to inherit the blessing, " but by me." Or, as the apostle has stated it, " All have sinned and come short of the glory of God; and we have redemption in Christ, whom God hath set forth to be a propitiation through faith in his righteousness for the remission of sins that are past, through the forbearance of our God." We thus, see—first, the blessing we have lost; secondly, our inability of ourselves to strike out a way back to it; and, thirdly, God's having revealed what man never could have discovered, the way that leads back to heaven, to happiness, and to the blessing. Now this blessing, with the way to it, is not obscurely taught in God's blessed word. It is taught, illustrated, and explained in almost every page of the Bible. The way to heaven is not *a* doctrine incidentally taught, but *the* doctrine constantly inculcated as the root of every branch and blossom, as the vital chord along which heaven transmits its influences to earth, as the central essential truth, the rejection of which is not the rejection of an ornament on the capital, but of the very foundation of the fabric itself. Having seen the blessing, the way to it, and how plainly it is revealed, let me tell you what the curse is, and the way to escape it, and how plainly it is told; showing that God has set both before us unmistakeable and plain. What is the curse? It is just this: " The soul that sins shall die." " Cursed is every one that continueth not in all things written in the law to do them." "Tribulation, anguish, and wrath upon every soul that doeth evil." "He that believeth not the Son shall not see life, but the wrath of God abideth upon him." It is, in other words, just the life of the worm that never dies; it is the inexhaustible fuel of the fire that is never quenched. God gave us the blessing; we wove for ourselves the terrible curse. There is no blame to be attached to God for our being laid under the curse; but all glory must be given to God, if ever we are restored to inherit the blessing. The constant and popular notion is, that God inflicted on us the curse; the real truth is, that we drew it down upon ourselves. And the real truth is, in reference to the blessing, that we lost and forfeited the blessing; and when God gives it, he gives it in his free sovereignty and grace. Now, what is the way to escape from this curse? The way to escape from the curse is just as plainly set before us in the Bible as the way to escape to the blessing. The way to escape from the curse, under whose projected shadow we are all born, is the way by which we arrive at the blessing—Christ the way, the truth, and the life. But a very common notion among mankind is, that we are not all born under a curse, and that to say so is fanaticism or extravagant language, and a universal denunciation. If there be truth in the Bible, we are born under the curse; for what does it say? "We are children of wrath, even as others." "The whole head is sick, and the whole heart faint." And the apostle repeats the phrase; "There is none righteous, no, not one." "All have sinned; therefore all are under condemnation." That is the plain, unmistakeable language of God's holy word; and, therefore, the idea that you sometimes meet with, that you must do some terrible enormity in order to be put under God's curse, is quite a mistaken one. You need do nothing; you are born in an eclipse; you are by nature children of wrath. I do not stop to justify this, or to explain how it is. I am

o

here merely as an ambassador, asserting, according to my credentials, that without exception, from the prince upon the throne to the peasant on the hill-side, we are born into a world in which, if we persist without a change, we must plunge into everlasting and terrible retribution. That is not a mere inference; it is plainly stated. Now, the way to escape from this curse is plain. Were we born under a curse from which we could never escape, that would be another matter altogether; but if we are born under a curse and remain in it by our own fault, from which we may escape by God's grace, then I will show, in the sequel of this statement, that every soul that perishes, perishes a suicide; while every soul that is saved, is saved by grace and by grace alone. The way to escape is Christ Jesus, who by his sufferings rescued us from the penalty of our sins, the curse; and by his righteousness entitles us to what we had forfeited, the blessing. So that by the death of that Saviour I am delivered from all I had incurred as a sinner, and by the obedience of that Saviour I have paid all that I owed as a creature. By the one I am redeemed from the curse; by the other, as a believer, I am entitled to the blessing. Having briefly explained what these are, and the way to escape from the one, and the way to reach the other, namely, Christ; and to walk in that way is just to believe God's word concerning him, to take God at his word, and trust in him as he is set before us; let me remind you that if you refuse the blessing, there is no alternative but braving and exhausting the curse. It is said here, there is a blessing and a curse set before you. Some people fancy that they can make a compromise; that they

need not be intensely Christian, as they are not, and
will not be intensely worldly; that they may strike a
compromise. But if they do so, it is really not an
alteration of their state, but a deception of themselves. There is no alternative between a blessing
high as the throne of Deity, and a curse deep and
terrible as the nethermost hell. If you reject the
blessing, you must take the curse ; you cannot choose
neither. You must take one—the sunshine or the
shadow—the evil or the good—the " Come, ye blessed,
inherit the kingdom ; " or the withering sentence,
"Depart, ye cursed, into everlasting fire." There is
no intermediate state, there is no intermediate condition here, and there is no intermediate one hereafter.
The Roman Catholic Church, stupid as it is in invent-
ing a purgatory, is not so stupid as many Protestants
are who suppose there is a sort of intermediate place
between what they would call the torrid zone of Protestant Christianity, and the frozen polar regions of
scepticism and infidelity,—that there is a sort of
equatorial temperature between them, in which they
may have all that is good, and risk nothing that is
evil. There is no point of consistency or rest between
the desperate atheism that defies the thunders and
denies the existence of a God, and the warm, glowing,
enthusiastic Christianity that counts all but loss for
the excellency of Christ Jesus. There is no point
between on which you can stand. The man that
hates the Bible with all his heart, and strives to exterminate it, is a great though a terrible consistency.
The man that holds the Bible, and loves the Bible, and
expends all he has to spread it, is a grand and a
blessed consistency. But anything between is im-

possible. You may fancy that you hold that moderate, quiet religion which is neither one thing nor the other; you are holding that which God from heaven says is neither cold nor hot, and therefore he will reject you. You are salt that has lost its savour, wandering stars to whom is reserved the blackness of darkness for ever. You are under the curse, whilst you believe you are inheriting the blessing.

Having seen what the blessing is, and what the curse is, and having seen how they are set forth plainly in God's word, I may add they are set forth very plainly, too, in the ministry of the gospel. What is the meaning of every sermon that is addressed to you? A blessing and a curse; and the way to escape from the one, and the way to reach the other. And that sermon that most simply, most plainly, most intelligibly sets forth this, has the highest excellence, the richest eloquence. And if you want to see the blessing and the curse, in all their tremendous development, look at the cross of Christ. Why that terrible suffering, why that agony and bloody sweat? Why that unearthly and piercing cry, " My God, my God, why hast thou forsaken me? " It was because our sins on him conducted down a terrible curse into him, and therefore he thus spoke. And why was that suffering on the other hand, needed at all? To express and convey the riches of God's love, the greatness of God's feeling, his determination to save to the utmost all that come to him, and to save you even at the awful expenditure of Gethsemane, the Cross, and Calvary.

But the part that I wish specially to discuss, and in plain, and simple, and I trust, very intelligible words, is, Is there anything upon earth that drives you irresistibly to the curse? Is there anything from heaven that draws you savingly to the blessing? Is there any excuse or apology that you can urge, or that men frequently urge, why they should not instantly enjoy the blessing, or why they should be doomed to continue another day under the curse? I answer at once, that there is no decree driving a man to ruin; there is no pressure from above like an incubus upon the soul and heart of any man; there is no impassable wall or impenetrable bulwark between the greatest criminal upon earth and a crown of glory, except, perhaps, that he thinks the gospel is too good to be true, and his own sins too dear to be abandoned and abjured. I have said there is no irresistible condemnatory decree. I appeal first of all to yourselves: Who has felt any such decree? Who at this moment is conscious of one? But you know, if I address any one that pleads this, you know that you contradict God's word, which in every sentence repudiates your thought; and that you contradict your own conscience, which, in every act you do, rebukes you for it. God in this book throws upon the sinner that is lost, all the responsibility of his everlasting ruin; and God in this book as plainly takes from the sinner that is saved all the glory of his everlasting deliverance. He repeatedly tells you in this blessed record, that you have ruined yourselves; that you are perishing, because you will perish. You know, if I address any such, that you are just what you choose to be;—you know that you tread the path that in your own taste and conscience you prefer; that in spite of infinite motives, of pressing protests, in spite of all the fears of the law, the forebodings of the judgment, the terrors of the curse,

the splendours of glory, you deliberately and know-
ingly, at this moment — it is no use disguising or
softening it—travel from God. No man goes to
hell, who does not open the door of it for himself;
and no man loses heaven, who does not, on the other
hand, shut its door upon himself. Your conduct is
therefore suicidal; your ruin is self-elected; you are
what you are at this moment, as unbelievers, just what
you choose to be; and that is the only reason why,
and there is no other. But you say, " Oh, are you
not aware of the doctrine which is contained in God's
word; the depravity of man, his total corruption, and
his ruin? Do you not hold that?" I answer, when
you tell me what that depravity is in its darkest
characteristics, when you portray it in its blackest
shadows, you do not in the least overcharge it. The
crimes in our calendars, the thoughtlessness of men
while others are plunging into endless ruin, appeals
from every pulpit disregarded, lessons from every
chapter of the Bible spurned away,—these things are
evidence enough of the height, the depth, and breadth,
and blackness of man's own ruin. But when you
have sketched man's ruin, when you have thus drawn
deep and dark man's depravity, you omit the feature,
the blackest and darkest of all. And what is that?
Just his unwillingness to get rid of it. The men
whose character you have thus sketched, are not de-
prived of minds to think, of hearts to feel, of consciences to absolve or to condemn. The greatest
criminal, as well as the greatest saint, has a mind
that thinks, he has a heart that feels, he has a conscience that acquits, absolves, or condemns. Then, what
is wrong with him? His conscience is seared, his

mind is blinded, his heart hates what it should love. If God took away from man by nature, mind, conscience, heart, then he might as well lay the obligation upon a savage, or still worse, upon a dumb brute. But when you know that you have a mind, a heart, a conscience, you know that it is your duty still to love the Lord thy God with all thy heart, with all thy soul, and with all thy strength; and after the darkest and the blackest portrait of man's corruption, our Saviour himself has added the last and the most terrible inscription, "Ye will not come unto me that ye may be saved."

Well, having disposed of that so far, let me meet another difficulty not unfrequently urged. You urge the sovereignty of God and his electing purpose from eternity; a doctrine I believe scandalously abused, often mistaken by true Christians, frequently misinterpreted by the world, made a road by many to eternal ruin. When any one pleads to me, "I cannot accept of the blessing, I cannot escape from the curse, because of God's decree or election;" I answer, I believe in sovereign election just as truly and intensely as I believe in justification by faith alone, in the righteousness alone of Christ Jesus. I will not stop now to say why, or on what grounds. But when you plead God's election or God's decree, as necessitating your continuing under the curse, and preventing you from accepting the blessing, let me ask, What do you mean by this election? What is your idea of God's everlasting decree? Do you mean something of this sort—is this your definition of it? God saves some, whether they believe in Christ or not; and condemns others, whether they repent or not; so that if elected, do what I like, I cannot be lost; and if not elected, do what I can, I never can be saved. Is that your interpretation of God's decree? Then it is no more the election of the Bible than it is a doctrine of Mahometanism; it is more probably a doctrine of Mahometanism, it is certainly not a doctrine of the word of God. If you, therefore, hold a dogma so terrible, if you honestly believe that do what you like, if elect, you cannot be lost; and that do what you can, if not elect, you never can be saved; let me ask, Do you in your conscience really believe this to be true, or are you making it a mere covert and pretext for pursuing your own plans and purposes? Have you studied that doctrine; have you really discovered it? If it be true, can you really sit so quietly under it? I wonder you can have a moment's peace, if you believe so terrible and awful a dogma. But at all events, if you are sincere, I ask you to be consistent. Your error I must reprobate, your misconception of God's truth I will not cease to condemn; but if I see you out-and-out consistent with what you have accepted as God's word, I will respect your candour, and I will only try the more to undeceive you. If then God's purpose be this, it includes the sparrow as well as the immortal soul; it descends to the very minutest, as well as grasps the most magnificent. If it saves the sinner, it takes care of the hairs of his head; and if it be good enough to sustain eternal life, it is surely strong enough to carry through this present temporal life. Then, if you are sincere, thoroughly persuaded of the definition I have endeavoured to give, do you ever go without food, because you know that if you

are elected to live to seventy, live you will, whether
you eat or not? Do you ever take a sip of prussic
acid or a dose of arsenic, because if elected to live to
seventy, whether you drink poison or not, you are
sure to escape? If your doctrine is good for the
greater, it is good for the less; if it is strong enough
to sustain eternal life, surely it is strong enough to
sustain this present. If good for the soul, why should
it be so bad for the body? Take care, lest you are
making the election of God a covert for indulgence in
the election of sin by your own sinful and pernicious
will. But let us examine this sovereignty in its own
nature, in its true nature, and see if it will bear such
gross and pernicious interpretation as you attach to
it. What is this election of God? At once I start
by saying, I do not see in Scripture what is called
reprobation; I do believe in what is called election.
And the principle that guides me is the principle that
I think so plain in the Bible, that God is the author
of all that is good, beneficent, beautiful, and just; that
man, and sin, and Satan are responsible for all that is
evil, sorrowful, depraved, and wrong; why or wherefore, I do not now pause to discuss,—this is not the
place. But let us look at this doctrine, the sovereignty
of God, which has been so much abused. May not
God now shower down blessings upon man, wholly
irrespective of that man's merits, and wholly because
of something done external to that man,—for him, not
by him? You will say, Yes. Well, on the other
hand, God never inflicts punishment except upon the
guilty, but he often sends blessings upon those who
have no merit at all. He gives his blessings where
there are no merits; but it would be unjust in God to

inflict any punishment where there is no guilt. If, therefore, it be no injury to the sinner that God makes willing to be saved, and that he saves, it will be no injury to the sinner that he *leaves*, not *makes*, him willing to take the way that leads to ruin, and leaves him alone. In your natural state, under the shadow of the curse, you are taking your own way. There is not an unconverted man who is not taking his own way; nobody is driving him, there is no load crushing him; he is going in his own way. If God just lets you alone, he does not interfere with you; you are still doing as you like, walking in the road that you yourself choose, and following every inclination that you prefer. And, therefore, if God lets you alone, he leaves you to follow your own will through all its legitimate issues. And if God makes a sinner willing to be saved, surely that person will be the last to complain that he has been made so, or to think that his will has been in the least degree interfered with. I cannot see, therefore, any injustice in this sovereignty, taking it in the strictest sense in which the Calvinist can take it; I cannot see any injustice to the saint, in that God makes him willing before he saves him; or to the sinner, in that he finds him willing and does not in the least intermeddle with him. And, therefore, in the doctrine truly explained, I can see no such consequence as that which has been attached to it. The fact is, you may talk of your weakness, you may speak of the decrees and the purposes of God, you may speak of the sovereignty of Him that rules in heaven, but you know that all these are not deep and solemn convictions, but mere pretexts, pretences, and coverts for your own sin. Let me ask you, Did you ever strive to enter in at the strait gate ? Did you ever pray as one that felt his ruin and needed a blessing ? Are you not constrained in the sight of God to say, what you will be constrained to feel at a judgment-seat if not changed, " I have tried often to muffle the remonstrances of conscience, to suppress the reasoning of my mind, to extinguish the deepest inspirations within me; and I have had very great difficulty in keeping my conscience quiet, whilst often passion and I were propitiating and pleasing each other ? " Is not that your state ? You know it is ; I need not quote texts ; I appeal to what you yourselves feel and know to be actual fact. If you can say at a judgment-seat, " I have read, but I could never understand ; I have prayed, but I never could get an answer ; I have striven against sin, but I never succeeded ; I have tried to crucify my passions, but I never was able; in short, I have done everything that a creature could, and sought Divine strength for what a creature could not; and yet I am ruined;" if you could plead this, it would be an apology that might be entertained at the judgment-seat. But as in the records of the last ordeal no such apologies are pleaded, I presume there is no ground for them. Then it cannot be that in God's decree, or in your depravity, there is anything at all that can necessitate your continuing under the curse, or to prevent you from instantly accepting the blessing. Do you, then, plead the necessities of toil, of business, the employ- ments, the pressure, the avocations of this present world ? These are, no doubt, severe in the days in which we live ; it would be wrong to underrate the pressure and severity of the competitions of this pre-

sent world. But granting it is all that you say,
granting it is worse than you say, are there no bright
interludes, no interstices for another thought, for a
brighter hope, for a holier and a better sympathy?
Are there no opportunities at all for what after all is
the very end of life—to make ready, and to be made
fit for another and a better? If this be so, is it sorrowful experience that wrings from your heart the
confession, "I have no time for religion"? or is it
delight in the smiles of the world that makes the pre-
tence, "I have no time for religion"? that is the real
question. Is it sorrowful experience that you would
thankfully be rid of, that wrings from you this confession; or is it a deceitful and delightfully discovered
excuse, forged by your preference of the sins and
wickedness of the world? And, besides, if martyrdom
were the only gate to heaven, better meet it than miss
the reward. If the loss of all were necessary—and it
is not—to the gain of heaven, better risk the loss than
lose heaven. " For what shall a man be profited if he
gain the whole world, and lose his own soul?" Do
you urge, in the next place, as a reason why you must
continue under the curse, and a stranger to the blessing, the great allurements of the world, the seductions
of ambition, the blandishment of honour, the praise,
the profit, the wealth, the fortune that ever glitter
before you, and tempt you to give yourselves wholly
to the world, and to withhold yourselves from God?
I answer, or rather, I ask, have these allurements of
ambition, of wealth, of power, of honour, have they
force to constrain you? Can they compel you to bow
down to them and worship them? You know they
cannot; they can neither compel nor constrain; all

they can do is allure. But it rests with you whether the allurement shall have success, or shall meet a disastrous repulse. The strength of money, the strength of ambition, the strength of sensuality, are not in things external to you, that force you; they are all within the heart; and if you were right within, all these would be absolutely powerless without. And therefore do not blame money, do not blame ambition, do not blame the love of pleasure, but blame the heart; and, then, when you blame the heart, let me ask you, do you lay it before God, and beg of him through Christ Jesus to give you a new heart, and renew a right spirit within you? Your want of power is, translated into plain language—want of will; it is not want of capacity to believe, it is simply want of will. If you were incapable of believing, it would be unjust in God to condemn you for not believing. For instance, if an idiot or a lunatic set fire to a house, you do not punish him, because he is not responsible. If God were to address the fowls of the air and the beasts of the earth, and bid them repent, and punish them for not repenting, it would be unjust; a brute is incapable of feeling, or of remorse, or of repentance. It would be tyranny alone that would punish you and me for want of capacity of feeling; but it may be only justice, and faithfulness, and truth, to punish men for want of will to believe and to accept the gospel. You cannot explain away your responsibility. If you should say, " But how can you harmonize it with God's purpose ? " I answer, that is no business of mine, and it is no great business of yours. The noble privilege, the precious opportunity, are for you in all their fulness ; and God tells you from heaven what preachers echo from the pulpit upon earth, that the reason why any are lost is, " Ye will not come unto me that ye may have life." I have often referred you to the last sentence at the judgment-seat : " Come, ye blessed," that is, those that have the blessing, " inherit the kingdom of glory prepared for you ; " it is meant for you, and you meant for it. But when he addresses the lost it is, " Depart, ye cursed, into everlasting fire, prepared," not for you ; you observe the studied alteration of the phrase ; the complete failure of the parallelisms. And why the failure ? It is obvious. " Depart, ye cursed, into everlasting fire, prepared for the devil and his angels ; " not meant even for the cursed — not meant even for the lost. Why then are they there ? They have elected ruin, when they might have accepted eternal life ; they have gone in the way they preferred ; and they now taste the bitter and everlasting fruits of the seed they have sown ; for they that sow to the flesh must inherit corruption.

I do not deny that there are difficulties in the way to heaven ; I do not deny that there are many obstructions. But what I mean to assert is, that God has removed, by the death and sacrifice of Jesus, every obstruction that man physically never could have removed ; and that now there is no obstruction between you and everlasting glory, for which you are not responsible in the sight of God and at the judgment-seat of the Lord Jesus Christ. The fountain is open, everlasting pardon is offered, the gates of glory are flung open, mercy without price is at your acceptance ;—what more can you have ? God is not straitened, you are straitened in yourselves. And let me remind you, every fear that springs up as you hear these truths; every solemn, tremulous vibration of the conscience that you feel at times to be within you, is God speaking to you. Every conviction that you feel, telling you, you ought to do this, and you ought not to do that, is God's Spirit striving with you. And if you can resist the fear, the feeling, the conviction, the conscience to-day, you will resist it with twice the ease next Sunday; and with four times the ease next Sunday; and with a geometric, not an arithmetic, progression you will increase your facility of resisting what, accepted now, would be your glory, your happiness, and your joy.

But there is another way by which some escape. You say, " I am satisfied "—and I am sure you must be satisfied, from these plain truths, that there is nothing in God to prevent you from having the blessing, nothing in God to prevent you from escaping the curse—" it is all true; and that it is my duty to be at this moment a Christian; " and you can be, for what is the way to be a Christian? " Believe on the Lord Jesus Christ and thou shalt be saved." " Yet if it were not for this little law business, if it were not for this business in my counting-house, I would accept it. If it were not that I have not yet reached that sum of money that I have resolved to retire with, I would accept what the preacher says in all its fulness." I have given you man's delusions, and I have tried to analyze them ; this is a more masterly one still, for that is the devil's delusion. Your passions say to you when you hear the preacher, " We must be indulged, or we will scourge you with scorpion effect; " your con-

science says, "It will not do to go on any longer."
You are in a struggle : conscience says, "Accept what
the preacher says;" your passions say, "Do not do
any such thing;" the devil steps in in the fierce
struggle and procures a delusive peace, that is only
the prelude to a more terrific war; "put off the matter
to a convenient season." Is such a season very likely
to come more convenient than the present? Is it
not true that the heart becomes less susceptible by
nature as you get older, and more averse by nature
to the things that belong to your everlasting peace?
Is it not true that the temptations that beset the
young man are not expelled from the heart of the old
man, but only changed? The temptation when young
is to plunge into every excess ; the temptation when
old is to hoard and scrape together the last farthing
in order to be rich. The temptation has been changed
in its character ; but it is as powerful in its action on
the old, as it is on the heart of the young. Besides,
the Bible will not give you more powerful motives
than it now gives ; the gospel will not be plainer than
it now is ; the preacher will not speak to you more
honestly or earnestly. Take care lest if our gospel be
hid, it is hid only to them that are lost. By putting
off to a supposed convenient season, you lose very
much present happiness, present peace, present opportunities of usefulness, present safety ; you gain absolutely nothing, and you hazard eternity itself. For
who knows what may be on to-morrow? Who knows
what a day may bring forth? Death strikes in the
peaceful capital just as it does around the walls of
Sebastopol. Death finds his prey in peace, just as he
snatches it in war. No man has any surer guarantee

that he shall see a week hence, than any soldier now in the high places of the field in the neighbourhood of the beleaguered city. " In the midst of life we are in death." And what, if while God is saying, " Now is my time ; " and you are answering, " To-morrow is our time ; " God may say, " Cut him down ; why cumbereth he the ground ? " And, my dear friends, a day will come when we shall look back upon scenes that have passed away in a very different light, and with very different emotions to those with which we gaze upon them now. Sunday we are so accustomed to, that we have come to feel it very commonplace ; preaching we are so accustomed to, that it comes to be as the sound of one that playeth well upon an instrument. But a day may arrive when you will look back, and say, " If I had only one of those fifty-two Sundays of last year to come back again, I would give the whole world, and all that is contained in it." The light in which we see the past from a death-bed, is intenser, brighter, clearer, than that in which we see the present. God has said, " Now is the accepted time ; " and should you persist in saying, " No, it is not," then take care lest the most awful words in the Bible ever be fulfilled in your case—" Because I have called, and ye refused ; I have stretched out my hand, and no man regarded ; but ye have set at nought all my counsel, and would none of my reproof : I also will laugh at your calamity ;"—what an awful expression !—" I will mock when your fear cometh ; when your fear cometh as desolation, and your destruction cometh as a whirlwind ; when distress and anguish cometh upon you. Then shall they call upon me, but I will not answer ; they shall seek me

P

early, but they shall not find me : for that they hated knowledge, and did not choose the fear of the Lord." My dear friends, scenes are coming from beneath the horizon, and crowding around our country, and even the world itself, when to be without the blessing, and to have only the curse, will be indeed to feed upon husks, and herd with swine, and be far, far from our Father's home. But still, in those scenes that are coming—scenes far more terrible, however respited for a little, than eye hath seen or ear hath heard—this one thought still remains ; whatever be the trials into which we come, that man in whose heart is God's blessing, has a little Paradise within him, if there should be almost a pandemonium without. Peace, the peace that passeth understanding in the heart, will still the waves and hush the winds, and be to you a little calm. If the blessing be upon you, sickness, and pain, and sorrow will have compensatory joys, and hopes that will sweeten its bitterest cup. And when you come to die, you will descend with unfaltering step into the valley of the shadow of death, not as into a strange place, but as a consecrated spot, every inch of which bears the footprints of Him that is gone before you ; and when you have reached its deepest depth, it will only be in order to ascend that level in which there shall be more than the splendour, and nothing of the evanescence, of Mount Tabor of old. Your last sleep will be to you everlasting refreshment ; and the first accents that salute your ear, after the sounds of time have died away in the distance, will be, " Come, ye blessed, enter into the rest prepared for you from the foundation of the world." In this world, come what may, there remains this magnificent thought!—nothing shall separate us from the love of God that is in Christ Jesus. If we have not the blessing, if we have only the curse which we have deliberately chosen, then the least thing will be painful, the least thing will be penalty, and there will be only the dark mountains on which our feet must stumble in the blackness of the shadow of death for ever. They that are blessed by Him who has the blessing to give, are blessed indeed. They know the joyful sound; the evening of their life will only precede the morning of a better and a brighter; and they will never regret that they trampled under foot the miserable sophistries which a fallen heart and a seducing tempter tried to incorporate into their minds; and that they flung behind them, in God's strength, the curse; and by his grace accepted, and rejoiced in, and now enjoy, the inexhaustible blessing.

May God rivet these truths upon our hearts; and to his name be praise. Amen.

CHAPTER XII.

WARNINGS. MONUMENTS OF IDOLATRY TO BE DESTROYED.
ROMISH NAMES. THE HOLY PLACE. JESUS THE EVERLAST-
ING TEMPLE. OFFERINGS. BLOOD NOT TO BE EATEN.

THESE laws were addressed to the children of Israel
whilst they were wandering in the desert, in the
prospect of their speedy and glorious entering into
that land which had been the burden of so many and
of so cheering promises. You can see the very great
importance of giving them these warnings, when they
were about to enter into a land, every grove of which
had been the temple of an idol, every association with
which in the past was linked with idolatrous practices,
and in which there might remain monuments of its
past superstition, that because of their architec-
tural beauty, or their venerable age, or because of
other associations, the Israelites might seek to perpetuate and to interweave with that service which
repudiates all idolatry, and demands all the affections
of the soul, the heart, and the mind to be given to
the Lord God. And therefore, to keep them pure
from that great branding crime of heathendom, the
worship of idols and images, and to preserve them in
the worship of the Lord their God, and of him alone,
they are told that when they shall come into this
land, "Ye shall utterly destroy all the places wherein

the nations which ye shall possess served their gods, upon the high mountains, and upon the hills, and under every green tree." They shall not only not be guilty of the offence, but they shall cut down and sweep away the memorials and vestiges of it; so that there may not be one relic left that shall remind them of the iniquities of the past, or be a nucleus for forming new and idolatrous associations for the future : —"Ye shall overthrow their altars, and break their pillars, and burn their groves with fire; and ye shall hew down the graven images of their gods, and destroy the names of them out of that place." This is a very important law : in this world, unhappily, names are often things; for whenever a party wish to get power, a party holding erroneous doctrines, the first thing they do is to establish titles; and when they have got titles, they soon follow them up by asserting realities. And therefore it is very wisely provided here, that not only should the scenes, the altars, and the groves, all be overturned, as having been desecrated by practices that were abominable in the sight of a holy God, but that even the very names that might remind of that superstition that had passed away should be expunged from their vocabularies, and not mentioned even in their conversation. What a pity it is that we do not expunge every name that reminds us of past sin. For instance, Christmas is a Romish name; the origin of it is, "The mass of Christ," the sacrifice of the mass; an abomination offered up in honour of Christ. It would be a much more beautiful idea to call it " Christ's birthday;" that would be very proper. And so Martinmas, known in Scotland—St. Martin's mass; and Candle-

mas—the mass of candles. All these are names of ex-
ploded superstitions ; but when we retain names, however inoffensive in themselves, very often the names
are the dry channels in which the tide of superstition
comes back with irresistible force. And so in the very
same manner, in all our service, in the names of our
churches, I would, if possible, alter all names that
savour of idolatry. I do not like saints' names applied
to churches — St. Andrew's, or St. Peter's, or St.
Thomas's. There is nothing sinful in those that give
these names, because they happen to have been long
the parish names ; I can understand that ; but why
should a new church be called after St. Andrew ? It is
not his church, he did not die for it, he did not make an
atonement for it, he is not the head of it, he is not the
glory of it. Christ church is beautiful ; Trinity church
is beautiful ; but St. Andrew's church and St. Peter's
church are names that, it seems to me, ought rather
to be expunged from the vocabulary of the Christian
church. The old names of ancient parish churches it
is scarcely possible to alter, but in the case of new
churches and chapels it is most inexpedient to prefix
such titles. I would not apply the names of ancient
saints or modern reformers to new places of worship.
At all events, we have here a remarkable proof of the
wisdom of God, in that he commands them not only
to take away the things, but the names, in themselves
perhaps innocuous ; but as associated with practices
that were corrupt, it was desirable they should pass
away, and be numbered with the things that were,
and that are to be no more again. At all events, I
cannot understand, unless there be a tendency in
human nature to take the least remains of evil and to

make it an apology for greater evil,—unless there be such a tendency in human nature, I cannot understand the minute and almost scrupulous warnings that are given in this blessed book to the children of Israel, to prevent their lapsing into idolatry or indulging in the practices and superstitions of the heathen nations; warnings not only about things, but names; so that in that land there might not be left a trace of ancient superstition that should not be overflowed with the springtide of righteousness, and peace, and truth.

After he had given these instructions, he adds directions about the place where they are to worship, and to which they are to bring their first-fruits, their heave-offerings, and the firstlings of their herds and their flocks:—" Unto the place which the Lord your God shall choose out of all your tribes to put his name there, even unto his habitation shall ye seek, and thither thou shalt come." And so he requires it again in another verse: " In the place which the Lord shall choose in one of thy tribes, there thou shalt offer thy burnt-offerings, and there thou shalt do all that 1 command thee." That place was Jerusalem; the very mountain on which Abraham was ready to offer up his son, his only son Isaac; and the mountain on which Jesus died a sacrifice for our sins. That was the only place where an Israelite might offer atoning victims, sacrifices, first-fruits, and heave-offerings; and the dispute, we may remember, with the Jews and the Samaritans was, whether the Temple or Mount Gerizzim was the mountain upon which they ought to worship. The Samaritans dissented, and took another mountain: evidently they were wrong; the Jews held fast the original place. But you say, If the place was so consecrated then, that only in that place was it legitimate to offer sacrifice; would not that be evidence that a place should be secured or exist now, in which only should worship be continually offered up? I answer, No; because then the place on which the temple stood, and the temple itself, were the type of our blessed Redeemer. He himself says, " Destroy this temple, and I will build it up in three days; this spake he of the temple of his body;" showing us that the temple on its site was the type of God dwelling in our nature; God's glory between the cherubim burning in the chancel of that holy temple, was the type of God living in flesh, and being manifest to mankind. The Jew looked to his temple when he worshipped; you remember Daniel opened his window and prayed with his face towards the temple at Jerusalem three times a-day; and every Jew still should turn towards that temple, if he be consistent when he prays; just as the Mahometan, retaining it as a superstition, looks towards Mecca. But now that the temple has been destroyed, and that the object signified by the temple has come—Christ Jesus; then just as it was right in the Jew to look to the temple of Jerusalem as he prayed then, it would be wrong for the Christian now, because the temple has passed away, and that which was typified and set forth by the temple is now come. Hence, a Christian, when he prays, looks neither east, nor west, nor north, nor south, nor to altar, nor to communion-table; but he prays looking to the only Mediator, and seeking acceptance for his prayers through his blood, and merits, and intercession alone. This shows, therefore, how what would be literal conformity to the words of Scripture here would be positively wrong; and what is not conformity to the words, but the acceptance of that which the words pointed to, is everywhere and always right. And, therefore, for parties now in the church, when they repeat a creed, or engage in any particular part of the service, to turn round and look in any one direction, as if that direction had any virtue in it, is Jewish; it is not Christian; it assumes that eighteen centuries have not passed away. Our blessed Lord is in the midst of two or three met in his name, invisible, but real. Faith looks to an invisible, but a really present Lord. But to make the eye or the body turn round in a given direction, as if in that direction there were virtue, is most absurd. If it be done for the sake of order, or uniformity, there is no objection to it; but if it should be done because there is some virtue in the east that is not in the west, a virtue we cannot discover, it is sinful.

Having thus specified the place, he directs them as to their offerings. He says, You are to bring the firstlings of all your flocks and your products to this place, and present these to the Lord—except the hart and the roebuck, which were destroyed in hunting, and could not probably be brought to the temple to be offered as first-fruits. He only makes this stipulation, that the blood of the animal should not be eaten. Now, the reason of this existed then in great force. The great lesson inculcated upon the Jews was, that the blood shed by the victim was the expiatory element. "Without shedding of blood there is no remission of sins," was the lesson taught throughout the length and breadth of Jewry; and, therefore, the Israelite was taught not to eat that blood; but to regard it as a holy, significant thing ; meant to remind him it was for expiation, not for nutriment. It was a purely ceremonial law: the ceremonial law ceased when the Christian economy began, except so far as it would give offence to Jew or Gentile. Then there was a reason for it; now, morally considered, there is no reason for it ; physically viewed there may be. But in the case of the Jews, it was meant to teach them that the blood was the expiatory element ; and they were prohibited, under the strictest penalties, from ever being guilty of eating it.

CHAPTER XIII.

SEDUCTIONS TO IDOLATRY. PENALTIES. MIRACLES, FALSE AND
TRUE. RELATIVE AFFECTIONS. MAJORITIES,

THERE is contained in this chapter the record of three distinct kinds of influences, of different kinds, employed to draw God's people away from the worship and service of the Lord their God, the only true and living God, to the service of the idols and the gods that the heathen nations then universally adored. You will observe that the penalty attached to each offence, to each of the three attempts to withdraw the people from their allegiance to their God, and to enlist their sympathy and service to the gods of the heathen, is a most severe one—nothing less than death. But for any one to quote this from this chapter as a precedent for persecuting with pains and penalties them that seek to make proselytes to error, though what they believe to be truth, is to misquote, misunderstand, and misapply the Bible. Just because it was law then, it cannot be law now. For, in our case, if a Roman Catholic attempts to make a Protestant a Papist, he tries to seduce him from what the one believes to be truth, to what the other believes to be truth; but he does not touch in that act, as far as it is a spiritual act, the obligations that they owe in common to their sovereign, to the constitution, to the laws, to their country. But under ancient Israel there was what was called a theocracy; God was not only their God, but he was also their King, their Sovereign, and their supreme Ruler; and to be guilty of idolatry was not only to be guilty of the spiritual offence, most heinous, most ruinous, unquestionably so, but it was also to be guilty of direct rebellion against their king, direct infringement of the public laws; it was therefore a national and political offence, high treason itself, justly punishable by the law laid down by God their Sovereign as well as their God. But we live now not under a theocracy, as they did; theirs was a combination of Church and State, the two welded into one; no doubt a most perfect constitution, but one that we know does not exist now as matter of fact. And, therefore, for prince or priest to quote this as a reason for persecuting those who seduce others from one creed, however excellent, to another creed, however superstitious and wrong, is to forget an essential distinction that subsists between the theocracy of the Jews and the ordinary social governments under which the nations of the world now live. Besides, wherever it has been attempted, persecution has never yet, I believe, won a conscientious adherent to truth, and it has never detached a sincere adherent from error. It is always found, that if you persecute men for what they believe erroneously, yet sincerely, to be truth, you add impulse and *éclat* to their creed; and you rivet the stronger the bonds of attachment that they feel to it. No man should ever surrender a conviction, that he sincerely entertains, to force; and you cannot but admire the man who says to you, " I shall be con-

vinced by argument; or, I shall change my mind
before satisfactory facts; but you never shall burn
out of my mind a conviction it has deliberately
cherished, or extinguish my attachment to a creed, by
force, which in my heart I believe to be true." And,
therefore, if ever the sword is to be unsheathed, let it
be by the enemies of the gospel, not by its friends;
if ever the fagots are to be collected, let them be
collected by those who know that their creed will not
stand the ordeal of a faithful analysis, not by us, who
submit everything we assert to the Scripture, to fact,
to evidence; and are abundantly convinced that
Christianity will emerge from the severest ordeal
only more glorified than before.

Now, in the first of the three instances there is
supposed a dreamer, and one, too, that gives a sign or
a wonder; and more, it assumes that the sign or
wonder may come to pass. Now there are two inter-
pretations proposed of this; and the one that seems
the most natural is that, of course, which you will
accept. The one is, that if this person perform what
seems a miracle, in order to seduce you from true religion, and if what he said turn out to be true; if he
prophesy, and the matter come just as he predicted; or
if he perform some sign, and the sign show itself just
as he commanded, then you have here either a miracle,
or the supposition of an accidental coincidence which
may be construed as a manifestation of his power
when it really is not. But I think the former is the
more probable thing; that it is quite possible that
bad men may then have done supernatural acts; and
I do not see how it is impossible that bad men may
not be allowed to do supernatural acts now. If it be

true, for instance, that Satan can enter my mind without my consent; if it be true that Satan can prompt and suggest what is evil unperceived, unnoticed, undetected at first by me, then that is a power so very supernatural that it does not seem straining possibilities at all to conclude that he may have the power to enable one of his own wicked partisans to do what is physically supernatural, as well as to inspire into the mind what is morally wrong and false. And hence it has been thought by many most competent critics, that it is not improbable, that amid all the foolish tales, and idle legends, and lying stories of the Church of Rome, there may have been supernatural things. Indeed, it is almost indicated that it will be so; for in the prediction of the Man of Sin, Scripture says, " He shall come with all lying wonders : " words that do not mean, as most people understand, false wonders, pretended wonders; but, as literally translated —" with miracles tending to prove a falsehood; " not false miracles, but miracles done to promote a falsehood. Recollect the prophecy, that towards the end there shall come false Christs and false teachers; and that they shall do such things, that if it were possible, they would deceive the very elect. But we read as a guard against this, that " If we," says the apostle, " or an angel from heaven preach to you any other gospel than that ye have received, let him be anathema." One single text from this book is stronger than all that the eye can see, than all that the ear can hear, than all that man can possibly perform. And, therefore, it says here, " Thou shalt not hearken to the words of that prophet."

The next assumption is, the influence of affection :

—" If thy brother, the son of thy mother, or thy son, or thy daughter, or the wife of thy bosom, or thy friend which is as thine own soul, entice thee." If the miracle fail, if the supernatural fail, then the next influence brought to bear upon you will be affection; and they will say to you, " You are my near and dear relative, my friend, my brother, my son, my daughter, my father, my husband; you surely cannot resist my advice." The answer must be, " Whoso loveth father, or mother, or husband, or wife, or sister, or brother, more than me is not worthy of me." In the realm of allegiance to God, not the highest saint in heaven nor the dearest relative upon earth must step in. In duties that you owe to him, you must be guided by his word; and not by the love, the affection, or the influence of any. You show the greatest love to a relative when you stand fast in the truth, and yield not one inch to any persuasion that does not rest upon the law and upon the testimony.

The third seductive power that is alluded to, is that of a whole city apostatizing from the truth. They are called here, " If thou shalt hear in one of thy cities that the children of Belial are gone out from among you." The word Belial is derived from the two Hebrew words which mean, " having not over one," or " not under any;" and it means simply an autocrat, a czar; one who defies all superior authority, and exercises a despotic and independent power on his own accord, and from his own spontaneous feelings. Therefore, it means one who will acknowledge no superior. He supposes a whole city to revolt. Now this is the argument of numbers. The first was the argument of miracles in

favour of error; the second was the argument of
affection; the third is the argument of numbers. The
meaning of it is this : " Why, how can you take up
such a religion as that ? Everbody else thinks differ-
ently. How can you be a Protestant ? Do you not
see that three-fourths of the Christian world, as it is
called, are Roman Catholics ? Great majorities are
against you ; you are a miserable minority." Your
answer to that, even if true, must just be the answer
that Luther gave when a similar argument was employed against him. He was told by a monk to whom
he was attached, " Luther, the whole world is against
you; how can you persist in the course you have
chosen ? " The answer of that great man was, " If
the whole world be against Luther, then Luther will
be against the whole world." His footing was on the
rock ; his convictions were taken from God's word ;
and it mattered not to him where the multitude was ;
he was resolved to hold what God had revealed.
And so, in the present day, truth is not always with
majorities. It is not multitude that is the test of
truth. On the contrary, we are told, " Thou shalt not
follow a multitude to do evil ;" the supposition that
multitudes may be against you. Every man in the age
in which we live must make up his mind as to what is
truth, upon the strength and evidence of this blessed
volume ; and then, if all the world should cry, " Great
is Diana," he must be satisfied to stand alone, and to
say, " Christ is all and in all."

CHAPTER XIV.

GOD bases all the prescriptions of his law, as the Great Lawgiver, on the ground that those that were to obey were his own chosen, beloved, redeemed, and sanctified people. He begins by declaring, first of all, their grand relationship to him as the Lord their God, the King of Israel. " Ye are," by adopting love, " the children of the Lord your God "—a covenant God; yours because he has given himself to you; yours because you have deliberately chosen him; and with a solemn oath have promised, " We will serve the Lord our God." Well, upon this strong ground, this sure foundation, as affectionate as it is sure, he says, " You shall not imitate the heathen by mourning for the dead as they mourn; " or, transferred from Judaism to Christianity, " You shall not weep for your dead as others weep, who have no hope; having a better, surer, nobler prospect, alike of the state of the soul, and the emergence from the grave of the earthly shrine it has left behind it."

Then God bases all this again upon the reiterated words, "Thou art an holy people unto the Lord thy God;" destinated to be so. The word *holy*, as often explained, means simply " set apart ; " and as used in Hebrew, and Greek, and Latin, in the corresponding words, it has a bad sense as well as a good sense ; the *kadosh* in the Hebrew, the ἅγιος in the Greek, and the *sacer* in the Latin, meaning, set apart to a good purpose or a bad purpose, as the case may be. In this instance it means set apart, or consecrated, of course to a holy and a sublime destiny, and to a present and a constant duty. " And the Lord hath chosen thee," by his electing love, " to be a peculiar people unto himself, above all the nations that are upon the earth."

Having thus declared their relationship to him, he lays down the laws of ordinary living. Some people at first, when they read all this, are disposed to say, " Is not all this unworthy of God, that he should not only declare those magnificent truths which we at this moment can appreciate ; and the nearer that we come to them, as to distant stars, the more beautiful and luminous they become ; but that he should descend from the magnificent, the glorious, the eternal, and lay down culinary laws, or prescriptions for eating and drinking ? " I answer, if this be your objection, is it not unworthy of God that he should descend from creating those stars, that are larger orbs than our own, and should be at the trouble of polishing a beetle's covering, or weaving the exquisite tissue of a bee's wing, or tinting the petals of a flower, as if he had nothing else to do ? Is not all in this chapter in perfect keeping with all that we know of God, that while he rises to the great, as if the great alone were within his province, he descends to the exquisitely minute ? And I question whether God is seen to be most glorious in creating the magnificently vast, or in watching over the ephemeral and the exquisitely minute. At all events, all that we know of God in creation, in providence, in redemption, leads us to see that he takes as much care of what the world calls, in its ignorance, little things, as he does of what the world thinks, in equal ignorance, great and weighty things. But there is another reason why God should lay down these laws. The Jews were a typical nation; they were typical of a higher body, that were to occupy a higher position—the church of the redeemed; and it was essential that the Jews should be separated from other nations, not simply by their moral and their spiritual excellence, but also by national, physical, and material characteristics; and we know quite well that the moral has much to do with the material. And therefore God hedges them, as it were, round from all the rest of the nations of the earth, that they might be a people marked off and sharply and clearly defined; a testimony for his unity, for his greatness, and for a divine revelation amid the nations of the earth, universally involved in surrounding darkness. And thus he lays down laws that would separate them, even in their ordinary diet, from the rest of the nations of the earth, as much as in their sublime and solemn ritual. And is not this law translated into New Testament usage; where, indeed, those ritual distinctions do not exist which the Jews felt obligatory upon them; but where we, nevertheless, are commanded, "Whatsoever ye do, whether you eat or drink," if you do not observe these laws, which are not obligatory, this you ought to observe, "do all to the glory of God"? But it is a very interesting fact, which physiologists have noticed, that these distinctions indicate, on the part of Moses, an extent of acquaintance with the animal economy, that either makes him out a most extraordinarily gifted man, or that proves to us that he was inspired and guided by God. It is matter of fact, that these distinctions, these generic laws, that he has laid down, are at this moment the best directories in reference to all that we should eat. It is the fish with the fins and the scales that are still the most wholesome; it is the animal that rechews its food, as the sheep and the ox, that are still best for food. Again, the swine, the hare, and others, that are what are called half-clean—that is, have one of the marks of clean animals, but not the two; the one dividing the hoof and the other not, but the one ruminating and the other not—are not so wholesome. And it may therefore turn out that those distinctions that we think so trivial, are yet after all, though not obligatory in their religious sense, most useful and important for wholesomeness and for health to mankind. And then, how comes it to pass, if these distinctions be not well founded, that we act upon them still? Men that do not believe in the Jewish economy, or even in a written revelation, show that they act in the main upon these laws at this day.

To show that these laws are not religiously obligatory, he says: The stranger that is in thy gates, or the alien, he may eat what the Jew should not eat. Now, that incidental remark, emerging in the midst of general laws, proves that whilst their physical wholesomeness should weigh with us, as religious laws they have ceased to be obligatory upon us, the Jewish economy having altogether passed away. But it is also worthy of notice, in the next place, and I think I made that remark before, that eminent physicians connected with the Board of Health, who have taken a very careful inspection of these things, have remarked that the Jews, who observe their laws, and rigidly too, during the time of epidemic pestilence, were generally spared. Now, that looks as if there were some connexion between the health of the people and these distinctions in diet, which, though not obligatory, are founded in the nature of things themselves.

We have, in the next place, the law that they were to bring their corn, and their wine, and the firstlings of their flocks, to the special place that God should appoint; and if the way should be too long, then they should turn their goods into money; God consulting the convenience of man, and not rigidly exacting what it was inconvenient to give.

Then he enjoins hospitality. He says, "Thou shalt bestow that money for whatsoever thy soul lusteth after." The word "lust," in its old sense, means simply preference or liking, and no more; it is not used in a bad sense—"for oxen, or for sheep, or for wine, or for strong drink." Now, at all events, here we see that wine and strong drink were in moderation lawful; if it were essentially poisonous, it would be positively forbidden. I cannot, therefore, under such a law as that, agree with the advocates of total abstinence on theological grounds. At the same time, I repeat here what I think it right to add, that the safe side is the side of total abstinence; and for a confirmed drunkard there is no cure in the world but total abstinence. I should feel that if in my congregation there was an individual who had sunk so below the beasts of the earth, that he drank wine and strong drink to excess, and if I felt that by my abstaining totally from tasting it on any occasion whatever, that I should be the means of making that individual abstain, then I should act upon the principle of St. Paul,—" All things are lawful, but all things are not expedient. If meat make my brother to offend, then I will abstain from meat." But when I do not find this best; but on the contrary, that the exhibition of using as not abusing is most useful — when I observe that the lawful in limit is the scriptural, I have always the impression that when men try to be holier than God's word, and take another rule of living than the Bible, they very often take another rule of believing than the Bible. I do not wish to say one word against those who think that total abstinence from wine in every shape and sense is a duty. It is perfectly lawful, if they are convinced it will be the most effective way to end drunkenness. I commend and admire them for it. It is no great sacrifice ; and if you could reclaim a sinner from his drunkenness by it, I think it would be dutiful and right for you to set the example. I am convinced, however, that to set the example that our blessed Lord prescribed is the true one ; and men that are bent upon the gratification of low, and wretched, and debased appetites, will make anything an excuse for it. John the Baptist came a teetotaller, neither eating nor drinking : and they said, " He hath a devil," because they must say something against him. Our blessed Lord came eating and drinking like other men ; and they said, " He is a wine-bibber, and a friend of publicans and sinners." And so, if you should come

totally abstaining from wine in every shape, they will
say you have a devil, you are mad, you are a lunatic,
you are a fool. Or if you come eating and drinking
wine like other people, they will say you are a wine-
bibber. The fact is, it needs the grace of God to
change the human heart; until He do it, all mechanical
arrangements must more or less necessarily fail.

CHAPTER XV.

WE have, in this chapter, some of those admirable temporal provisions for the earthly convenience and comfort of the land of Israel, which are to be found in the Bible, and in the Bible alone. If any one will compare the wisest legislation of heathen rulers with the legislation of this nomade race—a race of barbarians, as the Pagans would be disposed to call them —he will be struck with the contrast; seeing, in the highest pagan legislation, the evidence of the avarice, the tyranny of man; in the legislation of the ancient Hebrews, as communicated by their lawgiver Moses, that equity, that wisdom, that beneficence, and mercy, that prove the author of the laws to be the great Lawgiver, God. You will recollect, in reading this chapter, that it was a grand design of God to preserve that race in that same land as a standing testimony, as a nation of witnesses to the unity of God, to the obligations of his law, to the necessity of an atonement, and to be the family out of whom He that was to make the atonement was destined, in the fulness of the times, to spring. And many of those laws which seem to us occasionally supererogatory or unnecessarily minute, have, independent of their moral meaning, a special relationship to this grand design, of Israel as a distinct and protesting nation, destined to give birth to Him who should be the light to lighten the Gentiles and the glory of his people Israel.

Accordingly, it begins here with instituting, first of all, a seventh year, during which they were to sow no seed; during which the spontaneous produce of the fields, of the gardens, of the vineyards, were to be the common property of all that liked. But whilst they had this year so special, they had also special promises as well as special laws and commands to direct them in appointing that year. They lived under a theocracy; the highest possible type of a perfect government; for of all governments, the best, and noblest, and most effective would be a perfect despotism; that is, the ruler a perfect man, with a perfect heart, a perfect mind, and thereby perfect justice, perfect mercy. But as such, or even an approximation to it, is never realized amid fallen men, we must be satisfied to institute those checks, and restraints, and modifications which are found in their highest and best combination in the peculiar national polity under which it is our privilege to live. Under the Jewish economy, there was a seventh year, when the people had neither to sow nor to reap, and when a special blessing of God superseded their toil on that occasion, and supplied all the wants that the earth, and the vineyards, and the gardens might not be able to supply. They had the promise of special aid, and therefore they ventured, if I may use the expression, on a special sacrifice. We have no renewal of that promise; we have no command to this special institution; and therefore it would be as sinful for you not to sow every seventh year, as it would have been sinful for the Jew to sow and to reap every seventh year.

"Every creditor," was one part of this law, "that lendeth aught unto his neighbour, shall release it; he shall not exact it of his neighbour or of his brother; because it is called the Lord's release." That is— it assumes this, and in parallel passages it asserts—if the debtor should be unable to pay, only then at the seventh year the creditor should not exact his debt from him, he should not put him in prison, he should not sell his children to be slaves, he should not sell his little plot of land or disinherit him. It was to preserve the nation as a peculiar, distinct nation in the midst of the nations of the earth. If the debtor could pay, but would not pay, then he was to be made to pay; but if he would pay when he could not pay, then the creditor was not to exact the money. But whilst this was true of a brother Israelite, it did not apply to a foreigner; that is, a Gentile, or a stranger. There he might exact it. "But that which is thine with thy brother, thine hand shall release."

Then he prescribes laws for lending. "If there be among you a poor man of one of thy brethren within any of thy gates in thy land which the Lord thy God giveth thee, thou shalt not harden thine heart, nor shut thine hand from thy poor brother; but thou shalt open thine hand wide unto him, and shalt surely lend him sufficient for his need." Either give it him, if you prefer that as the better way, or lend him, if it is to help him during a year of pressure, when he has the fair and honourable prospect, as he has the open design, of repaying you what he has borrowed from you.

And then he guards against that mean, contemptible, most ignoble feeling that might spring up in the hearts of some who had the power of lending, but would not lend, by saying, " Why, we had better not lend this poor man a single sixpence ; for next year, or the next to that, is the seventh year, when, if he cannot pay us, we shall be compelled not to exact it, and he will be under no compulsion to pay it." It is against such men, that would assume unwillingness to pay where there might not have been ability to pay, and that would not run the risk of the poor debtor not being able to pay, and being therefore released at the seventh year,—it is against such men that this law is directed. It is, in other words, to do away with that uncharitable and that selfish monopoly that tries to seize all we can, and give nothing that we can withhold ; which makes man mean in the estimate of man, and sinful in the sight of God. Of all characters, I think that in itself, even viewed in an earthly light, is unspeakably mean, is that of the grinding, grasping, avaricious miser. Rather let me see the spendthrift, with all his extravagance and prodigality, than the miserable miser whose heart is with his gold, and would sooner part with blood from his veins than with it, if he will part with it at all. Now, against such a character there is a protest in every page of the Bible; against such a character in the Jews there is the most deep and decided warning in this very chapter; against the calculation of contingencies and of possibilities of failure to pay that which the individual that borrowed might be most willing to pay, there is that warning which shows it was the Master of the human heart that inspired it, and needed not to be taught what is in man, for he knows all that is in him.

Then, the next law that he lays down, is in reference to slaves. Certainly it never can be denied that, however horrible slavery may be, however condemned it is by the light, and spirit, and indirect influence of the New Testament, yet nobody with his eyes open can deny that a mitigated system of slavery did exist in ancient times; that one might sell himself, and be the slave, the bond-slave, of a master; his property, his time, his person, absolutely his master's. But whilst this existed, there were thrown around it such lights and modifications, that the slavery that existed in the ancient Jewish economy is not comparison, but contrast, to the system that has existed, and still exists in modern times and amidst modern nations. For instance, here is one of the great laws that altogether disinfect it of the horrors which have developed themselves where modern slavery has existed. It says: "If thy brother, an Hebrew man, or an Hebrew woman, be sold unto thee"—which admits the lawfulness of the transaction—"and serve thee six years, then in the seventh year thou shalt let him go free from thee." In other words, the slavery could not exist more than six years, and in most instances must be less. And then notice how he was to treat the slave he manumitted. "When thou sendest him out from thee"—what a tender sympathy is exhibited in this provision!—"thou shalt not let him go away empty; thou shalt furnish him liberally out of thy flock, and out of thy floor, and out of thy winepress; of that wherewith the Lord thy God hath blessed thee thou shalt give unto him. And thou shalt remember that thou wast a bondman in the land of Egypt.'' But if that slave should wish to come to you; if he likes his master; if your home has become, in his affections and sympathies, his home; if he wish to continue with you, not through life, mind you, but six years more, till the next jubilee, or till the fiftieth jubilee, which was the grand one of all, then you shall pierce his ear with an awl; and that shall be the signal and the sign that he has not availed himself of the seventh year, but prefers to continue a slave under the auspices of a good master, rather than to be a free man, tossed and buffeted upon a world in which he has no footing, and probably no hope. Well, so common was this, that the practice of piercing the ear went even into pagan nations; and it was a mark of a slave in ancient times, that he had rings in his ears, or a sort of ring in his ear, which indicated that his ear had been pierced by the awl, and that he was a slave, in pagan nations for life, in the Jewish nation till the jubilee.

The next provision we have, is, that all the first-lings of sheep and of oxen were to be consecrated unto God, as an expression of thankfulness to him for the increase, and as also an evidence that all that we have are not ours, but are gifts from God in his gracious providence, to be consecrated by us to his service and to his glory.

CHAPTER XVI.

WE have here, not indeed the institution of the Passover, which had been instituted before, but the recalling that beautiful rite to the recollection of the Israelites, as one of the most precious and significant of the whole of their ancient and remarkable economy. It is said that "in the month of Abib," that is, near the time, or about the time that we call Good Friday—"the Lord thy God brought thee forth out of Egypt by night; and thou shalt therefore sacrifice the passover unto the Lord thy God, of the flock and the herd, in the place which the Lord shall choose to place his name there." What really was the Passover? The word means simply or strictly transition, or passing over some that deserved to be visited, and smiting others that equally, and perhaps no more, deserved to be punished. The origin of it was this; that Pharaoh had slain the firstborn of the children of Israel, wherever his tyrannic hand could lay hold on them. God resolved to exercise a retribution that would make Pharaoh feel at least the social consequences, if he could not understand the moral wickedness, of such a deed. And therefore he told his own people—the children of Israel—that on a certain night they were to slay a lamb; they were to sprinkle its blood upon the doorposts and lintels of the house; and they were told that the angel of death, God's dread messenger of judgment, should pass through the length and breadth of the land of Egypt that night; and every home on the lintels of which there was no sprinkled blood, the angel of retribution should enter; but that into any home, however lowly, however humble, on the lintels of which was the sprinkled blood, he would not dare to enter. Now the predictions of God became soon the facts of history; for we find that the angel of death came that night and passed through Egypt; and there was a great wail amid all the children of Egypt, whilst there was great rejoicing in all the dwellings of Jacob. The poor Israelite father, mother, children, that were within the home, on the lintels of which was the blood of the slain passover-lamb, I have not the least doubt, when they heard the rush of the angel's wing, and the wail that arose from the door of their next neighbour, were themselves startled; even began to doubt, distrust, suspect the prophylactic efficacy of the great prescription under which they were. But you will notice, that the doubts of the Israelite within did not in the least affect his safety. His doubts affected his comfort, but they did not in the least affect his safety. He was just as safe when he doubted, feared, trembled, as another Israelite who had unflinching and unfaltering faith; because the safety of the home lay not in the strength of the inmate's faith, but in the efficacy of the sacrificial blood that was sprinkled on the lintel. Now, so it is with a Christian still. The best, the holiest, the most sensitive Christians, are not always assured of their safety. That they ought to be, is quite plain; that they are not, is matter of fact and of daily observation. But if you be true Christians, your doubts, your suspicions, may affect your comfort, and they do, which you know. But your doubts, suspicions, and even fainting faith, do not affect your safety; for your safety lies in the precious blood of the Lamb that was slain; not in the strength of the faith by which you lay hold on him. It is, therefore, very important to feel that your safety in reference to God does not depend upon the strength of your faith, but upon the perfection of the sacrifice of Jesus Christ the righteous. Your comfort is injured by your faltering and trembling faith, but your safety is not; your weak faith is your sin or your infirmity; but it is not therefore the perilling of your everlasting interests.

Now, this event was so important, in the deliverance of the children of Israel from Pharaoh, next their exodus from Egypt, that they were appointed by a solemn fast to call it into recollection once a-year. And how did they do so? The father of the family took a lamb, spotless and blameless, slew it, shed its blood; and then the flesh of the lamb was roasted, and the whole family gathered round it; and if one family were too few to eat it, other families were called; and thus a little church or congregation were collected. And when the head of the family was celebrating the feast' what did he say? His children were to ask him, "What mean ye by this service?" The word "mean" is not there; in the original it is, "What is this service?" And the father of the family was to say, "This is the Lord's passover." The question was, "What *mean* ye by this?" The answer is, "This *is* the Lord's passover." Now would an Israelite ever have dreamed that when the officiating person said so, the roasted flesh that was upon his table was transformed into an angel flying through Egypt, sparing the first-born of Israel, and striking down the first-born of Pharaoh? Did he ever dream of such a monstrous transubstantiation as that? And yet enlightened men, supposed to be well read, men in the nineteenth century, actually believe— and some men who subscribe Protestant articles believe it—that the moment the bread and wine are laid upon the communion-table—not altar, for we have no altar—and as soon as the officiating minister says what our blessed Lord said, "This is my body," clearly corresponding to, "This is the Lord's passover;" they believe—what the Jew never was so stupid as to believe—that the bread and wine actually undergo a complete transformation, so that the one ceases to be bread and the other ceases to be wine, and become both the flesh and blood of the Son of God. This is worse than the possible transubstantiation of the Jew; it is much more monstrous. The explanation of our Lord's words, when he said, "This is my body," is plain. At a feast instituted just behind the passover, that had then been celebrated, He transferred passover language to sacramental usage; and as the ancient officiating minister said, "This is the Lord's passover," Jesus said, "This is my body;" that is, in the first instance, it puts you, the Jew, in mind of your escape, it refreshes your recollection with it; in

R

the second, this puts you, the Christian, in mind of Christ our passover, sacrificed for us. And, therefore, adds the apostle, "Let us keep the feast." Now, this is very important, and I think it is one of those truths that we should never forget, that in the ancient passover there were two things. There was first the killing of the lamb, which was the sacrifice; then, subsequent to that, there was the eating of the lamb, which was the festival that succeeded; two distinct things; the first act was propitiatory, the second was simply festal. The apostle says, "Christ our passover is sacrificed for us;" that is, the atonement is made. And then what are we to do? "Therefore let us keep the feast." What feast? The Lord's Supper that commemorates it. So that the atoning part is done; and all that remains now is the festal act, or refreshing our minds with blessed thoughts, our hearts by divine feelings, our souls with bright hopes; leaning and looking to Christ that was, leaning still and looking forward to Christ that will be; our festival reminding us of a sacrifice, not being in itself a sacrifice.

Then, after he has given rules for the observance of this festival, and also on each of the three great festal days, on which three great occasions they should all appear before the Lord; he lays down laws for judges and officers. One strange expression occurs here: "In all thy gates." How is the word "gate" used in Scripture? Constantly as the place where authority and judgment are executed. The judges of old sat in the gates of the city; and we have the remains of this still. We speak of the Ottoman Porte, the Sublime Porte. It is the Ottoman *porta,*

the Ottoman gate ; Eastern usage retaining the
very name that used to be associated with the place
where the judges sat and administered justice. And
now when we come to that expression in the New
Testament, "The gates of hell shall not prevail
against Christ's church," we discover the meaning, by
referring to the fact, that the source of authority,
jurisdiction, power, was placed in the gates of the city.
And therefore the prediction, "The gates of hell shall
not prevail against the church of Christ," is not that
no portion of the visible church shall fall into error,
but that the authority, the power, the jurisdiction of
Satan shall not so prevail against the church of Christ,
as to extinguish and destroy it from the earth. In
other words, Christ is with it, and it will last and live
for ever.

Then, at the close of the chapter there are laws laid
down for the prevention of idolatry ; against planting
groves where the ancient pagans, like the Druids,
worshipped ; against erecting images in the house of
God, or doing that which God hates, and which was
fitted to seduce them from His love and pure worship.

CHAPTER XVII.

IN the first portion of the chapter I have read, we
have the prohibition of the sacrifice of animals that
were not in all respects without blemish, faultless,
and perfect. And this was designed not so much
because of any intrinsic excellence in their perfect
physical organization, but because they were types of
that spotless Lamb of God who needed to be without
blemish, that He might make atonement for the sins
of the people, and have no defect in Himself requiring
an atonement for it. It was therefore its typical, or
foreshadowing aspect, that alone required this exact
and scrupulous attention to the physical perfection of
the animals that were slain in sacrifice.

After this we have a command that seems to us, at
first blush, exceedingly severe—that idolaters should
be put to death ; that is, if any one should be found
in the land of Israel, man or woman, who had gone
and worshipped sun, or moon, or the host of heaven ;
or, what was the same thing, and what is repeated in
other parts of Scripture, had made images of the true
God, to worship God through the medium of them,
which was equally idolatry ; then they should bring

forth such persons charged with this heinous offence; and if there should be two witnesses, the guilty person should be put to death. Mark, first of all, the wisdom with which this trial was to be conducted. Circumstantial evidence was not accepted. It is accepted in modern times; it is thought by some to be most conclusive; often it is so; but yet we know that the innocent have sometimes suffered, and the guilty have sometimes escaped, in consequence of what is called circumstantial evidence only. In the land of Israel, therefore, and in cases affecting the life of the accused, circumstantial evidence was not enough; one witness was not enough; there must be two witnesses of the fact, before a party accused might be condemned and brought in guilty. The reason why this crime of idolatry was so heinous in the land of Israel was, partly, that God was their only King; a theocracy, their only government; and an act of idolatry, therefore, was not simply a spiritual sin, most heinous in itself, but also an act of treason and rebellion against the Supreme Magistrate of the land. If, therefore, in present times, a traitor, or one guilty of high treason, is worthy of death by the mildest codes of modern legislation; and if the idolater was then, by that very act, not simply a sinner as an idolater, but a traitor to his Sovereign and a recreant to his country; then the punishment of death was right and proper, as sustained by all the facts and judgments of the most civilized and enlightened nations. But just because an idolater was to be put to death in the land of Israel, therefore he is not to be put to death now; because we are not under a theocracy: idolatry, whatever be its grievous guilt in the sight of God, is not high treason to our country or to our lawful sovereign. And, therefore, when John Knox first urged the sentiment that idolaters should be put to death, he was utterly wrong—grievously wrong. He was not guilty of putting an idolater to death, but he did say they ought to be put to death; certainly, he took all the steps that he could to get rid of them from the land; but the sentiment he did hold that idolaters should be put to death. And this reminds me of a very important thought: it is not fair when our Roman Catholic fellow-countrymen taunt us with that—when we prove to them the proscriptive character of their creed, and they reply, " Did not Calvin sanction this in the burning of Servetus? did not Knox say, that idolaters should be put to death ? We answer, that there is a vast difference. In the first place, we belong to a church reformed and reforming, not assuming to be infallible, but capable of improvement; but they belong to a church assuming to be infallible—incapable of improvement; and what was sanctioned by its canons three hundred years ago, is just as immutable as its very existence. In the second place, we, the Protestants of the nineteenth century, deplore the errors of the Reformers, while we thank God for their excellencies. But the Roman Catholics, in the nineteenth century, glory in the deeds of their forefathers —Dominic, Innocent, and Hildebrand; and in their very prayer-books give consecration to the most atrocious conduct. In the Breviary, also, which every priest reads every day, and must read on the pain of mortal sin, it is actually stated, on the day appointed to commemorate Ferdinand and Isabella, that such was the excellence of these two—this king and this queen—that they carried the faggots with their own hands, and ignited them, in order to burn the heretics. Well now, I say, when such a thing as that is incorporated in a book of devotion, not abjured but cherished, the difference between John Knox advocating the extermination of idolaters—a course repudiated by us—and the Church of Rome insisting upon the burning of heretics—cherished by them—is so great, that one wonders that such a statement or comparison should be made at all. In the next place, we never admit that the Reformers were perfect; we do not believe that the Reformers were perfect. They were not our Popes; and we thank God that He used the Reformers not because they were perfect, but in spite of their grievous defects. And then, if John Knox, and Calvin, and Luther, and Cranmer in reference to the Anabaptists, did approve of persecution, at once we turn round, and say, in what school did they learn it? Just the school from whose teaching they came forth; for they were all priests and members of the Roman Catholic Church; and persecution for conscience sake was so indoctrinated into their very earliest thoughts, that the marvel to me is, not that the Reformers retained some of the smoke of the place from which they came, but that they got rid of so much of it, and that so rapidly.

The next lesson that comes before us in this chapter, is in reference to hard controversies. Now I am again forced to allude to a misconception of this passage. It is stated here, that when a matter of judgment, too hard for them, occurred, they were to bring it before the priest, the Levite, or the judge; and that the person that would not accept their decision was instantly to be expelled from amidst the people. The argument built upon this by the most able Romish controversialists is, that here plainly the Bible is not enough ; that you are to go to a judge, the priest, to get his opinion and his decision; and if you will not accept it, that then you are to be anathematized and expelled. But just mark a few distinctions that are overlooked in such a statement. First, it is not here a controversy about doctrine, but a controversy about blood, and plea, and stroke—civil matters. Secondly, when there is a controversy, it is not the high priest that is to decide it; but it is the priest, or the Levite—a layman, —or the judge—a layman also. And, therefore, if they will quote this passage as a precedent for Papal infallibility, deciding doctrinal discussions, and expelling them that will not submit to it, they ought to quote fully ; and if they quote fully, they will see it is not controversy about doctrine, but controversy about civil matters ; and next, that the controversy is to be appealed not to an ecclesiastic only, but to a layman as well. And, therefore, to quote this to prove that you are to go to Pio Nono—the least competent to explain the Scriptures of any human being, I should suppose, at the present moment—in order to get your controversies decided, is to misquote and misapply the plainest passages of Scripture.

In the next place, we read in this passage of the election of a king. And I wish to notice here, that God does not appoint the election of a king, but He assumes that in the lapse of ages they would, like other nations, have a king. The reason why there was not a king then, would not be a reason for us having a republic. It shows how people may misquote and misapply Scripture. God did not approve of the Jews having a king; but why? Because He was King himself, acting at the head of a theocracy—speaking by miracles and from between the cherubim ; and giving divine directions and divine laws throughout. And to argue, because God disapproved of a monarchy among the Jews, therefore we should be better with a republic in Great Britain, is like the Pope to misquote and misapply Scripture. In this passage God assumes that they would have a king, like the other nations; and, instead of prohibiting it —whatever were the wise and gracious ends He had in view in not doing so—He lays down laws for his direction. You will notice throughout the whole Old Testament economy, there were many things that God did not exterminate by a blow, but that He gradually and progressively superseded. For instance, polygamy existed among the patriarchs. God did not in so many words condemn it; but He made laws for its gradual extinction. Slavery, in a very mild type, existed among the Hebrews ; arrangements were made for its gradual extinction. And here is just the distinction between the modern revolutionist and the enlightened reformer. The revolutionist would upset the whole machine, and bring ruin and havoc; the enlightened reformer detaches proved abuses, adds to the efficiency of the machine, and escapes the risk of doing great damage. Well now, when this king was chosen, how was he to guide himself? God lays down the most wise and gracious laws. First, he should not multiply wives to himself, as had been done before. He should not multiply to himself silver and gold, lest his heart should be set upon it, and he should become avaricious; for a king may not only sin in the sense of being a great aggressor upon other nations, but he may sin also in being a hoarder of gold and of silver. In the next place, for his enlightenment, "when he sitteth upon the throne of his kingdom, he shall write him a copy of this law in a book." There was no printing then; the Bible was on parchment, required to be written out. And the king, even the king, was not to employ an amanuensis to do it, but he was himself to write out a copy of the law. And evidently the reason was, what you read rapidly, you forget rapidly; but if you sit down and write, and that carefully and in the best handwriting that you can, texts from the Bible, you will recollect them much more easily. And no doubt the object of making the king write it out for himself, was, that it might be impressed upon his mind and his heart the more. "And he shall read therein all the days of his life." Royalty is to bow at the footstool of God, to seek pardon for sin, direction for the future, grace and glory. And the result of the king regulating all his conduct by God's holy law will be, that he will prolong his days in the land, and his children in the midst of Israel.

CHAPTER XVIII.

HERITAGE OF THE LEVITES. MINISTERS TO BE DEVOTED TO
THEIR WORK. SINS SPECIALLY FORBIDDEN. THE PROMISED
PROPHET.

FIRST of all in the chapter we have read, we find
the portion assigned to the priests and the Levites,
whose function it was to minister before the Lord
after the ritual laid down in the previous books,
under the express commandment of God himself.
These priests and Levites—for every priest was a
Levite, though every Levite was not a priest—were
not to have a portion of the land assigned to them, for
their support, like the rest of the tribes of Israel; but
were to have a special provision made from the
service and sacrifices of the sanctuary, so as in a
sense to feel they were to be dependent upon God
alone for maintenance and daily bread. One can see
the greatest wisdom in this arrangement. It was to
prevent the priests and the Levites indulging in a
mercenary and avaricious spirit, or entering into
commercial pursuits, or becoming farmers, or taking
such an interest in secular concerns as should interfere
with their entire devotedness to the service of God,
and the ministration of His holy house. It is in some
degree with this thought before his mind that Paul
says, in his admonition to Timothy, " Give thyself

wholly to these things;" that is to say, do not try to combine the minister of the gospel with the farmer, or the minister of the gospel with the teacher, or with any other secular profession: but devote all your energies to the great work that is entrusted to your hands; and by doing so, you seek first the kingdom of God and His righteousness, and all other things will be added unto you. This is a most important provision at all times, that the ministry of the gospel should be thoroughly absorbed in its own peculiar province; not ignorant of other things, not inattentive to passing events; but consecrating all other things to the elucidation of the truth, the instruction of the people, the spread of that blessed gospel which is the wisdom of God and the power of God unto salvation.

We read, after this, of the sins that were specially to be avoided by the Israelites, coming into a land that had been polluted by all these sins, and worse than these; and among the things that they are specially warned not to indulge in, is divination, enchanting, or consulting familiar spirits, or a wizard, or a necromancer. Whether any of these things were real or not is not stated; it seems, as far as we know, that they were mere pretension, and not reality. But whether they were so or otherwise, they were to have nothing to do with them; and the ground on which they were to be resisted and rejected was, that God had spoken in His holy word; secondly, that He would give them a Prophet—the Prophet of his church—the Lord Jesus Christ—who should tell them all things whatever God had made known. And hence when the apostle alludes to that very Prophet, in his Epistle to the Hebrews, he says that "God, who at sundry times and in divers manners spake in time past to the fathers by the prophets,"—a succession of them,—"hath in these last days spoken to us by his Son, whom he hath appointed heir of all things, and by whom he made the worlds." We do not need, therefore, any revelation, additional to that which we have we cannot accept any revelation contradictory to that which we have; and, therefore, no evidence upon earth could convince me that God had spoken something new, that is not in the Bible, or that God has spoken something strange, that is contradicted by the Bible; because He tells us that this book is to be the only rule of faith, the only authentic and inspired document the only guide and governor of all we are to believe in reference to divine things; until the Author of the book come again, translate all its predictions into fact, and begin that blessed age in which there shall be no cloud, or obscurity, or mistake. And, therefore, nothing could convince me of anything being from God that contradicts this book; nothing could convince me that anything is requisite to my salvation that is not in this book. "If we or an angel from heaven," says the apostle, "were to preach to you any other gospel than that which ye have received, let him be anathema." And, therefore, when men tell us that spirits come up now from the other world to speak to us, I regard it as absolute delusion, as wickedness in them that believe it, absurdity in the thing itself. "For if they believe not Moses and the prophets, neither would men believe if one were to rise from the dead." Hold fast this blessed book as the standard of all truth, as the complete testimony of God; and be satisfied to test everything by it.

Whatever contradicts it, is a lie; whatever is not in it, is not necessary; whatever is added to it, is in the face of God's solemn prohibition—"If any one shall add to this book, to him shall be added the curses that are written in this book." Be satisfied with the Bible: you have not yet exhausted it; it has stores and treasures of thought, and hopes, and joys, that we have not yet touched. And we may depend upon it, that if we are not enlightened, it is not because the Bible is exhausted, or God's testimony dark; but because our minds have not yet explored it, and our study and labour have not yet been expended upon it.

Then he gives the prediction of a Prophet who was to arise—that is, our blessed Lord—who should speak to us all things that He should command him.

And then He lays down the test of a true prophet; that if a prophet speak in the name of the Lord—which he may do in that dispensation—and if the thing follow not, then it is quite plain that he has spoken from his own fancy, and not from God; but if the thing follow, then that is the test of a true prophet speaking in the name of the Lord.

CHAPTER XIX.

WE have already seen in the course of our readings
in the Book of Numbers, that remarkable ancient
Jewish institution called the cities of refuge, scattered
throughout the land of promise, to be asylums for the
manslayer, who had been guilty of accidental homicide
—not of deliberate and premeditated murder. We
can see the traces and shadows of this primal institution, in almost every land and century throughout the
world. Among the heathen, they had their asyla, into
which criminals might flee and find a momentary if not
a permanent shelter. In the Roman Catholic Church
they used to have their altars, which were bulwarks of
defence not always for the person accidentally guilty,
but very often for the most depraved and abandoned
of the age in which they lived. These institutions are
just the broken traditional fragments of a great
original, drifted like driftwood across the oceans of
the world, and testifying, by their existence, to a great
original, whose' record and history is here. In fact,
one of the most triumphant proofs of the originality
of these institutions, and at the date at which they are
recorded to have taken place, are just those traditional

remains, that are scattered throughout the length and breadth of heathendom, incorporated into the usages of almost all lands; and indicating that man is separated from some great original; and that the record of that original in this book, is the record not of a copy, but of a primal and original institution. These cities of refuge, as you recollect reading, in the account of their institution in the Book of Numbers, were to be six in number, three upon this side Jordan, and three upon the other side Jordan. And they were so distributed throughout the length and breadth of the land, that at whatever point a person guilty of accidental homicide might be, he could see from that point the spire or the tower of that city, shining in the sun. And roads were made to these cities, streams bridged, hills levelled, obstructions removed, so that the accidental homicide might flee with the greatest speed and the greatest certainty, till he crossed the threshold. And having done this, the avenger of blood might enter it at his heels; but he dare not touch him while he was within that city. If the avenger of blood were to smite the accidental homicide within the city of refuge, he would be guilty of premeditated murder, and also of the violation of a sanctuary—an offence only second to the first. The reason of these institutions seems to be this. First of all, their institution arose from a great law; and secondly, they were instituted to be an expressive foreshadow or type of a grand and precious shelter for all the people of God. The original law laid down to Noah was, that "Whoso sheddeth man's blood, by man shall his blood be shed." And that law, like all the laws of Moses, like the moral law, was not, and is not, to be interpreted loosely; it was so stringent, in its very letter, as well as in its very spirit, that in order that persons who were not guilty of premeditated murder might not be killed because they had shed man's blood, the original law was not modified, but a special provision subsequently originated, that he who had been accidentally guilty of manslaughter, or killing another, might not remain obnoxious to an offended law, but might have a temporary proviso that should save him from its terrible and its awful penalties. Such was the horror with which murder, or the shedding of man's blood, was regarded in ancient times, that rather than modify the law to suit subsequent circumstances, a new provision was made for the accidental violation of the law; that the law might stand in its integrity, and yet the man who had not by premeditation killed another might not be made obnoxious to its penalties. The atonement of Jesus is not a violation or suspension of law in order to save the law-breaker, but the magnifying of law, and yet mercy and absolution to him who flees to Christ our refuge.

It has always appeared to me, that that law justifies what I know many excellent and benevolent persons condemn—capital punishment for so great a crime as that of murder. I do not look at the expediency of the law at all, it rests with legislators to look at it in that light; but it does appear to me that there is one crime in the Bible for which capital punishment is the just, the divine, as well as the human requirement—the crime of murder. It seems to be the only crime that should be so visited; but when it is visited with that dread punishment, it is according to divine, as well as according to human law. It does not seem that there is any other offence that we know of that ought to be so punished; but that this law is obligatory through all ages seems to me plain from God's Holy Word. I know that the reply which some persons have made in ignorance is, that it was a Levitical law. It was no such thing; neither Levi nor Leviticus was in existence when that law was laid down. It was a law given in the days of Noah, and before the peculiarities of the Levitical law were in existence; and, therefore, both the Sabbath, and the law against murder, were not Levitical, but were instituted long before the economy of Levi—and evidently meant to be regarded as moral and not ceremonial obligations.

We read next, in connexion with this law, of a beautiful distinction :—" If any man hate his neighbour, and lie in wait for him, and rise up against him, and smite him mortally, that he die," then, even these cities, instituted for the homicide by accident or without premeditation, should not shelter him.

Then, there is a special law against the removing of a neighbour's landmark. In ancient times they had no walls, but simply stones to indicate the boundaries or marches of the different possessions of contiguous persons; and to remove a landmark in ancient times was equivalent to stealing, robbery, or plunder; and, therefore, there is a strict law against it, and a punishment attached to those that should be guilty of it.

We have here repeated what we read before, that very wise requirement, which all human experience shows to be so, that one witness should not be enough to bring in a person guilty of a crime; however clearly that witness might say he saw the hand and the crime, yet his testimony should not be sufficient to inflict condemnation on the person accused. You are aware, as I noticed before, that circumstantial evidence is, in our country and in its usages, accepted as conclusive. It is certainly, sometimes, as conclusive as if one saw with one's eyes, and heard with one's ears; but still it has happened that circumstantial evidence, which seemed to have the highest probability in distinguishing and determining crime, has proved to have failed; and occasionally the innocent have been punished as the guilty. And therefore God, in this provision, seems to act upon that most wise and humane law:— Better that ten criminals should escape, than that one innocent man should be condemned. And, therefore, it is laid down, that unless there be two, or even three, witnesses, no accused person shall be brought in as guilty of the crime laid to his charge.

The last verse of the chapter was constantly misconstrued by the Scribes and the Pharisees, and made by them to vindicate a system of personal and private revenge, instead of being the expression of a universal public law:—" Thine eye shall not pity; but life shall go for life, eye for eye, tooth for tooth, hand for hand, foot for foot." But this was not that any private individual was to take his revenge by inflicting upon his brother what his brother had inflicted upon him; but it was the judicial law of Levi; it was the public sentence, the public judgment, that was to be pronounced. And you have no more authority for private revenge from this text than you have, in the language of our country, for "taking the law into your own hands," and for a private person punishing the public criminal. But the Scribes and Pharisees, who had perverted God's law by their traditions, quoted this as the reason for private, personal revenge. And, therefore, our blessed Lord, when he explains the law in Matt. v., tells them, "Ye have heard that it hath been said, An eye for an eye, and a tooth for a tooth: but I say unto you, That ye resist not evil: but whosoever shall smite thee on thy right cheek, turn to him the other also." What our Lord lays down in that chapter, does not relate to special judicial dealings, but to private and personal arrangements. And hence, that clause so misunderstood by the Society of Friends, "Thou shalt not swear; but let your Yea be yea, and your Nay be nay," is a prohibition applying to private life, like all the rest of the requirements there; not applying to public and judicial investigation. The whole chapter was vindicating God's law from the misinterpretations and misapplications of the Scribes and Pharisees. And it is absurd to say, that because our Lord prohibits the law, "An eye for an eye, a tooth for a tooth, and life for life," as applying to private and personal revenge, therefore there should be no judicial punishment; and because our Lord prohibits private swearing, there should be no judicial oaths. To interpret it in this way, is altogether to misapprehend the meaning of our Lord, and to misapply the plainest texts of the Bible. Distinguish, in reading the 5th, 6th, and 7th chapters of the Gospel of St. Matthew, between what private Christians owe to each other, and what citizens owe to their country, and judges have to do in their courts, and legislators in the senate; and then you will escape the error into which the Friends, and some others, have fallen upon these questions.

CHAPTER XX.

WAR—LAWFUL IN SOME CIRCUMSTANCES. THE MINISTER MAY
BLESS THE SOLDIER. EXHORTATION OF THE OFFICERS. THE
COWARD SENT HOME. CHRISTIANITY AND HEROISM. OFFERS
OF PEACE. CANAANITES NOT TO BE SPARED. TREES TO BE
SPARED.

THIS chapter assumes a fact, which the eyes of man
must witness in every age, that war will break out,
whoever the guilty party may be that provokes the
war, or precipitates what all enlightened minds must
regret as a great and sorrowful catastrophe. Ever
since man fell, wars have smouldered or broken out in
the world. The real question for every one to solve
is not, is war sinful? It is sinful, of this there is no
doubt; on some one, wherever there is war, there rests
a heavy and a terrible responsibility. But it is evident,
on the other hand, that those who have the right on
their side, may in some circumstances engage in war,
and carry on that war, with all the energy and the
resources of which they are possessed. In other
words, the greatest lovers of peace must admit, that
war sometimes is inevitable, that sometimes on one
side it is lawful, or God would not have given us precedents of his people engaging in war, in His word, or
laid down laws to regulate that which is intrinsically
evil. For instance, there is no regulation of a breach
of any of the Commandments, because such breach is

in itself sinful; but there are here regulations laid down to guide a people precipitated into war, not by their own election, but by the force of circumstances; which show that while, on the one side, war may have all the guilt of a great crime, on the other side it may have all the heroism of a duty, of a solemn and inevitable duty. And hence the very commencement of the chapter is, "When thou goest out to battle"— not selectest battle for thyself, but goest to battle in the providence of God—"against thine enemies; and when thou seest vast preparations made by that enemy to meet you—a people of greater numbers, it may be, of more inexhaustible resources than you have—then be not afraid of them." Why? Because if your cause be right, if your course can be vindicated by Christian principle, then you my conclude that "the Lord thy God is with thee."

"And it shall be, when ye are come nigh unto the battle, that the priest shall approach and speak unto the people." I heard some make the remark—on a recent occasion when I was asked to give a lecture on the subject of war; not showing that war in itself is intrinsically a virtue, but that war in some circumstances may be justified, and become not merely an alternative but an absolute and inevitable duty— "How shocking that a minister of peace should be," as they phrased it, "the advocate of war;" he is not the advocate of war, for he deprecated it, deplored it, thinks it the most awful of calamities; but with this book before me, which is my rule of faith as well as my rule of practice, I cannot shut my eyes to what is transparent in every page, that sometimes war may be inevitable; that on one side to repel the torrent of war, however terrible and impetuous, may be a solemn and sacred duty. Well, now, the passage that would justify a minister of peace, not in making eloquent speeches against war when war becomes a duty, but in showing how, when war is a duty, it should be regulated, mitigated, directed, is what I find here,—that the priest of ancient Israel, the minister of God, was to go forward and say to the people, when they went forth to war, "Let not your hearts faint, fear not, and do not tremble, neither be ye terrified because of them." Now if the thing be intrinsically evil, could we suppose that God would thus consecrate and sanction that which in itself is sinful, and commission his high priest to appear upon the field, and to say to the soldiers going forth to the battle field, "Let not your hearts faint, fear not, and do no tremble, neither be ye terrified because of them." Of all plans to precipitate defeat upon ourselves, that will be the most successful which propagates the idea that we are engaged in an unjustifiable war, that the sooner we drop it the better, and that the sooner we retreat and take peace at any price the more Christian it will be. I say, such a prescription as that is calculated to give strength to the foe, to inspire fainting into the hearts of our own, even were it right; but as it is in itself positively wrong, I adhere to the more Christian, though, it may be, less popular precedent in this chapter; that the priest shall say to those engaged in a righteous war, "Do not faint; do not be afraid; do not tremble; the Lord is with you and goeth with you to fight for you against your enemies and to save you."

And then the officers, the colonels, the majors, and

captains, will catch the echo of the priest's words, and
they will go and say, gathering courage from what he
has spoken, and confidence from a sense of the presence
of God,—" What man is there that hath built a house,
and hath not religiously dedicated it?"—which was a
solemn duty—"let him go and return to his house."
What does that mean? That his heart would be
hankering after home; he would carry with him a
conviction that he had neglected some duty, or he
would be afraid that the house he had built would be
seized and occupied by another. It means, Do not let
us have in our battalions a half-hearted soldier, but let
us have one who is out-and-out devoted to his duty, to
his sovereign, and has a sense of the rightness of his
cause. And one man with a whole heart in the
regiment is worth a dozen with half-hearts only.
Then he goes on to say, "What man is he that hath
planted a vineyard?"—the very same;—"and what
man is there that hath betrothed a wife?" In the
ancient Jewish custom the betrothal of the wife
would be a year before the marriage of the wife; and
therefore such a one will be longing for peace, longing
to go home; and hence the best way is to let him go
at once, because his sympathies not being in the field,
but being left with his affections behind him, may
communicate the contagion to others, and make others
flinch from the battle. And then the whole is closed
with the admirable sentiment which embosoms the
highest knowledge of human nature, as well as much
truth: "In short, is there any man fearful and faint-
hearted, whether leader, officer, or private? then
let him go and return home; we are better without
him." As the illustrious Wellington said of some

foreigners on the field of Waterloo when they ran away—"Let them go ; we are better without them." That was a maxim sanctioned by Scripture itself. And so at this moment, if there be any in the service of our country afraid, faint-hearted, cowardly, timid, these men are not strength, they are elements of weakness. Cowardice is contagious; fear and alarm smites with electric speed a whole battalion, when it is generated probably only in a single heart. And therefore the best way for the commander is to say, "If there be any cowards in the regiment. let them go home." And how delightful it is to know, that amid the brave who have so heroically fought in the Crimea, and amid those who have so nobly fallen—where heroes have fought, so many saints have fallen! How delightful that in our army at this moment, there are more Christian men, officers and privates, than probably ever existed in the British army. But are there more cowards? The very reverse. I venture to say, if the great Commander who is there were just to repeat verse 8 of this 20th chapter of Deuteronomy to his battalions, and say, "What man is there among you fearful and faint-hearted? let him go and return home," that not half-a-dozen would fall out from the ranks and seek to return home.

Again: "When thou comest nigh unto a city to fight against it, then, here are the regulations that are to be observed. First of all, make offers of peace." That is our duty. To war for victory is inhuman; to war for peace is sanctioned by Christianity. And, therefore, before you use a single offensive weapon, you are to say to that city, "We are willing to come to terms of peace ; and the terms must be these, that if you submit, your people will be tributaries." In other words, " You must pay the expenses of the war, or you must pledge yourselves till the expenses of the war be paid." But if the city is obstinate, and trusts to its earthworks, and its battalions, and its immense resources, and its stores, and is satisfied that it will be able to repel you, then you are to take all the course that war dictates ; you are regularly to besiege it. " And when the Lord thy God hath delivered it into thine hands, thou shalt smite every male thereof with the edge of the sword ; " that is, with weapons in his hands, who has refused to submit with the rest of the inhabitants. Then comes in the relieving light of heaven amid the darker shadows of earth : " But the women, and the little ones, and the cattle,"—even the cattle ; God's mercies are over all his creatures,— " and all that is in the city, shalt thou take unto thyself; " thou shalt not put to the edge of the sword ; " and thou shalt eat the spoil of thine enemies, which the Lord thy God hath given thee."

But then there is an exception made of certain cities in the land of Canaan. This is a law applicable in all other cases ; but there is a special law applicable to the cities in Canaan—that they were not to spare them at all. Why this ? Because the Canaanites who were put to death,—not in the execution of private revenge by the Jews, but the fulfilment of a judicial sentence, pronounced by God, of which the Jews were the mere executioners, — the Hittites, the Ammonites, were a most debased, profligate, degraded race, whose very crimes had cried to Heaven for vengeance ; and their destruction was simply the punishment of a most guilty race by God's own command, and not the execution of the private revenge of the Jews against those that were their enemies. And, therefore, the exception was only to take place in this individual instance, and not to be carried out in reference to all sieges of all cities throughout the world.

In the next place: "When thou shalt besiege a city"—here is again God's mercy going deeper than even the brute creation—"wherever there are fruit-trees bearing fruit for food, spare them if possible. But where the trees are not fruit-bearing trees, then you may make them into timbers with which to help you to besiege the city."

Now read the whole of this chapter, and you will see it assumes that wars will come : and wars will arise till the Prince of Peace come and reign over a world first at peace with God, and through that at peace with itself. But secondly in this chapter, to regulate what should come, and to prevent those excesses into which evil passions would often precipitate people in moments of excitement, God interdicts unnecessary havoc, thus showing his providential government does not prevent the evil that sin has introduced, for it is right that the sinner should taste what the bitter fruits of sin are, but out of the evil educes good ; and over-ruling all the sins, the sorrows, the calamities that are the progeny of sin, to give greater glory to his name, and ultimately more enduring good to mankind.

CHAPTERS XXI.—XXV.

THESE chapters are not suitable for family reading, nor fitted to edify without offending a mixed congregation. "All scripture is given by inspiration of God, and is profitable;" but not equally to every person and in every place.

CHAPTER XXI.

In this chapter we learn that undetected murder demands expiation. The sin is so great, that if the perpetrator be unknown, it must still be washed out of the land.

The criminality of filial disobedience is here taught. The guilt remains, though the penalty is gone.

For one to "be hanged on a tree" was to be accursed. Jesus was made a curse for us.

In Judea and the East, women tinged their nails with beautiful colours; to pare them was to take away beauty.

CHAPTER XXII.

Among the heathen, females put on men's dresses, and evil and unholy practices ensued.

Parapet walls around the edges of the flat roofs on which the Jews sat and studied, were merciful provisions.

CHAPTER XXIII.

Nothing but sin now excludes from the Christian church. There is here beneficent provision for the poor traveller in a land of plenty.

CHAPTER XXIV.

Patience under a severe and trying state is better than incurring consequences of interminable evil.

In some of the minute provisions in this chapter there shines out the beneficence of God.

CHAPTER XXV.

PENALTY is necessary in every nation; yet mercy must be mingled with judgment. Forty stripes was the maximum; but to prevent excess, thirty-nine, or forty save one, were usually given.

CHAPTER XXVI.

DUTIES IN THE LAND. ALTARS. THANKFULNESS. OWNING
GOD. BENEFICENCE.

AFTER laying down innumerable minute laws on
the various modes in which sin may be committed
personally, socially, and nationally, in the sight of a
holy God, the sacred penman, inspired by the Spirit
of God, winds up all his directions by this great
national directory, which we read in this chapter.
He says to them, When you are come into that
land, the burden of many prophecies, the music of
many promises, on which your hearts have been
set so long, and set on it only as the type and foreshadow of a yet more magnificent one—" when thou
art come unto the land which the Lord thy God
giveth thee : " not which you have deserved, not which
your swords have carved out for yourselves ; "and
possessest it and dwellest therein ; " then what are
you to do ? To forget the past ? to give God no
praise ? to trust nothing in him for the future ? No ;
but " thou shalt take of the first of all the fruit of the
earth "—the first expression of the fertility of that
land—" and shalt put it into a basket, and shalt go
unto the place which the Lord thy God shall choose
to place his name there ; " his name hallowing the
place, not the place giving efficacy to our prayers or

commending his name. "And thou shalt go unto the priest that shall be in those days;" and you shall do what? Give it to the priest? praise the priest? confess your sins to the priest? No; but you shall say, "I profess this day"—not unto the priest, but "unto the Lord thy God, that I am come unto the country which the Lord sware unto our fathers for to give us. And the priest shall take the basket out of thine hand, and set it down before the altar." There is no altar in the Christian church; the very first and strongest proof of apostasy in a Christian church would be turning the communion-table—which being a table is for a festival—into an altar, which is for a totally different use, namely, for sacrificial offerings. If there be an altar in the house of God, materially and literally so called, then the Sacrifice is not complete; then the words, "It is finished," are a mistake; then Christ's atonement is not equal to all that we need; for we must still offer up sacrifices to propitiate God and make satisfaction for our sins. But the beautiful thought of a Protestant church is this, that we have a table, not an altar; a place in which we eat the feast that succeeds the sacrifice. The altar sustained its victim eighteen hundred years ago; the festival still continues through all the eighteen hundred years—not to repeat the sacrifice, but to commemorate the sacrifice already made.

No doubt, then, there was an altar, and consequently a sacrifice. But here is the mistake of some people. They transfer into the Christian economy the rites, the robes, the incense, the genuflexions, the lights, the altars of the Jewish economy. But this is to make the Christian church Jewish; that is to try and forget that eighteen hundred years have elapsed, and that Judaism is passed away. And, therefore, in modern times we bring our hearts into the sanctuary, and in the presence of the unseen Altar—Christ, who is Altar, Priest, and Sacrifice together, and in his name we present our thanksgiving and our praise, giving God all the glory of what we are, and praying for his guidance and direction throughout the rest of our life hereafter.

Let me ask, have you been prospered in the world; have things turned out brighter and better than you ever dreamed? Do you take a retrospect of all the way; and imitate the ancient Jew, whose imitation is excellence, and give unto the Lord thy God, who has brought thee into this goodly land, and made thy cup to run over, and caused goodness and mercy to follow you, praise and thanks, and own and confess it was not by might, nor by power, but by his blessing alone, that you are where you now find yourselves? If you do not, the Jew, under a darker economy, shames the Christian; for we, with greater privileges and mercies, are less thankful.

Well, then when the Jew should thus come into the temple, and into the presence of the priest, he was to say, "A Syrian ready to perish"—that is Jacob, called a Syrian—"was my father." In other words, he does not trace back his genealogy, to some illustrious hero who might have been; but to a humble, obscure friendless wanderer, ready to perish in himself, and kept only by God's mercy. And he says, "I was the son of a poor homeless father; he went down into Egypt and sojourned there, not with a mighty nation, but with a few: and they became a great nation, mighty and populous." And he explains how they became so. "When we cried unto the Lord God of our fathers, the Lord heard our voice, and looked on our affliction, and our labour, and our oppression, and the Lord brought us forth out of Egypt." In other words, the beautiful thought runs through the whole chapter, that whilst there is acknowledgment of greatness, and power, and prosperity, there is the constant undertone of thankfulness and praise ; only and exclusively to Him whose blessing prospered them, and whose right hand delivered them.

And they shall state : "And now, behold, I have brought the first-fruits of the land, which thou, O Lord, hast given me." Now, the first-fruits of the land, grew in the land of Palestine, just as they grow in the land of England. But the Jew of that day did not say : "It was those fortunate showers in May and June, it was this rich soil, and this scientific mode of treating it, that have made so bountiful a harvest ;" and yet these things need to be done But he looked above all secondary causes ; and gave the glory and the honour of the first-fruits to that God whose blessing had brought them there. I have often made the remark, which I think is so important, that there is just as great a proof of God's omnipotent power in making the seed germinate, grow, and be reaped as a prolific harvest, and made into bread for the nourishment of a man, as there was when he turned a few loaves into food, for five thousand persons ; only in the latter case it was contrary to the usages of nature, and we call it a miracle ; in the former case, it is according to what we term the usages of nature, and we call it ordinary. But in the one, as in the other, there is as much Omnipotent power; and if the other were to be the ordinary thing, and the now ordinary thing were to be the extraordinary thing, we should call the one which is now ordinary, miraculous; and the other which was then extraordinary, we should call the ordinary law of nature. The fact is, there is not a blade that grows, or a flower that blossoms, or a star that shines, or a harvest that is reaped, when nature sits amid her sheaves like a mother amid her children rejoicing, that does not prove God is there, and that does not suggest, to Him is due the praise, the thanksgiving, and all the honour, and all the glory.

While the Israelite does all this, he is also to rejoice : " And thou shalt rejoice in every good thing, which the Lord thy God hath given unto thee, and unto thine house." Now, here is the common sense of the Bible. An extreme monastic or ascetic spirit would say, " When you have got these good things, do not eat them, but put them away, or give them away to another." But the Bible does not say so. It tells the man, whose honest industry God has blessed, or whom God has prospered, elevated, and made great, that he is warranted in rejoicing in the good things that God has given him. And, therefore, those that have the good things of this life, whilst they trace them to their Author, whilst they take care that around them none shall starve while they are full; may, at the same time, thankfully enjoy and rejoice in the good things, whatever they be, that God has given them. See the exquisite sense that is in this wonderful book, the Bible. The one extreme is, you must live as an Ascetic, denying yourself everything; the other extreme is, you must live like an

Epicurean, enjoying exclusively a monopoly of every-thing; the prescription of the Bible is, Take the good that God sends you; thank him for it; rejoice in it; and let your surplus overflow, for a benefit and a bless-ing to others. You never, my dear friends, will see what a wonderful book that book, the Bible, is, till you come to study it thoroughly; and that man who studies it most thoroughly, will detect oftenest the outshining of that glory which dwelt between the cherubim, which still gleams in every text, and breaks forth from every chapter, and indicates that God is its author, and truth its essential matter.

After this the Israelite, while he rejoices, and gives of these good things to the fatherless, and to the stranger, and to the widow, and praises God, is to pray to him again: " Look down from thy holy habi-tation, from heaven, and bless thy people Israel; " not merely myself, but "thy people Israel."

And then he is reminded of the solemn fact, that God is to be his God; that we are to be his people; and to "shew forth," as Peter calls it, "the praises of him who hath called us from darkness into his marvellous light."

CHAPTER XXVII.

THE Law was ordered to be written on stone, in order to render it clear, incorruptible, and incapable of being effaced.

An altar of unhewn stone must also be erected, as if atonement must ever be associated with law. The Bible now takes the place of the former—Christ is our altar.

These curses descend on every one out of Christ. He is under the shadow of Ebal. The whole universe will echo, Amen.

None of these can touch the believer. " There is no condemnation to them that are in Christ Jesus."

CHAPTER XXVII.

From this chapter I extract for instruction these words—

" Cursed be he that confirmeth not all the words of this law to do them. And all the people shall say, Amen."

Verse 26.

Though this chapter was properly passed over in the ordinary course of our morning reading, yet it contains incidental lessons entitled to our special study and prayerful consideration. This 26th verse is referred to in various parts of the New Testament, and is evidently not a subordinate truth, ornamental but not essential, contains a vital and fundamental doctrine, lying at the very roots of the Christian economy—the permanency of the law ; that holy moral law which was proclaimed on Sinai amid lightnings and thunders. We read, in the 2nd verse of this very chapter, that " It shall be on the day when ye shall pass over Jordan unto the land which the Lord thy God giveth thee, that thou shalt set thee up great stones, and plaister them with plaister : and thou shalt write upon them all the words of this law, when thou art passed over, that thou mayest go in unto the land which the Lord thy God giveth thee, a land that floweth with milk and honey; as the Lord God of thy fathers hath promised thee." Now this was not so much to make the law clearer to the children of Israel as to indicate that in all its exactions, it was an unrepealed and permanent obligation. The idea of writing it upon stone was meant visibly to perpetuate it; so that every Jew might feel it was not a transient requirement peculiar to the desert, but a permanent moral obligation, of which he could no more get rid, than he could of his immortality, or responsibility in the sight of God. Yet this holy law, so intensely and entirely law, is based upon God's covenant relationship to his people and their covenant relationship to him; for it is written in the 9th and 10th verses, "And Moses and the priests the Levites spake unto all Israel, saying, Take heed, and hearken, O Israel; this day thou art become the people of the Lord thy God. Thou shalt therefore obey the voice of the Lord thy God, and do his commandments and his statutes, which I command thee this day." Thus God's relationship to them as a Father and a King, and their relationship to Him as sons and subjects, is made the basis and the motive ground from which their obedience was to spring, and on which they were to exhibit their obedience to that holy law which He had so clearly laid down and so permanently established. In our case the relationship is still clearer, and, if possible, deeper; for the apostle tells us in the Epistle to the Hebrews, "Not according to the covenant that I made with their fathers in the day when I took them by the hand to lead them out of the land of Egypt; because they continued not in my covenant, and I regarded them not, saith the Lord. For this is the covenant that I will make with the house of Israel after those days, saith the Lord ; I will put my laws into their mind, and write them in their hearts: and I will be to them a God, and they shall be to me a people." Thus God's covenant relationship is made the basis of the obedience of his people. The economy is not now, obey God in order to be made his son; but thou art a son of God; therefore go forth and obey him, and observe all his commandments. But even in this state, and amid these requirements, the idea of atonement is introduced; for in the 6th verse of this very 27th chapter it is written, " Thou shalt build the altar of the Lord thy God of whole stones: and thou shalt offer burnt offerings thereon unto the Lord thy God." Thus atonement is introduced in the very midst of the moral law; that the people of Israel might be pointed forward to that great provision through which the breaches of that law might be forgiven, and in which strength might be found for obedience. This altar was a great and essential part of the furniture of the ancient temple. But just because it was in the ancient temple, it is not to be in the modern church. In one sense it would seemingly be strictly scriptural to have an altar in the visible church; but in a higher sense it is most unscriptural. They had an altar, because it was a foreshadow of Christ, our Altar; we have no altar visible in the visible church, because Christ is our Altar, our Sacrifice, our Priest; we having no victim to offer, and needing none; having no atonement to make, because it was made eighteen hundred years ago, and its virtue endureth for ever. We do not serve a visible temple, with visible altar, and visible priests; but having a great High Priest over the house of God, who is passed into the heavens; having One who, by one sacrifice, hath perfected for ever them that are sanctified; and having Jesus Christ, the same yesterday, to-day, and for ever, our Altar, we serve him as justified, not needing an atonement to be made, as forgiven through an atonement finished, not waiting till one shall be accomplished.

That the blessing attending obedience, and the curse attending disobedience, might be clearly made known, Mount Ebal is the pulpit from which the curse is fulminated; Mount Gerizim is made the pulpit from which the blessing is proclaimed. And, therefore, it is written, " Upon Mount Ebal shall the curse be put, and upon Mount Gerizim shall the blessing be put."

The verse I have selected for our present remarks is an epitome of a great and fundamental truth; a truth that pervades and gives its colouring to every statement in the Gospel of Christ. It is quoted by the apostle in the Epistle to the Galatians, where he says, " Cursed is every one that continueth not in all things that are written in the book of the law to do them." It is quoted by the apostle James in other words, but substantially the same, " Whosoever shall keep the whole law, and yet offend in one point, he is guilty of all." Thus we have two apostles giving each a commentary upon this text; the one saying, " He that continueth not in all things; " denoting that obedience to be accepted must not only be perfect in itself, but comprehensive and continuous in its rendering; and the other apostle, St. James, saying that whoso shall offend in one point is brought in guilty of a breach of the whole law. This leads us to see that every precept of God's holy law is equally obligatory. The Fourth Commandment is as obligatory as the First, and the Tenth as binding as the Ninth; and he that is guilty of a breach of one is guilty, not merely of breaking an individual law, but of insurrection and rebellion, whether he intend it or not, against the great Author and Inspirer of the law —the Lord God of Israel. We thus learn that the breach of one precept is regarded by God as an impeachment of his jurisdiction and authority as King and Lord. Now, we very often view a sin as simply the breach of a law, and in that sense even we look on it too lightly; but throughout Scripture sin is viewed not as the breach of an isolated law, but as an insurrection against the great Lawgiver himself. And hence the sin of Eve and Adam in Paradise was not simply the sin of stealing, looked at it as an individual act, irrespective of any other relationship or aspect; but it was the breach of the law of the great Legislator; it was an insurrection against the King of kings and Lord of lords; and it therefore brought down upon the heads of Adam and of Eve the awful penalties of rebellion of subjects against their king, of creatures against their God. Now this truth, that " he that continueth not in all," or is guilty of the breach of one law, " is guilty of all," disposes of the principle accepted by the Pharisee, that excessive and scrupulous attention to one law was an atonement for daily disobedience to another law. The Pharisee selected the law that he had no temptation to infringe; and by excessive adhesion to it, he convinced himself that he made atonement or propitiation for the breach of a law to which his besetting sin or passion constantly inclined him; forgetting that the requirement of God is, " Thou shalt love the Lord thy God with all thy heart, with all thy soul, and with all thy strength ; " and through loving him go forth to illustrate, embody, and obey, that law which is the expression of his will, the holy and eternal law of God. Now, the great law and its sanctions are just as obligatory to-day as they were in the days of Moses, or when first enunciated from Mount Sinai. It is not true that the Atonement dilutes the law, or makes God accept an imperfect but sincere obedience now, instead of what He required of old, a perfect obedience, with all the heart, with all the mind, and with all the strength. God demands to-day a perfect righteousness as your title to heaven, just as He demanded when Adam fell. Only the difference lies here. It was exacted from Adam as a personal deed; it is paid for us by our great Substitute. The righteousness that is the title to heaven is the same; only Christ has paid it for us ; and we are entitled in him, and through him, and for his sake, to all the reward of a law magnified and made honourable. And God saves us now, not in spite of law, but according to law. God does not admit us to heaven though we have broken the law, but he admits us to heaven because Christ, our Substitute, has obeyed and magnified the law for us. Hence, under the ancient economy, as long as the law lasted which was in Paradise, man did, and therefore he lived ; now we accept what is done for us, and therefore we live. In either case is a perfect righteousness : in Adam's done by him, in ours done for us. And hence, under our economy, faith accepts, or believes, or trusts in, as given us, what

Adam had to do, accomplish, and perfect. And there-fore, while he was to be saved by his own continuous obedience, we are saved through faith in the obedience of another. Only let us take care not to fall into the error into which some fall who make the perfect corre-lative of this, " Do, and live ; " to be " Believe and live ;" putting "live " in each proposition as the same ; but in Adam's case doing, in our case believing ; and supposing that faith has merit now, just as deeds had merit then. But the truth is, faith has no more merit now than deeds have had since the fall. Then you say, why so ? Because if Adam was to be saved by a perfect obedience, which was true till he fell ; we should now be saved, if this interpretation be correct, by an orthodox faith ; and orthodox belief would have the merit now which a holy life would have had then. But this is absurd ; there is no more merit in faith than there is in any obedience that man can render. The meaning of faith is not that it takes the place of doing ; but that it accepts what is done for us, instead of our doing what the law exacts from every creature. And faith is thus preferred because it brings nothing, receives all ; as it is not the crea-tion of man, but the inspiration of God.

We learn in the next place, that on every one who fails to obey this law, the curse falls : " Cursed is every one that continueth not in all things." Now what a solemn truth is this, that all born into the world, are born in the eclipse, under the curse ; that on every human being there lies by nature a curse. All things are cursed to him, nothing is blessed to him. The prosperity of the rich, the health of the strong, the lands of the great, the titles of the noble, the sunshine, and the sweet flowers, and the fresh air, are never blessings, but necessarily curses to him who is not in Christ, and a stranger to his cross, his Gospel, and his Holy Spirit. On the other hand, he that is in Christ, has nothing cursed to him. Pestilence, plague, famine, war, battle, disease, death; these are not curses to him: all the curse is extracted before they touch him; and transmitted by the love that redeems us, they become ministering helps to them that are the heirs of God, and joint heirs with the Lord Jesus Christ. Let us ask in the very thought and idea of this, are we on that ground, on which everything falls a blessing; or are we standing on that ground, on which everything falls as a curse? Are we in the first Adam, in whom all was lost, and in whom all was cursed; or are we in the second Adam, the Lord from heaven, in whom there is no condemnation, and in whom there is nothing but blessing on our going out. and blessing on our coming in; blessing on our basket, and blessing on our store; blessing in things temporal, and blessing in things eternal; till happy is the people, or blessed is the man, whose sins are forgiven, whose transgressions are covered, and unto whom the Lord imputeth no iniquity.

Let us learn from this passage these important lessons:—First, the more thoroughly we study God's holy law, the more searching, inquisitive, and comprehensive we shall find it. The law, in word, seems to demand external obedience only; but when you read that law, as set forth by our blessed Lord, you find that a thought is sin, a desire is crime, an angry feeling rises to the guilt of murder. In reading the law on Sinai, the first impression is what Paul's was, that an outward life is a sufficient exponent of all it demands. But when you come to read that law, expounded by our Lord, and applied to the conscience by the Holy Spirit, you then find it takes cognizance not of words only, but of thoughts; not of deeds only, but of desires; not of the outward man only, but the innermost, the most secret and sequestered thoughts, desires, and imaginations of the heart. If this be so, the more we understand this law, and the more clearly we see ourselves in the light of this law, the more we shall be constrained to own, "Our hearts condemn us; and God is greater than our hearts, and knoweth all things." And the inevitable feeling that will be created by a sight of this holy law, brought near and close to our hearts and consciences, will be, "If this be true; if the law be what our Lord from the mount expounded it; if we be what we see ourselves, in the lightning clearness of that law; then if thou, O Lord, shouldest mark iniquity, O Lord, who could stand?" Then we shall be constrained to say, "Enter not into judgment with thy servant, O Lord; for in thy sight no man living can be justified." Then we shall feel in all its force, "By deeds of law no flesh shall be justified;" and in the light of this law, pouring into our hearts and consciences; bringing up into view the secret, seemingly expunged, but only hidden impressions upon our hearts, and memories, and consciences; we shall be tempted almost to despair. Satan's policy is to drive every one to despair; the law in Satan's hand drives to despair; the law in the Spirit's hand, leads to Christ. If you feel yourself under a conviction of sin, and in the sight of a holy law, fleeing from Christ, Satan has been preaching the law to you; but if you feel yourself under the conviction of sin, and in the light of this holy law, brought near to Him whose blood cleanseth from all sin, then it is the Holy Spirit; for "the law is our schoolmaster," not to plunge us in despair, but "to bring us to Christ." Guided and taught so, your next question will be, "What must I do to be saved?"—a question all heathendom asked for a thousand years; and which, finds its solution only in that blessed Book which, thanks be to God, is no more the monopoly of the priest, but the possession and privilege of all mankind. The answer to it is short and simple. "Believe in the Lord Jesus Christ, and thou shalt be saved." For what the law could not do, that God hath done, in that "he hath set forth Christ Jesus to be a propitiation through faith in his blood; that he might be just, and yet the justifier of them that believe in Jesus."

What joyous sounds are these: "God so loved the world, that he gave his only begotten Son, that whosoever believeth in him shall not perish, but have eternal life." "This is a faithful saying, and worthy of all acceptation, that Jesus Christ came into the world to save sinners." It is only from the depth of that ruin, in which a clear apprehension of the law, brought home to the conscience, lays us, that we can see the glory of that grand provision finished on the cross, through which God welcomes to his presence all that believe, blots out our sins, removes from us our transgressions as far as the east is distant from the west, receives us graciously and loves us freely.

CHAPTER XXVIII.

THIS chapter strictly and properly consists of two parts or divisions; the one pervaded by the promise of an ample blessing; the other full of the most awful and desolating curses provoked by the sins of men, and let loose by God in righteous retribution. But this part begins, first of all, with the blessing, before it unfolds the curse ; it begins by pronouncing the richest blessings upon them and theirs, that fear God, cleave to Him, and obey his commandments, and seek first his kingdom and his righteousness, that all other things may be added unto them.

These blessings, first of all, are manifestly national. It is to the Jewish people, as a nation, that God addresses these blessings, and adds these special and glorious promises. And this teaches us, that if a nation in its national capacity, through all its sections, and in the choice of its national representatives, fears God, hallows his name, reveres his sabbaths, promotes his cause and kingdom and glory, that all these blessings shall come upon it. We have no

U

right to suppose that these blessings were restricted
to the Jewish people, and that they cannot light
upon the Gentiles; but, on the contrary, we have
every reason for supposing still, by precedent, by
fact, and from Scripture, that a nation that is exalted
by righteousness, will endure and be prosperous for
ever. But, at the same time, whilst we state this,
it does not imply that a nation is cursed, when
afflictions, losses, bereavements, trials, descend upon
it. None of those things that are here predicted
as curses are real curses, if they light upon Christians; but all those things that are here predicted
as blessings, are no blessings to those who are
not Christians at all. By a great law, the moment
one's heart is renewed, and one is made a child of
God, everything that touches him is transformed
into a mission of beneficence, of goodness, and of
joy; and by the very same law, as long as you are a
stranger to this blessed Gospel, everything that touches
you, however beneficent in itself, becomes no blessing
to you. A man who is not a Christian, is not made
happy by having and accumulating wealth; and a
man who is a Christian, is not made miserable by the
absence of wealth. We must never estimate things
by their outer aspect, and say, this is good, and that
is bad, in the highest sense of the words; but we must
estimate every dispensation from the character of the
person who is the subject of it. And in the case of a
Christian the severest tribulation may be a higher
blessing than the greatest prosperity in the case of an
unbeliever. But, as applied to nations, it is still true
that the nation that honours God, God will honour.
He will not except it from trials, losses, painful

bereavements, and reverses; but He will sanctify the nation under them, sanctify these to the nation, and show that God never forsakes a people that refuse to forsake Him. We must never estimate a person by the thing that happens to him; but always estimate the thing by the person to whom it happens. When the tower of Siloam fell upon so many, and crushed them, the thoughtless Jews said, "What wicked men these must have been!" But our blessed Lord corrected the false view, when He said, "Think ye that those eighteen, upon whom the tower of Siloam fell, were sinners above all men? I tell you, Nay;" and instead of making such estimates, "Except ye repent, ye shall all likewise perish." And therefore, we are sustained under trials, reverses, and calamities that happen to us as a nation. Who can doubt that as a nation, just now, we are judged? Who can doubt that, amid the severe losses of 1855, God was not punishing, but no doubt He was chastening us? And if He be chastening, not punishing, we can still say as a nation, "What son, what daughter, is there whom the father chasteneth not?" If we be without chastisement, then our country would not be the daughter of God, but the alien and the enemy. Yet you are not to leap to the conclusion which one hears, and which many Christians give expression to, to one's deep regret—that such reverses prove that we are wrong, that such sufferings tell us, that we ought not to be there. I never can accept this. Always make sure that the cause in which we are engaged is a righteous one; and come thunder, come lightning, come bereavement, come reverses; these in a righteous cause, meeting those who are rightfully engaged in it, are not curses, they will not in the end be desolating calamities; they are God speaking still to the nation, "Fear me, and honour me;" and teaching us to remember that the race is not always to the swift, nor the battle even to a nation so strong as ours; but that, in our greatest strength, we need the deepest reliance upon the right arm and upon the blessing of Him, who only fighteth for us.

Now, if these blessings and curses light upon nations, we can trace, at all events in the case of the Jew, the curse scathing him wherever he is. Read over this awful catalogue of curses, that man may not pronounce, that the creature may not pronounce, that no being upon earth may dare to pronounce; and see, at this moment, if the Jew be not literally responding to the great majority of them. "He shall be a scoff and a byword." Why, who is the greatest proverb upon earth? The poor Jew: a byword for covetousness, for meanness; his very name, his very person, his very position a proverb amid the nations of the earth. And how true it has been in the middle ages, "Thou shalt plant vineyards, and dress them, but shalt neither drink of the wine, nor gather the grapes; for the worms shall eat them. Thou shalt have olive trees throughout all thy coasts, but thou shalt not anoint thyself with the oil." How true is that! You have only to read the history of the Jew in the middle ages of Europe, to see that whenever he had settled and was getting rich, the kings of the earth, and worse than they, the popes of the earth, were the first to interpose to make him poor. It was literally true of the Jew in the middle ages, that he planted vineyards, but he drank not the wine of them; and olive trees, but anointed himself not with the oil of them; and accumulated wealth, and the grasping and the avaricious Gentile, far more criminal in that respect than he, thought—wickedly or ignorantly thought—that in persecuting the Jew he was doing God honour, and Christianity great service. If God pronounces a curse, rest assured He will see to the execution of it; if God promises a blessing, you may be sure He will take care it shall light. He does not need your interposition to help him to fulfil prophecies; He asks you only to do the duties of justice, of mercy, and of truth. We are not doing God service, in trying to fulfil his prophecies, but we are entering into a province that is exclusively his own; and man's attention is withdrawn from the every-day duties that devolve upon him, to try to fulfil the prophecies in which he has no share, except to wait and hope for their glorious fulfilment.

That awful curse was executed against the Jews, " The Lord shall bring a nation against thee from far, from the end of the earth, as swift as the eagle flieth." And how often have we in Scripture, especially in its prophecies, the remarkable fact that while a nation is pointed out, some of its symbols are alluded to. We can see, for instance, the picture of the Turkish power, or of the irruption of the Saracens into Europe, by the use of what is called the horse-tail; where the Book of Revelation said, their power or jurisdiction was in their horses' tails. Now, when one reads that in the Apocalypse, at first sight, and you see the prophecy relates to the Saracens and the

Turks, you are puzzled what it can mean. But when you open the page of history, you find that when a leader of the Turks lost his standard, he cut off his horse's tail, hoisted it on a pole; that became the standard of the Turks, and it is their standard to this day; so much so that their pashas rise in dignity according to the number of tails—a pasha with two tails, or a pasha with three tails, and so on. You see, therefore, in the prediction of the Turkish irruption into Europe, a symbol that becomes suggestive and demonstrative of the nationality it refers to. So I showed you, in a lecture I gave you upon Russia, that Tarshish is a distinct nationality; that it was to oppose Meshech, and Rosh, and Tubal, or the Russian and German powers, that were to be united. I showed you that we could identify Tarshish as this great country, that takes its place in opposition to that Northern barbarism that would overwhelm all Europe. I indicated from other grounds, and very forcible ones, the remarkable fact that the lion is spoken of as its heraldic symbol; and that very fact would seem to prove the identification; and that Tarshish that is single-handed, as I then told you, to oppose the united forces of Northern barbarism, is identified as that great power singled out by God and predicted by Ezekiel, so many thousand years before. So here again, confirmatory of the same idea, we read in the 49th verse, " The Lord shall bring a nation against thee from far, from the end of the earth, as swift as the eagle flieth; a nation whose tongue thou shalt not understand." That was the Roman power, unquestionably. Now many of the Jews—the Hellenistic Jews—spoke Greek. The Latin was not a language that the Jews as a body generally understood. Then, the eagle was the great heraldic symbol of the Romans ; the eagle was on all their standards. And, therefore, specifying in this way indicates unmistakeably the power that was to make an irruption into Palestine and besiege their capital, Jerusalem, and desolate their country till they were scattered abroad among all the nations of the earth. And the prophecy contained in the 56th verse is very remarkable : it is said that the tender and delicate woman, the highest noble of the land, would be so reduced in the course of that terrible siege, that it is here predicted, what one would think absolutely impossible, that they should even feed upon their own infants. Just read the history of Josephus, where he describes as a Jew, writing seated on its ruins—writing on the very spot where the ploughshare of Titus and Vespasian forced its way ; and he will tell you, without thinking for one moment that what was taking place was the fulfilment of ancient prophecy, that the awful prediction here, which seems the very impossibility of nature, (for the greatest impossibility is stated in the Bible, when it says, " A woman may forget her infant that she bore," as if it were the merest possibility,) is possible ; and the instance in which it was most awfully fulfilled, as recorded by Josephus, was in the siege of Jerusalem by Titus and Vespasian, when the awful enormity took place ; and that nation learned amid the wreck of its capital, amid the quenched glory on its altar, amid their misery and sufferings at this moment in Poland, in Russia, in Italy, in Rome, over all the world—and they exemplify it to us as living witnesses, " Thy word, O God, is truth."

CHAPTER XXVIII.

" And thou shalt grope at noonday, as the blind gropeth
in darkness, and thou shalt not prosper in thy ways : and thou
shalt be only oppressed and spoiled evermore, and no man
shall save thee."—Chap. xxviii. 29.

ALL the blessings and all the curses relate exclusively, without a single exception, to the national
condition of the Jews from that day onward to the
present hour, and even the fulness of the times.
Both the curses and the blessings of this chapter relate
to that people, are applicable only to them, and have
been, as far as the curses are concerned, literally fulfilled,
painfully and terribly fulfilled, in their national experience. Nobody can fail to see that from the very
day when they cast off the only Saviour, and his own
received him not when he came to them ; when they
had shouted, "Away with him! Away with him!
his blood be upon us and upon our children!" that
from that day to this, every curse that they provoked
by previous sins descended upon them in greater fury
in consequence of that sin ; while the blessings pro-

nounced upon them that should fear, and love, and
worship God, remain unenjoyed by them, with few
exceptions. This verse is only one of numerous
others in the same chapter, all burdened with the
same heavy prophecy of calamity and distress and
tribulation to the Jews. When Titus and Vespasian
had completely mastered the Jews, and beaten down
the walls of their venerable and glorious capital, the
Jews, in the language of this text, swept and driven
from their country by a nation that they knew not,
have had no rest for the soles of their feet since.
A solitary attempt was made by the Jews to
rebuild Jerusalem some four hundred years subsequent to the destruction of their capital by Titus and
Vespasian. The Roman emperor sent his armies to
dispossess them, and they were cut down almost to
a man ; the few that were able to flee were scattered
over all the earth ; and from that day to this, the Jew
has been the greatest stranger in Jerusalem ; and in
every capital, and nation, and village besides, he has
been a byword, and a hiss, and a scoff among all
nations whither the Lord has driven him. We have
only to compare these predictions with facts to see
how exactly they have been fulfilled. In the 43rd
verse it is written, " The stranger that is within thee
shall get up above thee very high ; and thou shalt
come down very low." During the last few years the
Jew has been allowed to live in his own ancient
capital, and to dwell, as he is now trying, in the
ruined villages of Palestine. In each instance this
verse has been verbatim fulfilled. "The stranger
that is within thee shall get up above thee very high ;
and thou shalt come down very low." In Jerusalem

the Mahometan, the Arab, the Greek and the Latin monk, are very high; persons of importance, holding a definite position, ruling so far in the midst of the land; while the few aged Israelites who go to Jerusalem to spend their last days, and die within the precincts of the sacred city, are treated with universal scorn, or plundered, persecuted and maligned. "The stranger that is within thee"—the Greek, the Latin, the Turk, the monk, the Moslem, and the Arab—"shall get up above thee very high; and thou shalt come down very, very low."

In the same chapter it is written, at the 25th verse, "The Lord shall cause thee to be smitten before thine enemies; thou shalt go out one way against them, and flee seven ways before them; and thou shalt be removed into all the kingdoms of the earth." This text, and numberless others, threaten the Jews with a universal and unmitigated dispersion over the length and breadth of the habitable globe. Estimate at this moment the condition of the Jew. In what latitude or longitude of the habitable globe do you not find a Jew? In what capital of nations, savage and civilized, is he absent? Under the burning suns of India, amid the frozen ledges of Russia and Greenland, in Moscow, in Madrid, in London, in Paris, in Petersburg, in Pekin, in every city upon earth; amid all climates, under all circumstances, under republic, monarchy, and despotism, you will always find the Jew with the same marked and unmistakeable features, with the same grovelling meanness, and yet aspiring expectations; bearing visibly upon his brow the brand that was struck eighteen hundred years ago. And what is remarkable, they are not only dispersed and scattered over every land, in every latitude and longitude, speaking every language, drinking of every stream, but in every nation upon earth, and in every city almost upon earth, during the last eighteen centuries, they have been treated with unsparing, and ruthless, and savage barbarity. They have been persecuted by kings, and priests, and prelates, and popes, and popular outcries have led to their expulsion or destruction. Crusades against them have been blessed and consecrated by priests. And all this persecution has been dealt them for no reason upon earth except this, that they were Jews; and so far they thus presented the evidence of the fulfilment of the prediction that they should be pursued by their enemies, smitten by them, going out one way against them and fleeing seven ways; and removed into all the kingdoms of the habitable globe. Sir Walter Scott, in this matter a faithful historian, says, "Except the flying fish, there has been no race existing on earth, in the air, or in the water, that was ever the object of such unremitting, general and relentless persecution, as the Jew. Norman, Saxon, Dane, and Briton, however adverse their races were to each other, contended which could look with the greatest detestation on a people whom it was accounted a point of religion to hate, revile, despise, plunder, and persecute." Such is the testimony of one well-read in history. Even the Magna Charta of which we boast, and in the securities of which we feel free, did not contemplate the possibility of the Jew being a citizen, or regarded as a man, or as a responsible and intellectual person. Southey, the eminent historian and poet, in his Letters from Portugal and Spain, says, " Till within the last fifty years the burning of a Jew formed the highest delight of the Portuguese nation." And even to this moment Russia treats the Jew as a vagrant, and tolerates him only as long as he has anything worth taking from him ; dismisses him, or sends him to the mines in Siberia, when he ventures to think for himself, or to express a sentiment unpalatable to the despot over him. And the Turk vents his bitterest indignation upon the Jew, and spits upon him as the most contemptible and detestable of human beings. How can you account for this extraordinary treatment ? How can you explain it ? You do not find the descendant of the Greek, or of the Roman, or of any ancient nation, treated in this way. You do not find any other race upon earth singled out, because of that race, for special persecution, imprisonment, occasionally death. How and on what principles can you explain it ? That it is predicted is quite plain, for almost every verse in this chapter is a prophecy of it. In the 23rd verse, for instance, of this chapter, "And thy heaven that is over thy head shall be brass, and the earth that is under thee shall be iron. The Lord shall make the rain of thy land powder and dust ; from heaven shall it come down upon thee, until thou be destroyed." That very land at this moment is exactly described in this verse. It was once a land overflowing with milk and honey ; the vines upon its rocks, the cedars on its hills, the ores in its bosom, the rich vegetation in its valleys, the luxuriant pastures, the rapid and large produce of everything that was fit for man's food, gave it a value that had no parallel. But now this land, once so fertile, has the very dust on it for rain, the barren rock for its soil ; and though having capabilities in its bosom that show it might be the granary of the world, yet it is positively at this moment unable to grow enough corn for the nomad tribes that pitch their tents here and there upon its surface.

In the 33rd verse, "The fruit of thy land, and all thy labours, shall a nation which thou knowest not eat up; and thou shalt be only oppressed and crushed alway." The Jew in every land has been plundered; and in none more so than in our own land in ancient times. What he had accumulated for himself was taken from him; he sowed, but he did not reap; he toiled, but he did not enjoy it; he accumulated, but he was not allowed to possess. And in the 37th verse it is said, "And thou shalt become an astonishment, a proverb, and a byword, among all nations whither the Lord shall lead thee." "An astonishment," an extraordinary specimen, inexplicable except in the light of such prophecies as these. "And a byword." "Avaricious as a Jew;" "greedy, or mean as a Jew," is the proverbial expression almost in every country. Poets, dramatists, have all taken the Jew as the personation of what is mean, grasping and avaricious. Yet he is not more so, intrinsically, than we; it is circumstances that have made him so; it is persecution and ill-treatment that have crushed him. And all this is the fulfilment of prophecies old as the days of Moses, and yet not the justification of his persecutors.

Again, in the 49th verse, "The Lord shall bring a nation against thee from far, from the end of the earth, as swift as the eagle flieth ; a nation whose tongue thou shalt not understand ; a nation of fierce countenance, which shall not regard the person of the old, nor shew favour to the young." And again, in the 65th verse, "And among these nations shalt thou find no ease, neither shall the sole of thy foot have rest." Byron, in speaking of the Jews, calls them, without thinking he was quoting Scripture, "The tribe of the weary foot," the very language that is applied to them here. "Neither shall the sole of thy foot have rest; but the Lord shall give thee there a trembling heart, and failing of eyes, and sorrow of mind." How dramatically does all this delineate the history of the Jews from the period when they were scattered by Titus and Vespasian, and subsequently by the Emperor Adrian, downward to the present day!

All this teaches one or two very important lessons. First, we explain this severe and relentless persecution, permitted by God and predicted to fall upon them, on this ground, that they were set up as a model nation; they were endued with great privileges, they were invested with great glory, they were eliminated from the surrounding masses of heathendom, and made, and commanded to be, and enriched that they might be, a people alone, worshipping God, trusting in his word, reflecting his glory, obeying his commandments, doing his will, and in all their ways acknowledging and honouring him. This is what they were constituted, for this mission they were specially raised: they proved untrue to it; they became proud and forgot God; and the height of the privilege to which they were raised by the goodness and mercy of God, is the measure of the depth of degradation to which they have sunk on account of their misuse and abuse of great and distinguishing national privileges. Secondly, how impossible is it to escape the conclusion from all this that the Book of Deuteronomy is inspired! The predictions in this chapter, and in the ensuing one, are so specific, so literal, that they carry in their own bosoms the tests of their inspiration or the reverse. Had they been vague predictions that might have been fulfilled in the bulk, or the fulfilment of which it would be difficult and very delicate to trace, then we might have had our difficulties. But when these predictions are so specific, so literal, so exact, we must see by quoting history, either that they have been fulfilled and are true, or that they have not been fulfilled and are therefore false. Take the facts recorded by Volney the sceptic, by Gibbon the sneering infidel, or by Christian writers of all sects and parties; and without referring to these predictions, but simply recording what they find and the facts they witness, they record in history what is here predicted in prophecy. So really is the prophecy fulfilled, that the historian unconsciously, almost in the very words of Moses, declares the condition of the Jew in every land to which he has been banished. The historian writes to-day just what he sees; the prophet Moses wrote some three thousand years ago just what he was inspired to write. And when you come to compare the last eighteen centuries with the predictions of Moses, you find that the prophecy of Moses is transferred into the pages of Gibbon and Volney; and that Gibbon and Volney, who desired only to injure God's word, are made unconsciously, in his providence, the *amanuenses* who write down fully and faithfully the very fulfilment of the ancient prophecies of God. How true is it that he makes the wrath of man to praise him! how helpless is man when you see God taking the very sceptic, while the sceptic thinks not, and causing that sceptic to write down what he sees! and when future people read it, they find in Volney and Gibbon the fulfilment of the prophecies of Moses recorded. So much so, that the most eloquent evidence of the truth of the Bible may be found in the pages of the most inveterate disbelievers in it.

In the third place, is not this lesson very legible to us from the history of God's treatment of that nation: Be not high-minded, but fear? "Because of unbelief they were broken off; thou standest by faith, be not high-minded, but fear. Behold, therefore, the goodness and severity of God: on them which fell, severity; but toward thee, goodness, if thou continue in his goodness; otherwise thou also shalt be cut off." Now the Jews, raised to a great height, invested with great privileges, endowed with lofty and rich possessions, forgot the Giver; thought it was their might, not the mercy of God, that gave them all this; became proud in the imagination of their hearts; instead of living more holily they lived more licentiously, till at last their sins ejected them from their land; and that name which was the glory and the music of every tongue upon earth, has become a byword and a scoff amid the nations of the earth. We, as a nation, have great privileges, great blessings, a free gospel, an open Bible; liberty, every man, to give a reason for the faith that is in him, and every man to embrace and to profess that which he believes in his conscience to be true. These are great privileges. Spain, France, Italy, Russia, Austria and Prussia, have no such privileges. We have been made a great, a free, a powerful, a privileged nation; but it is by grace that we stand, it is by grace that we have been made so. The Jews occupied a position as lofty; they have fallen from it. Let England not be high-minded, but fear. Our candlestick may also be removed from its place; our height of privilege may also measure the depth of our ruin. Let us, therefore, be thankful for our privileges; let us brighten, not darken, the light that is kindled in the midst of us. And if we persevere in that righteousness that exalts a people, God, our own God, will bless us. It is not possible to escape the lesson of national responsibility while we read the history of the Jews. It was as a nation they were privileged, as a nation they were cursed, as a nation at this moment they suffer. And God deals with nations still as nations. Because the theocracy has ceased in Judea, it does not follow that national responsibility has ceased throughout the earth. Righteousness still exalts a people; and sin is still the ruin of any people. And if we cease to hallow our Sabbaths, to exalt our Bible, to acknowledge God in all the great assemblies of the land, and to legislate in his name, in his fear, and according to his will—the same degradation which fell upon the Jews will be meted out to us; and we too shall feel that sin is the ruin of a Gentile as well as it was of a Jewish nation.

How blind must the Jew be, seeing that he holds in his hand the predictions that delineate most graphically his present national experience! How can he explain the extraordinary fact that they are a people without a country, a family without a home; a church without sacrifices, without a priest, without a temple? How can they explain this? The very essence of their religion lies

in sacrifices of bulls and goats, and heifers and lambs.
Where is the morning and the evening sacrifice?
Where is the glory between the cherubim? Where
is the ephod? Where are the urim and thummim?
Where is the high priest? Where is the temple?
The Jew surely must often ask himself, Why is it so?
Why have not I my religion as I once had it? Every
nation has its religion; every people somewhere may
profess their religion. But the Jew in his synagogue
is a very different thing from the Jew in his temple.
There is no sacrifice in his synagogue, no altar, no
high-priest, no glory, no cherubim; nothing, in short,
that is essential to the very existence of the ritual
of Levi. Why has he had no sacrifice for eighteen
hundred years? Why, keeping the same faith, holding by the same law, the descendants of the same
people, tenaciously resisting every innovation, have
they not their religion in all its fulness? It is evident that they are the children of destiny; the subjects of a prophecy that cannot be broken; that their
desolation, their scattering, their separation from their
own land eighteen hundred years ago, and the cessation of all sacrifices, of all priestly offerings, is meant
to teach them in this desolating chasm, that Christ,
the end of the law, and hence of all propitiation, is
come.

We are warranted in indulging the blessed and delightful hope, however, that this nation, thus cut off,
debased, and cast out, shall one day be grafted in, and
their latter glory shall exceed the first. The same
apostle who tells us of their fall, says, "For I would
not, brethren, that ye should be ignorant of this mystery, lest ye should be wise in your own conceits; that

blindness in part is happened to Israel, until the fulness of the Gentiles "—that is, the times of the Gentiles, for it is that he is speaking of—" be come in. And so all Israel shall be saved." And again he tells us that " If the fall of them be the riches of the world, and the diminishing of them the riches of the Gentiles, how much more their fulness? For if the casting away of them be the reconciling of the world, what shall the receiving of them be but life from the dead?" All these passages show that the Jews are to be converted, and as might be shown from other passages, to be restored. It is as a nation they are depressed, as a nation they are scattered. It is because they are Jews they suffer; it is as Jews they are afflicted. It is as a nation they shall be restored; it is as a nation they shall be brought in. The dead and the dry bones, the types of the Jewish people, scattered through so many lands, buried in so many graves, shall hear the voice of God, and shall come forth, and form a great army; and restored to their own land, and divided again into tribes, they shall look upon Him whom their fathers pierced, and they shall mourn.

But because God has predicted that these curses shall light upon them, it does not follow that, like the Portuguese and the popes, we are to inflict them. God has predicted that the Jewish nation shall be the subject of such terrible curses; but he does not add to the prediction a command to the Gentiles to go and carry out the fulfilment—the very reverse. When God gives precepts, these are for us to obey; when he records prophecies, these are for himself to fulfil. But with a strange perversity man would rather leave the precepts, which it is inconvenient to flesh and blood to fulfil; and he would rather try to fulfil the prophecies, which gratify his pride of himself, and his hatred of them to whom those prophecies belong. But every declaration in God's word leads us to infer that they who bless Israel will be blessed, that they who help them will be holpen of God; that they who pray for them God will hear, and send back the prayer in responsive benedictions into their own bosoms. God will see to the fulfilment of the least promise and threatening; he asks us to see that we obey all his laws, by doing justly, loving mercy, walking humbly with our God; living soberly, and righteously, and godly in this present world; evincing thereby that we are the children of God, and that true faith in our blessed Redeemer, the only Messiah, worketh by love, purifieth the heart, and overcometh the world.

CHAPTER XXIX.

MOSES begins the chapter I have read by exhorting the children of Israel to that obedience to which they had been already pledged, amid circumstances so impressive as those through which they had come. He reminds them of the great trials that their eyes had seen, when God tested them in every circumstance and in every aspect, if they would persevere in obedience to that covenant he had made with them and with their fathers. He reminds them of the scenes they had witnessed; the pillar of cloud by day, and the pillar of fire by night; the opened sea forming a path for the children of Israel, and a grave for Pharaoh and his pursuing hosts; the rock rent and the waters gushing forth; the manna descending from heaven; and also great miracles that they had seen, healing their diseases, exercising and executing judgments upon the guilty. And what was the result of all this? "Yet the Lord hath not given you an heart to perceive, and eyes to see, and ears to hear, unto this day." Now what does this teach us? That no force of miracle, or splendour of sign, or multitude of wonders, will ever convert a single heart, or convince a single soul of righteousness, of sin, and of judgment. Now it is very important to notice that this people, who were fed by a continuous miracle, whose eyes were witnessing events the most stupendous and impressive—yet availed themselves of the least opportunity of declining from obedience to God, and of plunging into those deeds and sins of idolatry which have been so often branded and so solemnly forbidden. This only confirms what our blessed Lord said, when the rich man, in a state of misery and conscious suffering, recollecting that he had left sinful and unholy relatives upon earth, begged that some one might go and prove to them the reality of those things which they believed to be fancy ; the answer given was, " If they believe not Moses and the prophets, neither would they believe if one were to rise from the dead." This completely meets what people often say, " If we were to see a miracle we should be convinced." I answer, I do not believe that you would ever be convinced. Such is the ingenuity of man, such the sophisms that his fertile imagination can give birth to when his heart wants its services to screen it, that on seeing the miracle he would instantly proceed to explain it according to what he calls the laws of nature ; and after he had convinced himself that it was an incidental phenomenon, originated from natural causes, he would just settle down into his infidelity and scepticism only more confirmed than he was before. But suppose he were to see an actual miracle—what would be its effect ? If it be true that man's mind is to be influenced by conviction, not to be forced by power ; and if there be evidence more than overwhelming for all

that is written in this book, and of the inspiration of
them that wrote it—I do not see what you can reasonably demand additional to what you already have ;
namely, such evidence for all that is in this book as
would satisfy men impartial in their judgments, un-
biased by habits of depravity, and accessible to the
influence of truth, and of truth alone. And, besides,
if you saw a miracle to-day, would you not soon forget
it ? Do we not too well know that mere physical and
material impressions, however deep at the moment,
gradually lose their influence as they recede into the
distance of the past ? So much is this the case, that
these very people that saw such miracles a few years
before, now regarded and felt them so little that they
scarcely remembered that they had been done at all.
But might not the miracle be often repeated ? If it
were to be often repeated, you would explain it at once
as one of the natural phenomena of the world. We
live amid miracles in one sense. What is a miracle ?
It is not God more present in it than he is present in
the growing grass, in the blossoming flowers, in the
waving trees ; in the sunshine, in the cloud, and in
the storm : but it is God present in a formula or in
a shape in which you have never seen him present
before ; crossing and contradicting, as it seems to us,
what are the ordinary laws and phenomena of the
natural world. There is as much of God, there is as
much of God's power, God's wisdom, God's goodness,
in making those seeds cast into the earth in spring,
grow up into those golden harvests that we expect
soon to reap, as there was in turning a few loaves into
food for thousands, or in turning a few pitchers of
water into wine to refresh hundreds. Only, in the

one case, we are accustomed to the supply, and look
so much at the effect that we lose sight of Him who is
at the root of it ; in the other case it is so incidental
and so rare, that by its rarity it makes an impression
that would wear off just in proportion to the frequency
with which the miracle was repeated.   It is not more
light that we want, but life.   We do not need the
understanding more convinced, but the heart more
impressed ; not intellectual force or physical impression, but moral influence in the conscience and in the
heart, which the Holy Spirit can give : and unless we
have that, all the signs, the miracles, the wonders of
the past compressed into yet grander and more impressive ones in the future, will not convince one mind
or bring one sinner to the foot of the cross.

He exhorts them further by reminding them of
what God was, to keep all the words of this covenant ;
telling them, "Ye stand this day, all of you, before the
Lord your God ; your captains of your tribes, your
elders and your officers, with all the men of Israel ;
your little ones, your wives, and the stranger that is
in thy camp, from the hewer of thy wood unto the
drawer of thy water ; that thou shouldest enter into
covenant with the Lord thy God, and into his oath,
which the Lord thy God maketh with thee this day."
The expression, "Entering into covenant with God,"
is very remarkable.   It is one of those proofs of the
exceeding greatness of the love and condescension of
God which are so often scattered through the Bible.
He might command simply, and he might tell the
creature, "The obligation of that command is on you,
whether you like it or not."   But he asks man freely
to accept what eternally is his duty, to enter into

covenant with him ; that is, openly to say to him, " I accept that yoke which is easy, and that burden which is light;" and God says to the creature, "And I will cause to descend upon you all the blessings of the heaven above, and all the blessings of the earth below; and you shall know that they are a happy people who have chosen the Lord to be their God."

He then tells them that if that not rare and extra-ordinary character should appear who shall hear all the judgments pronounced in this book upon him that doeth wickedly, but shall say, " I shall have peace in my heart in spite of what God hath threatened, or of his power to execute what he has threatened ; and I will go on adding sin to sin, defying God's thunder-bolts and scorning his threats to execute his judg-ments upon me ; " then such a character of all men most provokes the righteous retribution of Heaven ; and on that man accordingly it is said all the curses that are written in this book shall descend. It is not only scepticism and atheism, but blasphemy united with both and developed in one character, when a man, knowing what God has said, defies him to his face, and takes his own course, and makes up his mind that he shall have what God alone can give— peace notwithstanding his sins and his crimes. And God says then that " If ye—the people that are about to enter into this good land—shall rise up and sin, and do all the things that are forbidden ; " then what shall take place ? " The whole land shall be brim-stone, salt, and burning, that it is not sown, nor beareth, nor any grass groweth therein, like the over-throw of Sodom." And when the nations come to see it they will ask, What is the matter with this land? It ought to be fruitful; why is it not so? And this will explain it: "Because its people have forsaken the covenant of the Lord God of their fathers." Now look at this moment at Palestine, and see if there be not upon the land all the evidences of that very curse denounced upon it in this and in the previous chapter. There is no land I believe, east, west, north, or south, that equals in capacities of fruitfulness the land of Canaan. The vines used to creep up its magnificent rocks and had no equals; its cedars upon Lebanon used to be the most renowned and beautiful in the world; their very remains creating yet impressions of what they once were. The land itself was able once to grow corn that could have made it the granary of Europe and of Asia. At this moment, when it is traced, tracked and explored, and colonies of Jews are now at the present time actually exploring and cultivating portions of it—as if the Jew was already taking an initial possession of it—it is found that it has capabilities beyond all belief. But why is the bare foot of the monk upon the one part; the Arab plunderer the only vision on the horizon in another part; that the miserable inhabitants themselves cannot grow corn enough to feed their own families; and the vulture and the eagle are heard screaming amid the rocks to which the vines used to cling, bringing forth all the clusters of Eshcol? How is it that the tombs of its inhabitants outnumber their homes; that of all cities upon earth, Jerusalem, the most beautifully situated, once the joy of the whole earth, is the most desolate, the most filthy, the most forlorn and miserable? There can be no reply to it except one: the sins of the people cast them out of it; the judgments those sins provoked have brought down a curse upon it. And when the nations of the earth, as they witness that land, illustrious for so many historic and traditional glories, ask, Why is it as we now find it? the few can say what the Bible helps them to say, "Because the people forsook the covenant of the Lord their God;" and they are now what they are described, and what we read in the previous chapter, a people that are a hiss, and a scoff, and a byword amid the nations of the earth; and are constrained to say, as the Jew in Poland and in Russia, under the autocrat, can say, where there are about two millions of Jews—when the morning comes, "Would God it were the evening;" and when the evening comes, "Would God it were the morning;" and as they can say in the Ghettos of Italy and Rome, "We are a people cast off and despised, and trodden under foot;" but a people, thanks be to God for the prospect, preserved to a splendid destiny; a people that have Palestine in title-deeds in comparison of which the title-deeds of our oldest nobility are but of yesterday; and who will be restored to that land; and that land again shall wave with fruit like Lebanon; and the nations of the earth shall group round it, and look from the Nebos and the Pisgahs of Asia and Europe; and they will say, "What a goodly land! beautiful for situation, the joy of the whole earth. If God cursed it for its sins, he has blessed it in his mercies; and again its deserts rejoice, and its solitary places blossom like the rose."

CHAPTER XXX.

CHRIST'S APPEAL. THREATENINGS. PROMISES. PERSISTENT LOVE. DISPERSION OF JEWS. WE NOT TO PERSECUTE. IMPORTANT ALTERNATIVES.

WE cannot but hear in the words of this chapter the tones of that most pathetic remonstrance addressed by our Lord to the capital of this same people: "O Jerusalem, Jerusalem, how often would I have gathered thee as a hen gathereth her brood under her wings, and ye would not!" This chapter is just the expansion of that most touching remonstrance, and so like it in its very expressions that one can see the authorship of the one in the writing and inspiration of the other. God speaks here, after he had told them in the previous chapter, and also in the chapter before that, which we also read, that they should be scattered among all lands for their sins, that they should be a scoff, and a by-word, and a hissing; that they should have no rest for the soles of their feet; that a nation of fierce countenance, which regarded not the person of the old, should make an irruption into their land; that they should all be driven away, because they had forsaken the Lord their God, and his covenant. God here introduces the practical thought that if they will not be guilty of the sins which he has so graphically enumerated and so unmistakeably condemned, that then as a nation his blessing, that those sins forfeited, will descend upon them, and God will bless them. But if they will be guilty of these sins with their eyes open, then as they were raised up to be witnesses for his unity, and to be the guardians of his word, and to be the model nation and church of Christendom, God will scatter them and curse them, and all the calamities that he had told in the previous chapters should descend upon them.

But he says, even after all this, "If when ye are scattered abroad amid all the nations of the earth whither the Lord hath driven thee, and if thou wilt return unto the Lord thy God, and obey his voice in all that I command thee, then God will have *compassion upon thee, and will turn thy captivity, and have compassion upon thee, and will return and gather thee from all the nations whither the Lord thy God hath scattered thee." How touching as well as beautiful is such a promise as that! A people so warned became, nevertheless, the most guilty of all the peoples upon earth. But even after guilt has abounded, and their hardness of heart and obduracy of nature have become aggravated and inveterate, even then God follows them, cleaves to them, remonstrates with them, beseeches them as a parent a child that they would bethink themselves and turn unto him; and all heaven is ready to shower down blessings upon them if they will only arise and go to their Father, and say in the land of their prodigality, "We have sinned against heaven, and in thy sight;" and behold, he will arise and have compassion upon them, and will gather them out of all lands, and will plant them again in their own land.

Now it is impossible to suppose that the dispersion spoken of in the commencement of this chapter was the captivity at Babylon, or any other dispersion subsequent to that event. It evidently contemplates that dispersion of which the Jews at this moment are the victims. They have been literally scattered into all lands, they breathe every air, they speak every tongue, they live under republics and despotisms, they are found in every capital, they are the money-lenders of every nation, they are essential to the working of the different nationalities of the earth. Wherever there is commerce, there is a Jew; wherever there is a prospect of profit, there he is. There is no capital, from the frozen ledges of Greenland to the scorching sands of Africa, in which the Jew is not. How can you account for a people, as I have often told you, retaining all their nationality unmistakeable, and yet a people that are without a home, a nation without a country, distinct, not blended with the nations, but separate from them, indicating that separation by the most unequivocal features,—how can you account for this except from what is said in the last three chapters we have read, and what is promised in the chapters of the prophets which we shall read, that God will look upon them, and restore them to their own land, and that they shall possess that land, and he will do them good, and multiply them above their fathers? It is impossible to conclude that this restoration here promised has been fulfilled, because nothing approximating to it has taken place from the captivity in Babylon onward to the present moment.

We then read in the next place that God will put the curse he denounced upon them upon their enemies if they will thus return unto him and obey his voice. It is very remarkable that God, whilst he denounces such severe curses upon the Jews, and tells them in the previous chapter that they shall be a hiss, and a scoff, and a byword amid all the nations of the earth, that never does he sanction the conduct of those that heap the curse upon them. Nothing was more absurd than the conduct of the superstitious monks, and priests, and prelates of the middle ages, who burned the Jew, persecuted him, plundered him, drove him into dens and prisons and dungeons, and pleaded as the consecration of their cruelty, that they were fulfilling the prophecies of God. Prophecy is not our rule of life, but precept. God reserves to himself the sublime prerogative of prophesying ; he reserves also to himself the equally sublime prerogative of seeing that prophecy fulfilled ; but he bids us take to ourselves the humbler but the more practical and useful duty of doing justly, loving mercy, and walking humbly with our God. No pretended fulfilment of a prediction by us warrants the least deviation from a plain duty, or the infraction of a single commandment.

He then proceeds to tell them, "I have set before thee this day life and good, death and evil." He warns them that these things were in the balance before them, and he says to them, "Choose life. My desire is that you choose life. I have no pleasure in the death of the sinner, but rather that he should turn from his wickedness and live." Now this commandment shows that if man has not ability to choose life, man has, nevertheless, responsibility for rejecting it. It is quite true we are not machines ; it is quite true we are not mere dumb, driven cattle ; and it is equally true that we have no power to regenerate, or sanctify, or save ourselves, and yet God addresses us precepts, and commands, and promises, treating us throughout as rational and responsible persons—responsible at a judgment-seat for our rejection of the truth; and the very man who feels most profoundly, "I cannot save myself," is just the very man that will pray most earnestly, "Lord, save me, or I perish." But you know quite well that the objection constantly urged, "We can do nothing," is not the expression of a deep sense of weakness, but an apology for indolence, and love of the world, and hatred of God. He that really feels himself perishing, really feels he cannot save himself, will lift up his heart to Him who can; and then he will be a living instance of what the world thinks a contradiction, what the apostle records as inspiration: "Work out your salvation with fear and trembling." There is your duty, choose life; but it is added, "For it is God that worketh in you to will and to do of his good pleasure."

CHAPTER XXXI.

THIS chapter contains the intimation made to Moses
by the Lord God of Israel, that the days of his pilgrimage upon earth were now about to end; and that
while he was not permitted to enter into the earthly
Canaan which had been the burden of his hopes, he
should nevertheless enter into a far brighter and better
Canaan, into which he did not expect so speedy and
so triumphant access. You remember, in the course
of the previous chapters which we have read, that the
angry words, mixed with pride, given utterance to by
Moses in smiting the rock, when the waters gushed
from it, had induced God to tell him that he should
not be allowed to enter that land to the margin of
which he had conducted the children of Israel. It was
a sin punished in the sight of all the tribes of Israel,
but chastisement only in its personal action upon
Moses; and though not permitted to enter the earthly
in consequence, he was not therefore prohibited from
an admission into the heavenly, through grace.

Moses begins the chapter by saying, "I am an
hundred and twenty years old this day." And what

a remarkable pilgrimage! Forty years in the court of
Pharaoh, becoming acquainted with all the learning,
the wisdom, and the experience of that remarkable
land; forty years in Midian, preparing for his great
office; and now forty years wandering in the desert,
before the Israelites entered into Canaan: the sum
total, one hundred and twenty years. This was the
age not of one of the antediluvian patriarchs, whose
ages stretched to an immense length, but of one who
lived long after the flood, and under circumstances
almost, if not altogether, similar to those in which we
now live.

This fact, that he lived to one hundred and twenty,
and that he was near one hundred and twenty
when he wrote the 90th Psalm, throws, I think, some
light upon a passage to which I have occasionally alluded; but which is often misquoted, and I think
misunderstood. Moses wrote the 90th Psalm, as the
heading correctly tells you. Moses says, in the 10th
verse, "The days of our years are threescore years and
ten; and if by reason of strength they be fourscore
years, yet is their strength labour and sorrow; for
it is soon cut off, and we fly away." Now, you ask,
how can you reconcile this; because in one passage,
he says the length of life is seventy; in his own biography he lived, not to an unusual age, but the usual
age of one hundred and twenty years? The answer
is, the normal length of human life was that which
Moses attained—one hundred and twenty: but the
abnormal length of life in the desert, and under the
afflictions with which they were visited, was reduced
to seventy; not reduced to that permanently, but in
the special state of suffering, affliction, and distress in

which they were. Moses says, substantially, instead
of our life being what it usually is, it is now only
seventy years of age : and that is evidence that we are
in a state of suffering and distress, so severe that we
cannot reach the natural length of human life ; a
length reduced by the heavy trials which it is doomed
to bear in the wilderness, not by a permanent fiat of
God.

There is no reason to believe that man's age ought
to be, speaking from physical considerations, and
from the intimations scattered through the Word
of God, less than one hundred and twenty. The
last reduction of human life was to one hundred and
twenty ; and if, speaking generally—speaking, I say,
generally—and according to human laws, and human
experience, if man does not attain the age of one
hundred and twenty, it is not owing to a fiat pronounced in Scripture that the limit of his life shall
always and everywhere be seventy ; but owing to
causes over which, more or less, the great majority
have in some measure control. What is very singular,
a very eminent French physiologist has recently written a work, which I have been reading, and been
deeply interested in, in which, by a singular coincidence, he bears out the conclusion that I have
gathered from the Bible, by stating a remarkable fact,
that in all animal life the law is that the animal lives
to five times the period it takes in reaching maturity.
It is true of the horse, the dog, the lion, the lamb, the
goat—every creature that we know lives, when
not suddenly cut short, or violently used up, to
five times the period that it takes in getting to maturity. He states that man takes five-and-twenty

years to reach maturity, and therefore, he argues, that man ought to live to five times that period, or to one hundred and twenty-five. But I will assume that man takes twenty or twenty-one years in reaching maturity ; then the law is that man's natural life is five times twenty or twenty-one, which will extend over one hundred years. And thus the very last reduction of life indicated in the Bible to one hundred and twenty, is the natural and proper length of life ; and perhaps, if we were in those sanitary and social circumstances that are favourable to human life, this age might be generally attained. But if it be true, as they say, that we eat incessantly poison mingled with every article; if it be true that we breathe an air made pestilential by the very streams that were meant in God's goodness to purify and sweeten it; if it be true that man sits at the desk till the brain is exhausted, and all his nervous energy paralyzed; if it be true that the excitements and competitions of business are what commercial men say they are—a violent and protracted strain and pressure on the mental and physical economy that bring to an early grave ; then the surprise is that so many people live so long— not that they live so few years, but that they live so many. But were all these social and sanitary arrangements what they should be, and what they might be, and what it becomes rulers and statesmen to take more care that they be—then I am quite satisfied that human life would be longer than it is ; and while it lasts, would be healthier, and happier, and better than it is. At all events, this seems to me clear, that the Bible gives us no evidence that human life is reduced beneath one hundred and twenty as its maximum; and we know that not a few do live to that age. Hence, this Frenchman says, that youth extends to five-and-twenty; that from five-and-twenty to fifty you have what he calls young manhood; from fifty to seventy, he says, there is, by the law of physical economy, the full strength and vigour of manhood; and that at seventy, not man dies, as we usually interpret it, but man begins to get old, to decay, to give way; and old age extends from seventy to one hundred, one hundred and fifteen, or one hundred and twenty. I quote it because it is very remarkable that scientific research should seemingly so completely fall in with what seems to be the indication of the Spirit of God in his own blessed Word. At all events, Moses lived to one hundred and twenty; a man tried, and vexed, and grieved, and thwarted, and at one hundred and twenty his strength was great; the eye was not dimmed: and he passed from grace to glory, from the desert to the eternal Canaan, there enjoying now the presence of God and of the Lamb.

When he thus saw he was about to die, he gives instructions to those that were to succeed him. He said to the children of Israel, " Be strong; be of a good courage; fear not." He calls Joshua, who was to succeed him, and he says to him, " Be strong, and be of good courage; and thou must go with this people; and fear not, for it is the Lord that is with thee." And then he orders the whole law; that is, the Pentateuch, the Five Books of Moses, commonly called, to be deposited in the holy place; and gives them these instructions:—All the people are to be gathered together on the great jubilee, once in seven years; men, women, children, strangers; and all this law is to be read in their hearing; it is to be taught "to thy children, to thy wives, to the stranger that is within thy gates;" so that all may be thoroughly acquainted with it. Now, what an evidence is this, that the Bible, in the tongue of the people, was the privilege and right of the people. And if a book, comparatively so obscure as the Old Testament then, was to be taught to women and children, why should the New Testament, so plain and perspicuous now, be withheld from woman or child? It seems the irresistible inference from all that Moses wrote, that the Word of God, instead of being the monopoly of a few, is to be and ought to be the possession of all mankind. And if it be so, it is implied that it is possible to understand it. Why teach children what they cannot understand? But the very fact that children were to be taught the Bible, implies that some of it, surely, children could understand. And we read of Timothy, "From a child thou hast known the Scriptures." And if Timothy, by no means a remarkable child, could understand the Scriptures in his day, and could learn their meaning from the teaching of his mother and his grandmother, Lois and Eunice, why should not children now be taught the Scriptures? and why is it impossible for them to understand the Scriptures? and why should it not be the duty of grandmother and mother to instruct children in the knowledge of the Scriptures?

Then Joshua is told by Moses again, to be strong and be of good courage. Moses predicts what the children of Israel will do after he is dead, and therefore composes that magnificent poem, which is contained in the succeeding chapter, the 32nd; to be a refreshment to their memories, a memorial of their mercies, and to remind them of the sins into which they would fall according to his own testimony.

CHAPTER XXXII.

SONG OF MOSES. ITS BEAUTY. THE LORD'S PORTION. GOD'S EDUCATION OF HIS OWN. THE HEN AND THE EAGLE. INGRATITUDE. NATIONAL PROSPERITY. DEFINITION AND DESCRIPTION OF GOD.

In the previous chapter there was allusion made to the song that Moses was to sing, or rather to compose, while inspired by God, for the instruction and the edification of all the children of Israel. It has been well remarked by Bishop Louth, a very competent judge of all that is beautiful in writing, that there is not a more eloquent or more impressive poem in any language, considered merely as a human composition, than that sublime one which we have now read. It begins with an appeal addressed to heaven and earth, or a summons to every intelligent being to come and listen to the grand truths which the inspired poet is about to unfold in this truly inspired poem. And he tells them, in the very commencement of it, "My doctrine shall drop as the rain, my speech shall distil as the dew, as the small rain upon the tender herb, and as the showers upon the grass;" not like the thunder shower, which ploughs up the earth, devastates the soil, breaks the branches and scatters all the foliage; but like the dew that saturates the soil, not by the quantity that falls at once, but by its continuous falling, and fertilizes while it saturates also.

"Because I will publish the name of the Lord: ascribe ye greatness unto our God." Then he describes him as the Rock; "their Rock," the ground of their confidence, "is not as our Rock, even our enemies themselves being judges." His work is perfect; earth was perfect when he made it. If imperfection has scathed it, it is not from him but from the curse and sin subsequently introduced into it. "Just and right is he" in all his dispensations and economy. When they seem to you most uneven, it is not his ways that are uneven, but your judgment that is wrong and your perceptions that are dark.

He then speaks of his people Israel that "they have corrupted themselves;" he has not done it, but they have done it; they have requited with ingratitude the Father that fed them, the Rock of their salvation; they have disregarded and forsaken him who gave them their inheritance. A very beautiful expression it is: "The Lord's portion is his people; Jacob is the lot of his inheritance." God looks down upon earth, and of all things that are beautiful above, of all things that are fragrant below, he selects none to be his special portion, his favourite possession, save souls that are redeemed by precious blood, and sanctified and made fit for glory by his Holy Spirit. How remarkable that God should pass by the angels that fell, even the angels that abide in glory, and should select as the bride of the Lamb a people that have forgotten him, forsaken him, provoked him, corrupted themselves, and should make them a glorious church, and present it to himself without spot or blemish, or any such thing. When man loves or selects a creature for himself it is because in the creature there is something beautiful or attractive; when God selects a creature for himself it is in spite of its defects, its corruption and its sins, in order to make it beautiful with imperishable glory and perfection.

He describes how he found him—" In a desert land, and in the waste howling wilderness." And the way he treated him was, as the eagle stirs up her nest, to rouse the fully-fledged eaglets to take flight and search for food for themselves, stirring them up when they are disposed to sleep and slumber, and continue under the domestic shelter of the nest, and takes them abroad, and trains them to fly; and when the eaglet, weary on its wing, falls, she darts down, catches it upon her wings and carries it back to the nest, to rest a little and be refreshed for a stronger and more successful flight. So did God deal with his people. What an exquisite figure! I know not which is the more beautiful, the figure of the eagle in this passage, or the one used by our Lord: " As a hen gathereth her brood under her wings, so would I have gathered you, and ye would not." Perhaps the domestic hen is the meeter symbol in the Testament of love; the eagle the more appropriate, but not less expressive, symbol in the Old Testament economy.

He then speaks of the reception that all his goodness received from them. He says, " Jeshurun waxed fat," describing his people under that epithet; that is, they turned the mercies of God to their own advantage, enjoyed the blessings, but smote or forgot the hand that bestowed the blessings upon them. They were guilty of this great sin: "Of the Rock that begat thee thou art unmindful, and hast forgotten God that formed thee." He then specifies some of the judgments that he will pronounce upon them if they should continue in that state and not return to him; and he tells them what is still true, that if a people be wise, if they be right in their relationship to God, that one shall chase a thousand, and two put ten thousand to flight. Now that lesson lives still. "Some trust in chariots, some in horses; but we will trust in the Lord our God." There is no doubt that a nation's faithfulness to God in honouring his Sabbaths, in revering his word, in hallowing his name, in acting under a sense of responsibility to him through all its national organs, will receive a blessing; and that a nation, as such, waxing fat and kicking against him; forgetting the Rock that begat them, and God that formed them, will find that they will not succeed in the field of conflict, or prosper in the sunshine of lasting peace. It is a law lasting as the very existence of nations themselves, that righteousness exalteth a nation, and that sin is the ruin as well as the shame of any people.

He closes this beautiful chapter, after continuing the song descriptive of what his people had made themselves, with a description of himself: "See now that I, even I, am he," that is the translation of the word Yehovah, who is and will be; "I kill, and I make alive;" none can fall where I give not permission; none can live unless I sustain. "I wound and I heal: neither is there any that can deliver out of my hand. For I lift up my hand to heaven, and say, I live for ever." What a magnificent portrait of Deity, sketched in the splendour of his own glory! " I am that I am." And now I might well ask you, Whence did these illiterate, barbarous, rebellious, quarrelsome Jews in the desert get this idea of God? Take Greece, not contemporaneous Greece, but Greece in its meridian glory, in the days of Pericles, when it reached its culminating greatness in arts, in literature, in poetry, in music, in history—in all that are supposed to be the attainments of a great people. Read the idea entertained by the most enlightened Greeks, or heathen rather, of God, and you will be struck with its monstrous puerility. But read the apprehension of Deity entertained by the most barbarous Jew, who had never shaped a piece of marble into any beauty, who had never touched the canvas, and made it glow almost with life, whose music was poor, whose literature was low. Ask the Jew to define God, and he tells you God has defined himself: " I am he, and there is no god with me : I kill, and I make alive ; I live for ever; I am that I am." Now, how do you account for this difference ? Not by the attainments of the Jew, for he had none. The Greek, with all his literature, bowed down to a miserable idol, or inscribed upon his altar, " To an unknown God." The Jew, without any literature, or science, or attainments of an æsthetic kind at all, had ideas of God that the deepest philosophy has not yet exceeded. Now whence the difference? The answer is, the Greek struck out from his heart, corrupted by the fall, his apprehension of his god; the Jew received direct from heaven, as a revelation, his comprehension of God. Therefore, the definition of God entertained by the Jew, as contrasted with the ideas of God entertained by the most enlighthened Gentiles, alone is fitted to demonstrate that this book is the inspiration of God.

GOD'S CARE OF HIS OWN.

THE following words in the song of Moses are selected for special illustration. They are beautiful and expressive :—

"For the Lord's portion is his people; Jacob is the lot of his inheritance. He found him in a desert land, and in the waste howling wilderness; he led him about, he instructed him, he kept him as the apple of his eye. As an eagle stirreth up her nest, fluttereth over her young, spreadeth abroad her wings, taketh them, beareth them on her wings : so the Lord alone did lead him, and there was no strange god with him."
—DEUT. xxxii. 9—12.

How exquisitely beautiful the imagery under which God sets forth the affection that he bears and the care that he exercises towards his believing and his beloved people! Israel in the desert was the type of the Christian in the world; and all that the one received from God's providential and paternal care during forty years in the desert, the other, that is, the Christian, derives from God in all his wandering up and down throughout the pilgrimage of life, his years of threescore and ten or more here below. Whatever was written in the Old Testament is written for our learning. "These things," says the apostle, "happened unto them," literally translated, "for types," or, as it is in our translation, "for examples."

The human heart was the same, and God's love was the same, in the desert, that the one and the other are now in the world. Forms have varied, circumstances have changed, but the substance, the essential substance, of man by nature and by grace, is now what it was in the desert, when man moved with the burning flame of the pillar of fire for his guide, and miracles as the means of his daily nutriment. Now, here it is said, in speaking of God's people, whether in the desert or in the world, " He *found* him." Then, if God has found us we were lost, and if God has not yet found us we are now in the condition of lost. Lost—what does that mean ? Lost to God, of no service to him; lost to ourselves, for we have missed the grand end of life; lost to others ; we are banes, not blessings ; injurious, not benefactors ; and so entirely lost is the best and the most upright or all that are not yet washed in that Saviour's precious blood, that he has no more strength to recover himself and to restore his nature to communion with God, than he has strength to put forth new wings and take a flight to the nearest or the remotest star. We are lost just as the Israelite was in the desert when he travelled away from the camp and company of the people of God, without a star in the sky, without a taper upon earth, without a footpath home, or a friend to lead us from the intricacies of the labyrinth back to our Father and our God. Each of us is by nature the lost sheep that must either die of hunger or be torn by the wolves, the lost coin that the woman has not yet found, or the lost son, feeding upon husks, far from his Father's home, and serving a stranger in a strange land. Such, then, is our state by nature. Now, it is not the abject criminal that is so, but it is all who are unrenewed who are so. What a solemn thought, that we are each of us by nature lost sinners, lost sheep, lost sons, a lost coin; that we are of no use to any one; that we are perishing; and that if we continue in the state in which Adam and the fall have left us, we never can be admitted, if there be truth in the Bible or fixity in God's law, into that happy presence into which only recovered sons, recovered coins, sheep that have been borne upon the Shepherd's shoulders home, can be admitted and made welcome for ever.

This expression, "He found us," not only implies we are by nature lost, but it also hints to us the blessed thought that God missed us. Now, when one thinks of this, one is struck with the greatness of the wisdom, the width of the knowledge, the depth of the sympathy of God. This world itself is no larger, amid the multitude of orbs that are strewn over the infinite plains of the universe, than a grain of sand is amid the sands on the seashore; and one sinner in this world is the merest atom when counted with the numberless millions that now inhabit this globe; and yet God, who has millions upon millions beyond all calculation and beyond all comprehension continually to minister to, misses that one lost sheep from the fold, that lost coin from his treasury, that prodigal son from his home. The least is not beneath his notice, the mightiest is not beyond it; and there is not one lost sinner whose case, condition, and character are not at this moment as clearly before the eye of God as if God and that lost sinner were the only two in the universe. We think of God too often

as a Being great, but distant ; grand and glorious, but
little interested in us. But the truth is, he is as much
interested in each as he is in all, and he as thoroughly
comprehends, and sees, and fathoms each, as he sees,
comprehends, and fathoms the angels and the cherubim
that are about his throne. But, secondly, God missed
us the instant that we became sinners ; and, thirdly, the
expression " found us " implies, not that we sought
him, for then it would have been, we found him, but
that he sought us ; and therefore it is written that he
found us ; in other words, the doctrine of election,
or of sovereign grace, or of grace, which so many
quarrel about, is simply this, that God came after
us whilst we were fleeing from him ; that the first
movement that reconciled us to Himself did not
originate with us but with him. He missed us, he
came after us ; not we missed him, we first sought
him ; and, therefore, it is written that Jesus went
after us as the shepherd the lost sheep, and sought
it until, it is beautifully written in that parable,
he found it; and it is written again, " God so loved
the world, that he sent or gave his only begotten
Son ;" and again it is written, " He came to seek and
to save them that are lost." What is the whole
economy of Scripture but God's sovereign love
stretching from heaven to earth in quest of lost
sinners ? What are all the institutions of His
ancient law, what are his promises and types, but
lights hung out in the sky that we may see where
our home is, and what is the way back ? And what
are all his promises, and gracious invitations, and
thrilling remonstrances, but voices, the voice of our
heavenly Father sounding in the desert, bidding the

z

lost son come home, seeking the lost sheep to bring it back to the fold, searching with the lighted candle for the lost coin, that, repolished and restamped with the image of God, it may again take its part in the currency of heaven. We thus read then, first, that we were lost; secondly, that we were missed; thirdly, that we must have been sought out; and, lastly, what is the crowning point, that we are found. "He found Israel in the desert." God has found us if we be Christians. Found us. Blessed thought! whatever God undertakes he accomplishes. You remember in Luke xv. the shepherd went after the lost sheep, how long? Until he found it. Wherever God sets his heart upon the restoration of any, he persists in the process until that process is crowned with triumphant success. The means he uses are various. It may be the storms of affliction, to remind you by the contrast of a peaceful home; it may be the thorns, the briars, the wolf in the desert, to teach you and impress upon you your peril; it may be gleams of sweet sunshine, as from your Father's presence, to remind you that in his "presence there is fulness of joy." But, whatever be the process, whether the preaching of the word, the reading of the word, the incidental perusal of a chapter, afflictions, trials, bereavements, sorrows, poverty or wealth—all of these are the evidences in the desert that your Father is seeking after you; and if he has set his heart upon you he will not cease to seek until he has found you. You say, But if God be omniscient, omnipresent, omnipotent, why does he not seize the lost, and carry it home at once? That is, in other words, Why does God not treat us as if we were stones, or dumb, driven cattle, instead of rational, intelligent beings. God has not made us cattle, but human beings; and therefore God will, and by the very law of his own being he must, treat us as capable of motive, capable of conviction, capable of persuasion. No man is driven to heaven; many are drawn to it. No man is carried there by force; every one that goes there is made willing in the day of God's power; and therefore God stands at the door and knocks—it rests with you to open. God goes after you, and seeks you, and finds you, and he so subdues you by a sense of the misery you have incurred that you are too happy to be laid like the recovered sheep upon the shepherd's shoulder, whilst the good shepherd carries it home, all the way rejoicing.

The place that he found Israel in is described here as a " desert place." It was in Israel's case literally a desert; it is in a high sense—this world is, in a high sense—a desert to us still. I do not mean that there are no bright views in it, that there are no beautiful flowers, that there is not plenty of literal bread, plenty of common water. All these things were absent in the desert of Sin, but they are present with us. But then man does not live by bread alone; and whilst in reference to his lower wants this world may be a perfect paradise, yet in reference to man's higher wants, and as a being treading a loftier level, this world is to him a desert. There is no living bread in it except what is rained from heaven; there is no living water in it except what gushes from the stricken rock; there is no guide through its intricacies and its tangled paths to glory except by the shining

pillar of fire by night, and the pillar of cloud by day ;
and we are taught in every nook, and cranny, and
winding, and alley of it, " This is not our rest ; there
remaineth far beyond it a rest for the people of God."
So much for the statement here that God found Israel
in the desert.

Then when he had found him, what did he do with
him ? It seems almost strange, and inexplicable,
that, instead of instantly taking him home, he should
lead him about. " He found him, and led him about."
How remarkable ! If you will take Bagster's Pocket
Bible, or any other form of that excellent edition of
that Bible, and look at the wanderings of the children
of Israel through the desert as they are there marked on
the map, you will see that when they had almost touched
the margin of the promised land, they were conducted
right back again till they almost fell back upon the
very borders of Egypt. In other words, God did not
lead the Israelites by a straight line as the crow flies,
or as an arrow goes, but zigzag, backwards and
forwards, right and left ; or, in the expressive words
of this passage, he " led them about." And God
leads his people so still. No one in this world is
carried direct, without a trouble, without a deflection,
without an obstruction, without an interruption, to
heaven. Your own experience often has been that
you have been turned you knew not why ; that
instead of going straight forward you seem to have
been proceeding right backward ; that instead of
going to the right, you have suddenly, through
some influence which you could not explain, been
constrained to go to the left. Your whole course
has not been a continuous progression, you have had

your days when you have stood still, you have had
days when you felt you were going backward, when
your light seemed to be quenched, and when all the
love that was once kindled within you seemed to
be extinguished for ever. And next day that light
has been kindled, your lamp has burned the more
brightly, your love has attained its first fervour; and
your experience must be, if you be a Christian, that
your whole Christian course has been morally what
the whole terrestrial course of the Israelites was
geographically, not right onward as the arrow cleaves
the air, but zigzag, or, in the language of my text,
" led about." And so He says, " I will bring the
blind by a way they know not; I will lead them in
paths they have not known." But in the midst of
all this,—often to us inexplicable at the time, for very
often the Christian wonders how it is so, and thinks
he is forgotten or forsaken when he is not; and he is
cast down frequently on the supposition that he
is cast off, which cannot be—God is instructing
us : " He led him about, and he instructed him."
He instructed him because he led him about.
The leading about was just for the purpose of instructing him; and hence, when the explanation of
this leading about is given in Deuteronomy, in that
most interesting chapter, the eighth, we are there
told that " He led thee about, fed thee with manna,
that he might make thee know that man doth not
live by bread only, but by every word that proceedeth
out of the mouth of the Lord. He led thee these
forty years in the wilderness, to humble thee, and to
prove thee, to know what was in thine heart, whether
thou wouldest keep his commandments, or no." In

other words, the end of his leading about was just that he might instruct his people. And have not you learned often lessons from the cloud that you never derived from the sunshine? Have you not very frequently gained instruction in affliction that you never reaped in prosperity? Have you not found now, when you have gained a new stage in your progression Zionward, that it was good for you that you were led about, that it was well that you were not carried right on to the end that you had in view, and that pulpit, and platform, and press, and Bible have all instructed you; and sick bed, and sorrow, and bereavement, and loss, have all wrought for your good; and that as God has found you, and as God has led you about, so God has been teaching you, and you have learned that happy lesson, " All thy people shall be taught of thee, and great shall be the peace of that people." But in the midst of all this teaching, leading about, and instructing, you were always safe; for " he kept thee as the apple of his eye." What a magnificent simile is that! " He kept thee as the apple of his eye." The eye is a member, or a part and parcel of the human body, and therefore the image denotes our union to God. We are members of his body ; we are in God, united inseparably. " Who shall separate us from the love of God that is in Christ Jesus?" But the figure rather suggests to us protection. There is a most exquisite provision in the human organism that, while I am unconscious, let the minutest mote in the sunbeam approach my eyeball, instinctively, without design, the eyelid closes upon it, and is its shelter and defence. God's everlasting attributes close, as the eyelid on the eye, around the humblest believer, and he that touches you must first touch, in his own language, the apple of his eye. The protection of a believer is therefore complete. The eye is the most sensible, the weakest, the most easily injured organ in the human frame, yet so washed, so watched, so purified, so sustained every moment, that it seems the organ in which is concentrated most of the wisdom, the power, and the beneficence of God. And, in the next place, it would denote sympathy. I have quoted already that passage, " He that toucheth you toucheth the apple of my eye." That is, just as a man would feel the least thing touching the eye as most acutely painful, so God feels when the humblest believer is maltreated, ill-used, suffers, or is assailed. Hence, when Saul persecuted the Christians, a cry came from heaven which showed that the apple of his eye was touched, when he said, " Saul, Saul, why persecutest thou me?" as if these words were to remind Saul of the statement in that book which he then believed—the Old Testament—" He that toucheth you toucheth the apple of mine eye."

And then it is added, as an explanation of all God's dealings with us, that " as an eagle stirreth up her nest, fluttereth over her young, spreadeth abroad her wings, taketh them, beareth them on her wings: so the Lord alone did lead him." The image is exquisitely suggestive. The eagle may be noticed in those northern districts and mountain ranges where her eyrie is found, and when she is training the eaglets, or the young eagles, to fly. After they are fully fledged, and ought to begin to leave their own home, and to seek another for themselves, the eagle, the mother eagle, will rise above the nest, spread her broad pinions, fly round it in narrow circles; and when the young eaglets will not come out and spread their wings upon the wind, she will go and gently push them, and strike them, and stir them up, in the language of this text, till at last they try what they can do. Those who have watched in the Highlands may have seen the eaglets being thus trained. The instant that a weary, young, just full-fledged eaglet has ventured too far, or its pinion becomes too weary to sustain it any longer, and it begins to fall downwards like a stone, the mother eagle will dart down with the speed of a thunderbolt, catch the eaglet upon her back or broad pinions, and bear it back again to its nest, where it is gently tended till it is strong enough to fly. So, it says, God does with us. He trains us; not merely tells us, but he trains us. He places you in circumstances where you will be sorely tried, but he will not let you fall. He will place you upon ice so thin that it can scarcely bear you, but just when it gives way he will seize you, and shelter and protect you. He will put you in troubles so sore that you think you will sink under them, but when your need is sorest his presence will be nearest. "As an eagle stirreth up her nest, fluttereth over her young, spreadeth abroad her wings, taketh them, beareth them on her wings : so the Lord alone did lead him." And the eagle is the meet type of the Christian. It should breathe to him, suggest to him, a very instructive lesson. When the eagle flies the highest he does so gazing at the noonday sun. His eye is able to bear the intense splendour of the meridian sun, and his flight is always highest when his bright eye is fixed most vividly upon the meridian sun. A Christian's progress will always be highest and speediest when he runs the race or pursues the flight set before him, looking unto Jesus, the Sun of Righteousness, the author and the finisher of our faith. By so doing we shall mount, as the prophet says, with eagle's wings; we shall, as the psalmist sings, renew our youth like the eagles; we shall run, and not faint; we shall walk, and not be weary.

Now such are we—helpless, poor, feeble, needy; such is God—missing us, coming after us, finding us, feeding us, leading us, instructing us, training us all by grace. And these grand blessings we thank God for, we praise God for, we commemorate in all their fulness, when we rejoice and glory in the opportunity before the wide world itself of taking into our hands those memorials which tell the world that we glory in the cross, that we derive all our blessings through it, that we look for eternal joy because of it. We thank God at a communion-table for these his blessings in the past, we trust in him for his promises for the future; and eating that bread and drinking that cup we hereby show forth, and we delight to show forth, we are not ashamed to show forth, the necessity of his death, the preciousness of his death, the nature of his death, the purchase of his death : God our portion, and we the people of his inheritance.

CHAPTER XXXIII.

THE BLESSING OF MOSES.   BLESSING ON EACH TRIBE IN
SUCCESSION.

THE patriarch Jacob blessed his sons upon his death-
bed, and pronounced their inheritance for the future,
in words full of poetry and of truth. Our blessed Lord
left the world also blessing, as he had continued in
the world blessing; and Moses, who was the type
and symbol of that true Prophet, departs from his
arduous post, and resigns the solemn mission that had
been intrusted to his hands, partly predicting the
future destiny of the tribes, partly pronouncing
blessings upon them as they then existed in the
world.

It begins by stating, "This is the blessing wherewith Moses the man of God blessed the children of
Israel before his death." Often had they ill-treated
him, often had they grieved and vexed his meek and
magnanimous spirit; but yet in his last moments he
forgets all the insults, the reproaches, the misconstruc-
tions to which he had been recklessly exposed by the
very people on whom he had poured down benefits;
and he leaves the world, not retaliating on them curses
for their crimes, but pronouncing on them, like the
blessed Master whom he served, blessings in spite

of their sins and their great defects. He begins by praying, "Let Reuben live," that is, being a border tribe, and apt to be merged in the others, let him live as a tribe; "let him not die; and let not his men be few." And then the blessing that he pronounces on Judah, the tribe especially in connexion with Benjamin, from which our Lord was to spring, is very full and rich. "He said, Hear, Lord, the voice of Judah, and bring him unto his people." The common idea, and it seems a just one, is that the "him" that he here refers to is the great Messiah,—"bring him unto his people." "The sceptre shall not depart from Judah until Shiloh come." Moses, therefore, prays that God would bring him of whom he had spoken in a previous part in the prophecies and benedictions of Jacob on the children of Israel. He prays that that Shiloh may be brought to Judah; and this practice of alluding to our blessed Lord by the word *him*, the pronoun *him*, instead of mentioning his name, is kept up in a very remarkable manner by John, when he says, "Behold, what manner of love the Father hath bestowed upon us, that we should be called the sons of God; therefore the world knoweth us not, because it knew *him* not;" and yet he has not been speaking directly of our Lord. Then he goes on to say, "Beloved, now are we the sons of God, and it doth not yet appear what we shall be; but we know that, when *he* shall appear," that is, Christ—it is not the Father who appears, but Christ—"we shall be like *him*, for we shall see *him* as he is. And every man that hath this hope in *him* purifieth himself, even as *he* is pure."

John assumes, what Moses seems dimly to indicate,

that Christ was so dear to every Christian, so valued, so appreciated, that there could be but one *him* in a Christian's heart, who must occupy all supremacy within him, and be the nearest and the dearest object of his adoration. Although I may remark, in reading that 3rd verse of 1 John iii., that many persons often misconstrue it: "Every man that hath this hope in him purifieth himself, even as he is pure." Many persons read it as if the *him* referred to "every man," every man that hath this hope within himself. But it does not; it refers to Christ. "Every man that hath this hope in him of whom I have been speaking—even in Christ—purifieth himself, even as he is pure;" and then he says, "*He* was manifested to take away our sins. Whosoever abideth in *him* sinneth not." So Moses, very much in the same spirit, and thinking of the great object of the hopes of Judah, the great promise that was made to Judah, speaks of the Messiah as *him;* and says, therefore, "Hear, Lord, the voice of Judah, and bring *him*," the Messiah, "unto his waiting and believing people."

Then he refers to the tribe of Levi, the sacerdotal tribe, from which the priests and the Levites sprung; and he says, "Let thy Thummim and thy Urim," literally, "Thy lights and thy perfections," "be with thy holy one, whom thou didst prove at Massah, and with whom thou didst strive at the waters of Meribah." Levi forfeited these; or, rather, when Christ came, the true light and true perfection, then the dim twilight—the Urim and the Thummim of Levi—passed away, and were lost in the splendour and glory of the greater. Moses promises that "Levi shall teach Jacob thy judgments, and Israel thy law;

they shall put incense before thee, and whole burnt
sacrifice upon thine altar;" and therefore he prays
that his substance, which was set apart to him as a
divine substance, living by the temple, and not out-
side of it, should be blessed to him.

And of Benjamin he says very beautifully, "The
beloved of the Lord shall dwell in safety by him; and
the Lord shall cover him all the day long."

Then of Joseph he says very touchingly, "Blessed
of the Lord be his land, for the precious things of
heaven, for the dew, and for the deep that coucheth
beneath." There is something exquisitely poetical
in this. He recognizes Joseph as having great
temporal blessings—a fertile land, a prolific seed, a
balmy clime; and he expresses all these things in
language exquisitely poetical: "The deep that
coucheth beneath." What a perfect picture is
that! representing the great sea like a wild beast,
when calm, couching, waiting, or peacefully slumber-
ing beneath. "And for the precious fruits brought
forth by the sun, and for the precious things put forth
by the moon, and for the chief things of the ancient
mountains, and for the precious things of the lasting
hills." It seems at first absurd to speak of precious
things put forth by the moon; but the moon is not
simply for giving us light by night, it has an influence;
and farmers say it has an influence in ripening their
corn. It has an influence upon the tides, so necessary
to the health and so advantageous to the wants of
man. And, no doubt, independent altogether of its
dim light in the absence of the sun, to give which it
was originally located in its present relation to our
earth, it has an influence, and that influence is spoken

of as the precious things of the moon, as well as
of the sun.

Then of Zebulun, which was a seafaring tribe,
Moses speaks in the 18th verse thus : "Rejoice,
Zebulun, in thy going out," that is, upon the paths
of the ocean ; and, " Issachar, in thy tents. They
shall call the people unto the mountain; there
they shall offer sacrifices of righteousness : for
they shall suck of the abundance of the seas,"
that is, its merchandise, its commerce, its traffic, its
yield of fish, and all the abundance that the seas
contain ; "and also of treasures hid in the sand."
Now, this seems at first sight a very useless thing,
because if there be any one thing that we associate
with barrenness more than another, it is the sand.
We speak of " the barren sand." Nothing will grow
upon the sand of the sea-shore, and if you dig deep
nothing but the salt sea-water can be found under it.
Then what can Moses mean by speaking of treasures
hid in the sand ? It is reserved to a subsequent age
to discover that the barren sand is most fertile in
one respect, and that it contains all the materials
of that exquisite creation, glass, which admits the
light of heaven, and excludes the cold, in our homes
and dwelling-places ; and hence it has been thought
that the treasures hid in the sand were known to
the Egyptians, and therefore probably to the Israelites ;
and that glass is not so recent a discovery as history
seems to us to indicate. At all events, the only
treasures that we know that were long hidden in the
sand are the materials that constitute that bright and
shining medium for the transmission of light which

we now feel the advantage of in our dwellings so much.

And of Gad he said, " Blesseth be he that enlargeth Gad ; he dwelleth as a lion, and teareth the arm with the crown of the head." And of Dan he said, " Dan is a lion's whelp ; he shall leap from Bashan." And every one of the allusions, I may mention, has some reference to the name that was given to the tribe.

Of Naphtali he said, " O Naphtali, satisfied with favour, and full with the blessing of the Lord ; possess thou the west and the south."

And then of Asher he speaks in very glowing language : " Let Asher be blessed with children ; let him be acceptable to his brethren, and let him dip his feet in oil. Thy shoes shall be iron and brass," not soon to wear out ; " and as thy days,"— the trials that beset thee, the troubles that meet thee, the storms that descend upon thee, the cold thou hast to bear, the heat thou hast to encounter ;—" as thy days are, so shall the supply of thy strength be."

Then he closes the chapter in language exquisitely poetical : " The eternal God is thy refuge." What a magnificent thought is that ! That God who is the same yesterday, to-day, and for ever, is thy refuge, thy shelter, thy sure defence. " And underneath thee," the humblest individual of the tribes of Israel, " are arms that never become weary, that never relax their embrace, that are strong as omnipotence, and everlasting as eternity." " And he shall thrust out the enemy from before thee." Surely all these promises have never yet been realized. Israel

is now the weary-footed wanderer, under the curse
that we read in this book pronounced upon it for its
disobedience. But Israel is the heir in reversion
of a restoration that will be more than a compensation
for all its past ruin.

" Israel then shall dwell in safety alone : the
fountain of Jacob shall be upon a land of corn and
wine." The same Hebrew word that means a
fountain of water means also the human eye. We
cannot understand the meaning of the passage, " The
fountain of Jacob shall be upon a land of corn and
wine." The Hebrew word which means *fountain*,
means also the *eye*, and ought to be here translated,
" The eye of Jacob shall be upon a land of corn and
wine," then the meaning is perfectly plain ; that is, he
shall be the possessor of it, and shall look across it
and say, " This is mine." There is a very beautiful
allusion to it by Jeremiah, " Oh that my head were
waters, and mine eye a fountain of tears." Now
when you think that the Hebrew word for *eye* and
fountain is the same, nothing can be more beautiful.
" Oh that mine eye—which means a fountain—were
indeed a fountain giving forth tears."

" Happy art thou, O Israel : who is like unto thee,
O people saved by the Lord,"—happy as long as
thou wast loyal to God ;—"the shield of thy help,"
—to defend and protect thee ;—" the sword of thy
excellency !"—to make room for thy progress. " Thine
enemies shall be found liars unto thee ; and thou
shalt yet tread upon their high places," at that day
when the mountain of the Lord's house shall be
established in the top of the mountains.

THE HAPPY NATION.

In one verse of this eloquent chapter we have a portrait of great beauty.

"Happy art thou, O Israel: who is like unto thee, O people saved by the Lord, the shield of thy help, and who is the sword of thy excellency! and thine enemies shall be found liars unto thee; and thou shalt tread upon their high places."—Deuteronomy xxxiii. 29.

We have read in the previous parts of this expressive prophecy, of good things to come to all the tribes of Israel; the blessings pronounced upon each tribe, together with a special prediction of its future glory, magnificence, and repose. After Moses had prepared to die upon the mount which God assigned, he pronounces these blessings, as the dying patriarch did on a former occasion; and as became one whose heart was with his people in the desert, even while his spirit was worshipping with God beside the throne.

He closes the summary of all these glowing predictions of approaching blessings by saying, "The eternal God is thy refuge;" no temporary shelter, no transient protection, but the everlasting God who faints not, neither is weary, whose days have no end,

2 A

and whose strength has no decay; even he is thy refuge. And Israel therefore may sing what Luther sang so nobly three hundred years ago, "The eternal God is our refuge and our strength: therefore will we not fear, though the hills be removed, and though the mountains be carried into the midst of the sea; and though the earth shake with the swelling thereof." And he adds, "Underneath are the everlasting arms." As the arms of a mother sustain her infant, so the everlasting arms of God, wearying not, neither fainting, bear up, and preserve, and keep from falling and from perishing the very humblest believer. "And he shall thrust out the enemy from before thee; and shall say, Destroy them." Then he predicts, "Israel then shall dwell in safety alone," each man under his own vine and under his own fig tree, with no internal quarrels, with no external aggression; a people, happy, not because they are numerous, nor because they are physically strong; but strong in that strength which outlives all strength, and safe in that refuge which is surer than battlements and ramparts, the eternal God their refuge, and underneath the everlasting arms. Fertility also shall follow their preservation; for "the eye of Jacob" here translated erroneously "fountain," the Hebrew word for "eye" and "fountain" being the same; "the eye of Jacob shall be upon a land that waves with corn, and that produces wine, and that shall have the early and the latter rains; the heavens dropping down dew." Then, looking around at these, the pledged and promised national blessings bestowed upon a people that trust in God; Moses exclaims, with his dying lips, "Happy art thou, O Israel: who is like unto thee,

O people saved by the Lord, the shield of thy help, and who is the sword of thy excellency!" We may here observe in what the happiness of a people chiefly consists. It consists not so much in temporal as in spiritual and eternal blessings. The temporal are the fruits, the eternal relationships are the roots on which they grow. Israel was happy in having temporal blessings, but still more in having that which is the spring, and root, and source of them, spiritual and eternal mercies. "Who is like unto thee, O people saved by the Lord?" We have often noticed in reading God's holy word that the most startling and splendid deliverances of a national kind, secured apparently by the heroism of those that fought for them, or by the wisdom of those that planned the campaigns, are ascribed, never to Israel's sword or Israel's skill, but invariably to Israel's God. When a people, however successful in their efforts, however much they may see to applaud, to admire, and to appreciate, take the glory to themselves, and withhold it from Him to whom it is most justly due; their right hand will become palsied; victories will be followed by defeats, and skill and success by "confusion worse confounded." Let it always be our character as a nation, when we are blessed with evident tokens of success, to be thankful to those that achieved the victory; but while we give thanks to them as the human instruments, let us lift our hearts still higher, and give the glory and the praise not to the bravest soldier or to the greatest general, but to that God who taught the one to fight and inspired the other to devise; and who alone has the praise,

the honour, and the glory. This was the case with
our nation at the fall of Sebastopol. Victory
mingled with song; but while all were thankful at
a great and magnificent result that crowned toils,
and tears, and blood, and suffering; yet there was
mingling, as we all know, with the general congratu-
lation, a deep under-tone of sorrow and distress;
homes made desolate; presences that were familiar,
familiar no more; and names that were as household
words, registered only on some cold stone, or on the
resplendent tablets of them that fell in their country's
cause. But if there was a great victory, and nearer
prospects of at least a temporary peace,—and we
must be thankful for a temporary one, for in this
world there is no such thing as an eternal peace
among nations; all peace must from its very nature
be temporary, transient,—let us not, while sympathizing with them that weep, while lamenting
the terrible price at which it has been procured,
take to ourselves the glory, but let us feel that
if we are God's people, we are happy as a people
saved by the Lord, who alone is the shield of
our help, who alone is the sword of our excellency.
And if our enemies, who boasted that they would
sweep our troops from their soil, and take Europe
itself for a prey; if they are found to be liars, let
us give the glory to Him to whom it is due; and
thus praising Him we shall learn, "Them that honour
me I will still honour;" and a nation that gains victories and gives God the glory will gain more. A
nation that gains victories, but takes to itself the
éclat, and neither thanks God publicly nor privately,

will reap no blessing from the past, and it is sowing only for disasters in the future.

But there is a sense, lower in the estimate of this world, but really higher in a Christian's estimate, in which Israel is a happy people. Whatever happened to Israel happened to them as ensamples. We therefore look upon this verse not simply as the declaration of the happiness of a nation, nationally victorious, nationally blessed; but as a portrait, a sketch, at that day of God's people; still a happy people, a victorious people; and of whom faith can say, if sense and sight cannot see it: "Happy art thou, O people of God; a people saved by the Lord; the shield of thy help, and who is the sword of thy excellency!" In other words, is it true that Christians are a happy people? In the first place, it would be very odd, it would be very strange, if God, even in this world, should make his enemies happy, and his own people miserable. It would be most unnatural that the only miserable people should be those that love, and serve, and honour God; and that the only happy people should be those that do not. Is it therefore true that God's people are a happy people? I answer, they have reason to be so; they are so, in proportion as they realize and appreciate what God is to them, and what they are made by God; and if they are ever unhappy, their unhappiness does not come from religion, but from the want of it. God's people are a happy people! And they are so, first, because they themselves are consciously the subjects of God's sovereign, unbought, undeserved, disinterested love. It is happiness to a man on earth to know that he is loved by somebody; there is a certain portion of unhappiness in feeling that you are hated by anybody. To know that another hates you in some degree makes you feel unpleasant; you would rather it were otherwise. To be sure that a person loves you, is at least a contribution, however minute, to that stock of happiness, of conscious happiness, that you have within. Now, if that be true in the human, it is still more so in the divine. To be conscious that one is the object of divine love, the subject of divine and unfettered love; to be sure that we are kept by that love for a divine destiny; to know that our names are written in heaven, and ourselves visible, and our race not strange to God, the Saviour,—why this is a new atmosphere, a holy light, a heavenly sunshine, a spring of conscious happiness, just in proportion as we feel it and know it to be true. And in the next place, God's people are happy, inasmuch as if they are sure that they are God's people, if they know that they are his sons, they have learned that all things work for good to them. Can you conceive an intenser spring of earthly happiness than this?—to know that whatever happens to you, in some way, sooner or later, is ripening into good for you; to be sure of this, that not *some* things but *all* things; and that all things are not dead, inactive, but active, operative, working; and that all things good and bad, painful and pleasant, are not discordant, but work together in harmony; and that all these things working, and working together, have a beneficent issue—work together for good; to know that, takes away from pain its chief sting; gives to enjoyment its greatest zest; is more than a compensation in sickness, more than consolation in sorrow,

and must make the person happy in proportion as he
feels the truth and reality of it; that all things work
together for good to him; and that his light affliction,
which is but for a moment, even when longest, works
out for him a far more exceeding, even an eternal
weight of glory. Another element of the happiness
of those who are the true Israel is that they have
peace. There are various sorts of peace. The half
animal, half vegetable, the connecting link between
two kingdoms, has what may be called a peace; that
is, perfect quiet. The dog, and the horse, and the ox,
have a sort of peace, but it is insensibility, not real peace.
And so a worldly man may feel peace, peace as long as
he does not think, or his conscience is not awakened,
or his eyes not opened; he has peace; but it is described by the prophet as "peace, peace," apparently
great peace, when really and truly there is no peace
at all; it is quiet, not peace; insensibility, not the
peace that passeth understanding. But in the case of
a Christian, the heart has found its rest, the intellect
its inexhaustible study, the soul its sublime aspiration, the conscience its ease; because it has found
that truth which feeds every faculty and inspires every
affection of the soul, and enables man to look above,
around, below, behind, before, and to feel, "justified
by faith, I have peace with God, through Jesus Christ
my Lord." Then a Christian, too, has special happiness, because he has hope. He has hope beyond the
grave. The world has wishes, desires, sometimes
expectations, but never heavenly hope. Hope is
based upon truth; and separate from truth it is not
a hope, but a wish. And the Christian's hope maketh
not ashamed. It is not a mere wish, not a mere

desire, but it is an assured expectation, based upon
the strongest ground; and that, in the experience of
the Christian, maketh not ashamed. The Christian,
in the next place, has happiness because he is sure
of victory over all opposition, internal and external.
" This is the victory that overcometh the world, even
our faith." "They shall be more than conquerors
through him that loved them." The eternal God
is his refuge. " The sun shall not smite thee by
day, nor the moon by night." " What shall separate
us from the love of God that is in Christ Jesus our
Lord ? Neither death, nor life, nor any other
creature."

Having noticed these elements of his happiness,
let us add, the happiness of God's people is a present
possession. The world seeks happiness; the Christian
has found it. The world ever is to be blessed ; of the
Christian it is said, " Happy art thou,"—not will be—
" O Israel, saved by the Lord, the shield of thy help,
and who is the sword of thy excellency !" The world
is looking for happiness, but it goes to the wrong
source. The Christian is looking for happiness, and
he applies to the right source. His happiness, therefore, is not only in reversion but it is in possession.
It is not, " Happy *will be* the people that know the
joyful sound;" but, "Happy *are* the people that
know the joyful sound." And this happiness, in
the next place, is real, substantial, solid. It is not
the delirium of excitement, or the fever of a momentary
joy, but a permanent, real, substantial happiness,
which grows in intensity as he grows in the realization
of his grand destiny, till the present happiness is lost
in the eternal happiness that awaits the people of

God. This happiness is permanent and enduring. Add eternity to the least happiness, and it is most weighty; let the greatest happiness be temporal, and it loses half its weight and half its value. Sin has its pleasures as well as holiness; but they are but for a season. True piety has its happiness; but it is a happiness that endureth for ever.

But you ask now, after hearing these remarks, Are Christians never unhappy? We answer now, as at the beginning, they are. But this arises from their losing sight of their relationship, their failing to realize what they are; and their unhappiness arises, not from their being Christians, but from their momentary suspension of the enjoyment of Christianity. An incidental illness happens to a healthy man; incidental sadness happens to a Christian. But it is not his religion that is the spring of sadness, for it is the spring of joy; but it is the want of it, or the suspension of his enjoyment of it. It is a cloud in his sky, not the extinction of his sun in the firmament.

But do not Christians meet, you say, with losses, bereavements, trials, griefs, sicknesses? Unquestionably they do; but the happiness of a Christian does not consist in the absence of these things, but in spite of these things. Christian happiness is not the happiness of men that have never fallen, nor the happiness of men that have never sinned; nor is it the happiness of men who are delivered from the possibility of falling; but it is the happiness of men who are in tribulation, who are exposed to trials, to bereavements, to a thousand afflictions; but their happiness flourishes in spite of them. "In the world ye shall have tribulation, but in me ye shall have peace."

And of all these tribulations it says, "If needs be."
And it is said, "If ye be reproached for the name
of Christ, happy are ye." What an expression is
that! If you be called nicknames, if you be derided,
caricatured, despised, maligned, then, what says the
apostle? Not, you ought to be very sorry; but,
"Happy are ye." But why happy? "Because,"
he says, "the Spirit of God and of glory resteth upon
you." Just as the dove could find no rest for the
soles of its feet at the flood save in the ark, so, says
Peter, the Spirit of God selects the persons reproached
for Christ's sake as the special place of his dwelling.
And, besides, to a Christian what affliction on earth
can have any real and lasting pain? If he loses
his friends, his relatives, it is only for a season; if he
loses earthly riches, he knows it is only that he may
get a better and a firmer hold of heavenly riches; if
he loses health, it cannot destroy his everlasting
prospects. The worst that happens to him is the
April shower that refreshes and makes fertile, not
the winter storm that devastates and destroys. But,
you say, are not worldly men really happy? I
answer, they may be mirthful, they may be excited,
they may be merry, but they are not often happy.
Their mirth is as the crackling of thorns in the flames;
it is a transient excitement, the fever of a moment,
not that growing happiness that, like the shining
light, shineth more and more unto the perfect day.
There is no doubt, then, that this religion is fitted
to make happy as it is to make holy, and that
God's people are not only a holy, but a happy people.
The very definition of Christianity indicates it. For
what is its definition? "The kingdom of God is

righteousness," that is, character ; secondly, " peace," that is, privilege ; thirdly, "joy," that is another privilege. Two-thirds of Christianity are peace and joy, one-third, the first third, is righteousness. It is quite plain, therefore, that if Christians are not happy, it is not Christianity they ought to blame, but their comparative want of it.

CHAPTER XXXIV.

THIS chapter closes the last of the five most remarkable books contained, perhaps, in any record, or even
in the Old Testament Scripture itself. Conceive that
these five books, forming the Pentateuch, from which we
have so profitably and delightfully read, were expunged
from the recollections of men, and from the records of
eternal truth ; what a blank would there be, what a terrible unfilled chasm ! The past would be all obscurity ;
the most wondrous and glorious facts and phenomena
in history would all be hidden ; we should be in utter
darkness as to the creation of the world, as to our
own formation, as to our fall, as to the prospects, and
hopes, and promises of a recovery. In short, the
blank would be intolerable. What would supply
its place ? Would the laws of Confucius, would the
institutes of Menu, would the writings or the traditions of Zoroaster, would the laws of Lycurgus, or
would even the boasted republic of Plato supply the
place of this most precious record—the five books
of Moses ? They could not.

If you will study modern legislation you will
find that it grows in purity, in mercy, in excellence, just as it draws its inspiration from these,
as infidels would call them, obsolete and antiquated
records of a past and an uncivilized race. Many of
the laws here have a purity, a mercy, and indicate a
knowledge of human nature, its wants, its frailties,
its sins, its ruin, that show that the inspiration of
God guided the pen of the writer. And those
very things that seemed at first to us useless, turn
out on maturer experience to be most important;
and little laws that a hundred years ago we could not
explain, time, and experience, and history, and events
have enabled us more fully to appreciate the wisdom
of. These five books have been translated into every
tongue, they are read at this moment in every language; and, take the fact as it exists, there is no
book so extensively read, that has so deeply impressed,
and toned, and coloured the history and condition of
the human race, as this book, and these five books in
particular.

The last chapter of it, which we have now read,
obviously was not written by Moses; clearly it was
added either by a subsequent writer inspired and
directed to do so; or, it is, as I think it ought
properly to be, the first chapter of the book of Joshua.
Probably, by some mistake in the arrangement of
the books, this last section, which describes the
death and burial of Moses, has been transferred from
the preface to the Book of Joshua, to occupy the
place of the postscript of the five books of Moses.
Obviously, Moses could not have written it; the
rest of the book was written by him, and he closes

all that he had to say in the 29th verse of the previous chapter: "Happy art thou, O Israel: who is like unto thee, O people saved by the Lord, the shield of thy help, and who is the sword of thy excellency! and thine enemies shall be found liars unto thee; and thou shalt tread upon their high places." Then this chapter begins the description of his departure to the heights of Abarim; his death there, with the glens, and plains, and mountains of the promised land sparkling in the distant sunshine. He there dies, and is buried, "No man knowing his sepulchre unto this day," a period subsequent to his burial.

You remember the occasion of Moses being refused entrance into the promised land. He spake unadvisedly with his lips, he lost his temper, and his deep sense of responsibility to God; he omitted to glorify Him in the presence of the people as he was commanded to do; and for that offence he was expelled from the land that had been the burden of his hopes, the great object of his prayers; but he was admitted into that better and brighter Canaan, of which the earthly one was but a dim type and foreshadow. And this was inflicted as a chastisement; first upon himself, secondly, as a lesson to the mighty hosts he was leading through the desert, and not as a punishment by an angry judge upon an offending criminal.

It is said, "The Lord said unto him," when he showed him all that land, "This is the land which I sware unto Abraham, unto Isaac, and unto Jacob, saying, I will give it unto thy seed: I have caused thee to see it with thine eyes, but thou shalt not go over thither." This was requisite, not so much

for the information or the sanctification of Moses, as
for leaving a lasting and impressive lesson behind
him, which should show the children of Israel that, if
judgment should thus begin at the house of God, and
in the person of the most illustrious leader of that
house, what should be the end of them that obey not
the gospel.

When he died, " the Lord buried him in a valley
in the land of Moab, over against Beth-peor: but no
man knoweth of his sepulchre unto this day." Now,
was there any wisdom in this, or can we suggest
any reason for it? The reason is obvious. So beloved was he, so venerated, that if the Israelites
had only ascertained his sepulchre, they would
have carefully collected his ashes, and they would
have given that homage to the dead dust of an
illustrious leader which is owing only to the living
God who raised up that leader. For the fact is,
Romanism is not a creation of the last two or three
centuries: it is indigenous to corrupt human nature;
and the Jews needed to be guarded against the errors
of that system naturally and instinctively springing
up in the human heart. And, therefore, in the
exercise of a wisdom the most profound, the tomb
of Moses was hidden from the knowledge of his
people, and they had, therefore, no pretext for
giving to the dead the adoration that was due only to
the living God.

We read that " Moses was an hundred and twenty
years old when he died; but his eye was not
dim nor his natural force abated." Forty years
in the court of Pharaoh, forty years in Midian,

forty years in the desert, making in all one hundred
and twenty years.

The children of Israel, when this aged and venerable
leader died, wept thirty days. How fickle is poor
humanity! At times they blamed him, at other
times they even cursed him; they then assailed him
again, "Hast thou brought us here to die?" But
when he left them, then they learned what we also
need often to learn, that we do not know our blessings
till we lose them.

Joshua, then, was full of the spirit of wisdom, for
Moses laid his hands upon him, and he was consecrated
to finish what Moses began. You may remember
that I called your attention to the remarkable fact,
that God consecrated a soldier to close and finish
what the legislator had begun; and I inferred from
this, in a previous chapter, that if war be in all circumstances unlawful, as some say, if the soldier be the
exponent of a condition of things that we should
never accept, it is difficult to account for this fact,
that God himself selected a soldier to terminate what
the peaceful legislator had begun; girt the sword
around him, and anointed and consecrated him for
his dread mission. It is plain, therefore, that
however to be deprecated war may be, however
unnatural, however truly the fruit of sin, yet it
is sometimes lawful; and an enlightened and Christian nation will never engage in it except when it
is clearly justified by the emergency that has arisen.

And then we read as the character of Moses,
"There arose not a prophet since in Israel," for
Christ himself was a prophet like unto him, "like
unto Moses, whom the Lord knew face to face,

in all the signs and the wonders, which the Lord sent him to do in the land of Egypt to Pharaoh, and to all his servants, and to all his land, and in all that mighty hand, and in all the great terror which Moses showed in the sight of all Israel." *

* For a fuller estimate of the character of Moses, see " Voices of the Dead."

THE SINS OF GREAT SAINTS.

"And the Lord said unto him, This is the land which I sware unto Abraham, unto Isaac, and unto Jacob, saying, I will give it unto thy seed : I have caused thee to see it with thine eyes, but thou shalt not go over thither."—*Deuteronomy* xxxiv. 4.

MOSES committed a great sin in the sight of all the children of Israel; and for this one sin he was forbidden to enter the land of promise. He died gazing on its glories, but not a partaker of them. The biography of Moses is a most remarkable one. His deeds, his eloquent words, the writings, inspired but still his, which he has left behind him; all his supernatural gifts, his wonders, his miracles, his whole character, are rare and resplendent. His renunciation of all the splendours of a court for the sake of his people Israel, choosing affliction with the people of God rather than the pleasures of sin, which are but for a season; his embassy from heaven, his advocacy of the oppressed, his heroism when the people forsook him, and urged their return to Egypt and its flesh pots; arguing that they had better have died there than be brought up to die in the desert; his successful march to the borders of Canaan; his appointment of Joshua to take his place, and to finish what he had been privileged to begin,—altogether

constitute the marks of a character that has no precedent and no parallel in the Old Testament; and it
is so remarkable and so recognized in the New, that
in the songs of heaven some notes from the strain of
of Moses are perpetuated; for "they sing the song
Moses and of the Lamb."

Amidst all the circumstances of trial and depression
to which he was constantly exposed, one does not
wonder that he should on one occasion have been irri-
tated beyond what he should be; that he should have
spoken words that did injury to his cause, and reflected discredit upon Him whose minister and servant he was; and that it should be written of him as
part of his otherwise glowing epitaph, " He spake
unadvisedly with his lips, and he believed not God, to
sanctify him in the presence of all the people." For
this one offence he was forbidden to enter into that
land on which he had set his heart, which he longed
to see, into which he thought he should be privileged
to conduct the people he loved; whose plains he was
suffered to behold only from afar; but he was admitted, however, into that better land, through the blood
of the everlasting covenant, where there shall be no
cloud, and no change, nor weeping, nor crying, nor
sin, nor sorrow, any more. Having alluded to most
of these interesting facts in the history of Moses;
having noticed in previous discourses his preferring to
suffer affliction with the people of God than enjoy the
pleasures of sin for a season; his esteeming the re-
proach of Christ greater riches than all the treasures
of Egypt; his forsaking Egypt, not fearing the wrath
of the king; for he endured, as seeing him who is
invisible; having also called your attention to his

keeping the Passover, and the sprinkling of blood, and his accomplishment of the passing through the Red Sea,—I turn now to one trait in this most remarkable biography, subject very much to misapprehension in the minds of some, turned into an argument against Christianity by the perverse ingenuity of others ; namely, the one great defect in his character ; and, along with this, the defects that appear in the most illustrious saints whose names and histories are recorded in this Book ; and to show in what light we should regard such flaws in the sainted witnesses of God ; flaws that have never been absent in any one case, in any one dispensation, or in any one century of the history of the Church of Christ. We have seen in Aaron a great sin punished or chastened, as was the sin of Moses : we have seen in Abraham and Sarah, and in Rebekah and Jacob, sins recorded that brand at least one spot in the history of each ; quoted by those who seize that spot as if it were the description of the whole character, as a reason for discrediting the narrative, and doubting the inspiration of the Sacred Volume. There is certainly not one illustrious for his piety, recorded in this Volume, Enoch probably excepted, who had not some defect registered and recorded against him ; not as a precedent for us to imitate, but as a beacon to warn us to avoid.

In weighing the sin of Moses, in connexion with the sins of the ancient patriarchs, prophets, apostles, evangelists, I would endeavour to show that the record of these sins proves, not disproves, the inspiration of the Scriptures ; and secondly, that the existence of these sins, so far from being a presumptive disproof of the truth and reality of the persons themselves, is, as recorded in Scripture, a proof of the authenticity, the genuineness, and inspiration of the whole. The very first reflection is, the faithfulness of the historians that record these sins. A Jew loved his country to excess. He gloried in its founders, he was zealous for the weight and the splendour of the impression they should make upon the Gentiles who were around him. And such was the bigotry, or nationality of the Jew, that his disposition and his strong temptation was, to tone and shade down the defects of his illustrious founders; and to bring into the foreground and make brilliant, impressive, and absorbingly prominent, their virtues, their excellencies, and their good. Now, then, if Moses was a Jew,—if all the writers of the New Testament and the Old Testament also were Jews, how do you account for it that these men so overcame the prejudices of sect, the prepossessions of country, the partialities they felt as zealous for the law and the prophets, that they have recorded with undiluted and uncompromising faithfulness not only the virtues, but the sins, the flagrant sins, that cleave to the character of their most illustrious founders? If the Jew had been left to the influences of his own historic prejudices, he would have carefully passed by the defects in Abraham, the sin of Sarah, the treachery and misrepresentation of Rebekah and Jacob; he would have carefully passed by the fall of Peter, the wickedness of Paul, the great crime of David; and he would have brought forward their heroic virtues in the most brilliant and prominent re-lief. Then how did he so overcome the temptations of

sect, and nation ; the pride of country, and his own
traditional history, that he records these sins, and records them without a single word of defence, or
excuse, or apology ? Is not this so far a presumption
that they were inspired by God as faithful historians,
to describe character as it was ; not to dress up character as their prejudices and passions might incline
them ? In the second place, is not this evidence of
sin and defect in Abraham, in David, in Moses, in
Aaron, in all the illustrious leaders of Israel, only
in keeping with universal experience ? Perfection is
in reversion, not in any in this fallen world a present
and a universal possession. What countenance is
faultless ? What crystal in the rock, what gem in the
sea, has not its flaw ? What flower in the garden,
what fruit on the tree is perfect in its form ? Where
is there gold without alloy ? where is silver without
dross ? iron without rust ? a raiment without a moth ?
a plant without a worm to gnaw its root ? The sun
himself has spots ; the angels in glory are charged with
imperfections. The fact, that the saints of the Bible
had their sins, their defects, their great sins, is only
proof that they belonged to the general class of humanity ; and that, like all besides, they were not yet
perfect, but aspirants towards a perfection that will
one day be, when Christ will present his church to
himself a glorious church, without spot or blemish, or
any such thing.

But you must recollect, in observing these defects of
God's most eminent servants, that their predominating excellence of character renders the incidental
sins, however aggravated, that cleave to it only the
more sharply and clearly defined. It is because they

were men of such prevailing excellence ; it is because
their whole mission, character, and career, was so
spotless, that we come incidentally upon a great fault,
a grievous sin ; and the very splendour of the embo-
soming character makes the incidental sin the more
flagrant, dark, and conspicuous. The principles they
held, the profession they avowed, the law which they
wrote, and pronounced in the hearing of all the
people ; their responsibility, their duties, their obligations, their own enlightenment,—all combined to make
the incidental sin, flagrant enough in itself, appear
the more flagrant to us. And thus, when submitted
to carping, and cavilling, and partial judges, the very
excellency of Abraham becomes his misfortune, as you
go to estimate his sins ; and the very spotlessness of
the character and conduct of Moses renders the incidental and exceptional sin into which he fell only the
more palpable and unmistakable.

What renders the sins of these illustrious persons
more conspicuous is, the Author of the portrait, or
the Inspirer of the record that describes them. He
who describes and records the sin of Abraham, of
David, and of Peter, is the Holy, Holy, Holy God.
He has no sympathy with sin, no disposition or
temptation in any shape, for that is impossible, to
make apology for it ; he sees the sin in its first dawn-
ing, in its full development ; and describes it with an
accuracy, an exactness, and a fulness, unattainable
by a human writer. And, therefore, the sin being
more fully described by reason of God inspiring the
writer, it is made more palpable to us. And were
the least sin of those that deride the sins of ancient
Scripture as set forth in the light of God's counte-

nance, delineated by the pen which records the sin of Abraham, and of David, they would see their sins swell into a portentous magnitude that would dispose them to be silent on the sins of others, and to kneel at the footstool of the heavenly grace, and to cry aloud, with no feigned lips, " Enter not into judgment with thy servants, O Lord, for in thy sight no man living can be justified."

While stating these facts, important to know in estimating the sins of these illustrious stars in the ancient Jewish firmament, it is neither our duty nor our disposition to palliate in the least degree the iniquities of the greatest saints that stud the firmament of the past. Abraham and Sarah were guilty of falsehood, unmitigated falsehood; it must be called and branded by its name, and by no other. Aaron sanctioned, not only connived at, but sanctioned and promoted absolute idolatry, in its worst and most unhallowed form. David was guilty of a complication of crimes, to brand which language may be exhausted, and justly exhausted, of its severest epithets. John and James, when they called down fire from heaven, fostered a revengeful, a popish, and persecuting spirit; and Peter was guilty of the basest ingratitude, spoke the greatest falsehood, when he denied that blessed Master who had followed him with mercies, taught him when he was ignorant, and showed him the way that leads to heaven and to happiness. We should never attempt to palliate these sins. It is a great mistake in the minister to say it was because of this, or because of that, or because the temptation was great. No; Scripture does not do so. Scripture does not say, Abraham was overcome by fear; and, therefore, so much per cent. is to be deducted from his criminality. Scripture does not say, Peter lost his self-possession, and, therefore, he was as much to be pitied as to be blamed. The Bible does not state that David was liable to all the sins of humanity; it makes no such attempts. It states the sin, in all its blackness and its aggravation; makes no excuse to lighten it, no apology to soften it. We do best when our sermons are copies of the Bible, and our judgments echoes of its verdict, and when we describe the sin even of an Abraham, a David, an Aaron, and a Peter, just as sin is, and as sin ought to be delineated and described.

But do these recorded sins in the great men and the good men of Scripture weaken the claims of that religion of which they were raised up to be the promoters? Does it prove the Bible is not inspired, and that our religion is not a revelation from God? The very reverse; for the book that records the sins, in every instance condemns them in most unsparing language. This book faithfully delineates what facts are, and writes facts just as they are; setting down nothing in malice; diluting nothing through exaggerated and partial preference, but delineating the occurrence of the sins which in every page it denounces as the fruits of the flesh and of the Wicked One. Read the life of the most excellent man you can select; and you will see how his biographer studies to make an apology for his defects; how he explains away his sins; how he exalts, magnifies, and makes prominent his virtues. I do not know a biography that is exempt from this; and I do not know a more profitable exercise than comparing the best human biography ever written, with the biographies in the Bible of any of the saints of God. You will see in the biography that is human the partialities of friendship, the evidences of a sense of fellow-feeling of sin; but in the biography of the Bible, all the severity of an impartial judge, all the purity of a spotless and exalted censor; the evidence that the limner of character in the Bible is the just, the holy, the faithful God; the evidence that the sketchers of the lives of great men and good men in this age and in this world were beset with temptations such as their subjects were previously liable to. But suppose now, that all the characters that are recorded in this blessed Book—Abraham, and David, and Paul, and Peter, and Moses, and Aaron—had been described as absolutely faultless, would the objections of the sceptic have then been mitigated, neutralized, or removed? I conceive it would have been all the very opposite. For then the sceptic would have said, "Why these persons in the Bible seem totally different from Christians in every age of the world. Living Christians," they say, "we find characterized by many defects; but these Christians who are recorded as they were in the Bible seem to have been characterized by unmitigated excellence and perfection, and to have had none of the faults, the failings, and the defects, incidental to our common humanity." And hence the impartial reader would have said, "Either these sketches of Abraham, of Moses, of David, are not authentic and correct; or religion has lost its power, and cannot give birth to such exemplary, moral, and excellent characters in the nineteenth century as in a darker and more imperfect dispensation." So that it seems that, if all these characters had been described as the sceptic, in his objection to the actual record, prefers, instead of being an argument in favour of our religion, it would have been an argument altogether against it. But it has been objected, that if religion has so little power in preventing sin as it had evidently in the case, they say, of these illustrious men; we should be as well without it, and might as well fall back upon Paganism, upon reason, or natural religion, as take a religion which leaves so many defects in characters it records as its most illustrious ones. I answer, you do not say, we can see the stars better with our naked eye, because the telescope does not enable you to see them all, and to see them perfectly. You do not say, the constitution of our country is bad, because it does not do all we could wish, but leaves a great deal undone that we should prefer to be perfectly and accurately done. So this religion tells you it is itself progressive; its influence on the individual, like its influence on the wide world, is as the shining light, that shineth more and more unto the perfect day. And to expect that it shall make perfect character in an imperfect dispensation, where perfection is utterly unknown in every department of social, of moral, of political, of intellectual life, is to expect of the Bible what it was not meant to create, and what it is unreasonable to demand. But we are willing, quite willing, to test Christianity by its fruits; and we ask you, therefore, if you think it does not produce better characters than religions that are corrupt, or than natural religion? We ask you to try it by its fruits. Let a Christian country, where there is an open Bible, freedom of speech, an enlightened and wise constitution, where there is a predominating tone of public sentiment, evidently the inspiration and the creation of the Christian religion, be compared with a country where there is no open Bible, or no Bible known ; where religious freedom is neither permitted nor understood ; and the contrast is so striking that you will see at once the fruits of the open Bible, and that free access to its blessed truths, elevates, dignifies, ennobles ; and the results of the reverse degrade and debase mankind to the very lowest. Compare our country at this moment with Russia, with miserable Naples, with restless Spain ; compare it even with France, or, in short, with any country upon earth ; and you will come to the conclusion that the tone of civilization, of enjoyment, of moral glory, rises high just in the ratio in which there is an open Bible, a faithful Gospel, and universal freedom. Or, if you will take individuals, let Moses, that servant of God, be compared with the impostor Mahomet ; let David be compared with Alexander the Great ; Solomon, with all his sins, with Nero and Domitian ; and what will be the result of that comparison ? That the Scripture characters shine resplendent like lights in the firmament, notwithstanding their defects and blots ; but that the latter characters are huge blots and stains upon humanity itself, degrading the age, and injuring the noblest interests of those that were placed beneath their sway. It is not fair to seize the sin of Abraham ; and, like Zoilus in his treatment of Homer, gaze upon it, and shut your eyes, with most inveterate and passionate prejudice, to all the excellencies that shone in that magnificent character. And when you select the great sin of David, or of Peter, or of Abraham, and instantly say, "See what Christianity does!" you are reasoning most unfairly. You only see in the sin of Abraham and of David what Christianity has left undone, not what Christianity has done ; and you should estimate how much it has done, that you may form a right estimate of how much of corrupt nature remains, which the Gospel of Christ has not yet removed, and washed away. And perhaps if we saw Abraham's heart and David's life as God saw them, we should be struck with astonishment at the magnificent results that grace achieved in them ; and instead of wondering that one sin remained, we should wonder that so little sin remained in so originally depraved and fallen a heart.

We have, in the record of the sins of these men, a very striking evidence of the truth and inspiration of this book. We have, in the record of these sins, evidence of the severe and righteous judgment of God. Suppose this book had been got up by an impostor, or a merely bigoted, uninspired, and prejudiced Jew, had been writing it ; I have said before, he would have left out these sins ; but I might add also, that his temptation not to record the sins of these great saints, would have been greater from this fact,—that really, if they were not written here, not one would have known of their occurrence thirty, forty, or fifty years after they were committed. David's sin would have remained absolutely unknown, unless a special providence of the very God whose inspiration you impugn in recording it, had revealed it. And, in the next place, Rebekah and Jacob's conspiracy against Isaac, was a secret conspiracy. It would never have been known if the very God that inspired the writer to record it, had not, in his providence, made it known; and instead, therefore, of it being an argument against inspiration, it is an evidence of it. Peter's denial of Christ was in the presence of a maid-servant, and one or two private individuals only; it would have been forgotten six years after it was uttered. Then why is it written? Why is it hung up like a beacon in the bright sky? Why is it conspicuous before all nations, and audible in all tongues? God need not have recorded it; it would not have been known beyond Peter's day, if He had not recorded it. But God has recorded it, and prominently and emphatically; and, therefore, it indicates inspiration in the record, certainly not the absence of it. Thus, the very sins that never would have been known, as branding the biography of the most illustrious saints, patriarchs, apostles, psalmists, and evangelists of the New Testament, God himself has deliberately inscribed as on monuments of brass; he has hung them up conspicuous before all nations; and, so far from being afraid lest the statement of truth would substantially injure the claims of Christianity, He saw that truth is always strength, that the *suppressio veri* is just as bad as the *suggestio falsi;* and that, to state the truth and the whole truth, about saint and sinner, is, in the long run, the way to glorify Himself, vindicate his ways to men, and do the greatest good to the souls of sinners.

These recorded sins in Moses, Abraham, and David, have encouraged many a believer to seek forgiveness who otherwise would have despaired. Wicked men may quote the sins of each of these as precedents for them to imitate. But we all know well that the abuse of a thing is no argument against its legitimate use. The Bible itself may be abused; the doctrines of grace have been abused ; men have said " We shall sin because grace has abounded." Justification by faith alone might be abused. But, because one sinner shall abuse the statement of David's, and Abraham's, and Aaron's, and Moses' sins, are the whole company of God's people to be denied the comfortable inference, that there is forgiveness with our God, that he may be feared ? Would you rather that David had been refused forgiveness ? Would you rather that Moses, and Aaron, and Peter, had been condemned to ever-lasting ruin ? Would you not rather wish to hear what Scripture actually records,—that they were accepted, and pardoned, and glorified, not in conse-quence of their sins, but in spite of their sins—through that grace that abounded more where sin had so sadly abounded.

These instances have made Christians not only less liable to despond, but they have also made them more careful and circumspect in their conduct. They have served to the Christian as beacons on life's intricate and stormy sea, revealing to him the rock, and the sand be-neath, on which others almost made shipwreck. Peter's confidence has made many a presumptuous man pray. " Take heed, lest ye also fall." Abraham's, and David's, and Solomon's sins, have made many a Christian pray more frequently, " Lead us not into temptation, but deliver us from evil." And thus we see, from all these considerations, that the recorded sins of the most illustrious examples in God's holy Word, when looked at in the light and splendour in which they are re-corded, are full of suggestive lessons of practical guidance, of comfort, instruction, warning, direction in righteousness; that the man of God may be perfect, thoroughly furnished unto every good work.

And now, what is the inference we draw from the whole of these thoughts? First, how clear the inference—there is no salvation by works. Abraham would have been condemned, if tried by what he had done. Jacob, and Rebekah, and Isaac, and David, and Solomon, and Peter, and Paul, if to be acquitted or to be condemned by their works, would have perished everlastingly. We have, therefore, irresistible proof that by deeds of law no flesh can be justified. Neither the royal Psalmist, nor the princely Solomon, nor the faithful Patriarch of Mamre and of Ur, nor the heroic apostle Peter, " by deeds of law could be justified." " Enter not into judgment with thy servant, O Lord; for in thy sight no man living can be justified." What a blessed thought, then, that we are saved, not in consequence of sin, but in spite of sin, through the precious blood that washes it all away. There never was but one way to heaven from the days of Adam to the present moment. Adam was a Christian, exercising prospective faith; we are Christians exercising retrospective faith; but both Adam, Abraham, and David, and you, and I, and all that believe, are admitted into heaven, not by anything we have done; and, thanks be to God, we shall be excluded from heaven not because of anything we have committed; because our trust and confidence, and only hope of an entrance into glory, is in this blessed truth: " The blood of Jesus Christ his Son, cleanseth us from all sin." The greatest saint in the days of Abraham, the greatest sinner in the days of

Ahab, needed to be washed in that precious blood; and there is not a saint in heaven that owns he got there by his own deeds; for, we are told, that each and all cast their crowns, the evidence of their dignity, before the throne of God and of the Lamb; saying, "Unto Him that loved us, and washed us from our sins in his own blood, and hath made us kings and priests unto our God; unto him be glory, and honour, and blessing." If Abraham could not be saved by that beautiful biography notwithstanding its incidental defects, how much less we! If David, the sweet singer of Israel, whose strains of praise and penitence have found an echo in every heart to the present hour, could not be saved by what he was, how much less we! If Peter, who denied his master, and Paul, who persecuted his servants, were both constrained to disown their own righteousness, and to hold fast the only righteousness of Him who was made sin for us that we might be made the righteousness of God by Him, how much more we! Each of these biographies tells us, in the most emphatic accents, that there is but one hope, but one way to heaven, but one name in which we can be saved; the only name given under heaven, the name of the Lord Jesus Christ. A second lesson from all these considerations, is, that there is but one spotless, perfect, holy, beautiful character presented to the eyes of men; and that character was God manifest in the flesh. An evidence of the Deity of Christ results from the contrast of all he said, of all he thought, and of all he was, with the most excellent and sainted of all the patriarchs and prophets, who preceded or went before him. His whole life had perfectly

2 c

beautiful proportion. Around Jesus of Nazareth there was a halo of sanctity that was never shaded nor placed in abeyance. His were all the wants of humanity, his were none of its sins; his all the agonies and sufferings of a martyr; his all the spotlessness in spite of them, of the holy, holy, Holy One of Israel. If the best and the most illustrious saints beside have stains, defects, and grievous sins, and He only stands out so perfect, so pure, so spotless— either He was God manifest in the flesh, the very likeness of God; or the conception of such a character, and the record of such features, and the sketch of such an ideal, carried out and executed by the fishermen of Galilee, is a miracle so stupendous that there is nothing writ in the whole Bible to approach or parallel it. But we know that He who is our perfect example is God manifest in the flesh; and you have only to contrast and compare the lives of all who went before, with that holy, harmless life of the Son of David, to be able to say, " Truly this was the Son of God." And very remarkable it is, and what you must often have noticed, that in all the onslaughts made upon the Bible, and upon its characters, by sceptics and infidels, they have never dared to impugn the spotlessness of the Son of God. It is said that when the Romans burst into the Jewish temple, and saw the unutterable splendour of the Holy of holies, the fierce Roman soldier fell back, and would not dare to lay a rude hand upon that holy and resplendent carved work. It seems as if all the sceptics of the world who have assailed the outworks of Christianity, the instant they have approached that holy, spotless character, the Son of God, have fallen back, and reverently adored instead of trying to strike down; till at last the most exquisite delineation of the spotlessness, the beauty, the perfection of the character of Jesus is found in the writings of Rousseau, the notorious sensualist and sceptic of the eighteenth century, in France.

How glorious is that grace, manifested to us, which forgave the sins of these men, and forgives the sins of all still, that seek forgiveness through the blood of Jesus!

But whom are we to follow? This Bible gives us the prescription that prevents mistake. Paul records it in words that should never be forgotten: "Be ye followers of us—how far?—even as we are of Christ." In a magnificent passage in the Epistle to the Hebrews we read: "Seeing we are compassed about with so great a cloud of witnesses, let us run the race set before us in the gospel, looking"—not to the witnesses, αφορωντες, looking away from the witnesses by whom we are surrounded, and "looking to Jesus, the author and finisher of our faith." And, it seems to me now, that if Moses could speak from the crags of Abarim; if Aaron could again become eloquent from his stony grave on Mount Hor; if Abraham could only be heard from the land of Ur, or from beneath the oaks of Mamre; if Peter could speak from the shores of the Sea of Galilee, or of Gennesaret they would all, with one voice, with one consent, bid you pity them, for they were sinners saved by grace; and look to, and lean on, and imitate, and seek salvation through—not the loftiest angel, or the purest saint—but the Lamb of God, who taketh away the sins of the world.

THE DEATH OF MOSES.

" So Moses the servant of the Lord died there in the land
of Moab, according to the word of the Lord. And he buried
him in a valley in the land of Moab, over against Beth-peor :
but no man knoweth of his sepulchre unto this day."—*Deuteronomy* xxxiv. 5, 6.

LET me direct your attention to the death of Moses,
and his burial in a valley in the land of Moab, and
his sepulchre that no man knoweth. Moses died.
There is nothing new in this. Every man believes
that all must die ; but few live as those who are
really strangers and pilgrims, passing through a
world that is not their home, and looking for one
beyond the stars. The Christian is not exempt from
death, any more than the worst or the most wicked
of mankind. Death has passed upon all : " The wages
of sin is death." " It is appointed unto men to die,
and after death the judgment." Only in the case
of the unconverted, the unregenerate, the unbe-
lieving, death is penal, the infliction of a righteous
Judge on a guilty criminal ; in the case of a Christian death is paternal, its sting and bitterness are
gone ; and it is made, though often painful, the transference from grace to glory ; from the outer court to
the Holy of holies, where he is made to serve and
worship within.

There is a word that here determines the fact, and

time, and manner, and place of each man's death. "Moses died, according to the word of the Lord." And what occurred in his case occurs in that of every Christian. All three—time, place, and manner— are fixed in the word of the Lord. Moses died not one minute sooner than was appointed. And so in the case of Simeon; "Lord, now lettest thou thy servant depart in peace, according to thy word." "Moses died in the land of Moab, according to the word of the Lord." "It is *appointed* unto men to die." Here then is a higher power interposing, and disposing of man's existence upon earth. We often think it was this or that cause, or this unhappy inci- dent, or that unexpected infection, that carried such a one to the judgment-seat. So far that is true; but above all, and superintending all, sits enthroned He without whose permission a sparrow cannot fall to the ground, nor a hair drop from one's head, still less a soul quit its terrestrial tenement, and go unsent for to the judgment-seat.

Men rarely die possessing all they desire. Moses was taken at the close of a protracted life, but in the midst of unfinished plans: in spite of ardent aspira- tions to cross the Jordan, and see the Land of Pro- mise, and taste of its milk and its honey, he is denied the very thing that he had set his heart upon; the thing that he thought of all things the most sure and certain upon earth, he is forbidden to see, be- cause he spoke once, at Meribah, unadvisedly with his lips. Not a Christian dies who can say, on the eve of death, "I have attained all I attempted—I have finished all my plans; I have reached the very point to which I soared." On the contrary, every one feels, as one looks back, that we are here to-day amid unfinished plans, broken-off projects, unattained ends, many disappointments ; but all, in some shape or in some way, good and expedient for us.

Moses reached a great old age—a hundred and twenty. If he had felt all the weakness and the infirmities of old age, such a weight of years would have been a burden rather than a blessing. But to him was this privilege given, that he should see the utmost limit of human life, but enjoy to the very last breath all the freshness, the strength, and the vigour of his earlier days ; and appear more glorious and joyous in his autumn than even in his spring-time and summer. Old age is indeed delightful when it is passed in this condition ; but when the grasshopper becomes a burden, when desire faileth, it is well that man goeth to his long home, and that the mourners soon should go about the streets.

What a strange, conflicting experience was that of Moses ! He is denied one great blessing, but he is vouchsafed many others ; and probably the great blessings that he did enjoy made him feel they were compensation, in some degree, for the great desire that he had long cherished, being balked and disappointed ; and his not being allowed to enter into the Land of Promise, towards which for forty years he had been travelling in the midst of the deser.

The death of Moses was solemn. He died not in the midst of sorrowing friends, sympathizing relatives whispering words of hope or of consolation in his last moments ; he is carried to a mountain-top, the top of Nebo or Pisgah ; and there alone, without a companion to close his eyes, or a single friend to bid him farewell, he wraps himself up, and gives up his soul to Him that made him; and he was buried in a sepulchre, no man knew where. This seems to us severe in one aspect; but after all it is the universal experience. Friends can go with you into the Valley of the Shadow of Death up to a certain point; but by-and-by the ears become dead to terrestrial voices, the eyes dim to earthly and sensible sights; the soul retires .into the recesses of its earthly tabernacle, and is alone with God. The last transaction of the soul on earth is to be alone; its first transaction in eternity is to stand alone at the judgment-seat. And all salvation, we gather from every page and passage of holy Scripture, is the individual transacting with God the things that pertain to our eternal peace; and he who has not believed alone, is not fit to die alone or to be judged alone; for thus and then he meets God for the first time at death or at the judgment-seat, and must meet him as his Judge, and not as his Advocate, his Mediator, and his Friend.

The death of Moses was sudden. He knew that he must soon die; that on that very mountain he should die; but when, was not revealed. All in one day, without a warning stroke, the soul leaves its earthly tenement, and is with Christ in God; and finds itself in happy company with Aaron, who had preceded him from mount Hor; with Abraham, and Enoch, and Isaac, and Jacob, and the fathers that believed, and suffered, and went before him. We know not in what way our death may be; whether it shall be the result of pining disease, or of a sudden cessation of the pulse of life; but we are quite sure of this, that he who is united to Christ, in the exercise of living, personal trust and faith, need be in no respect anxious about the mode of his death. If it shall be sudden death, it is sudden glory; it is being spared a thousand pains, and toils, and pangs, and agonies; if it be protracted suffering, there will be the peace that passeth understanding, and the everlasting arms, and the presence and the consolations of God's Holy Spirit. If to die be Christ, it matters little whether that death be sudden, or whether it be otherwise.

Moses' death, though it was a chastisement, a public visitation of a public sin perpetrated in the public eye of all the hosts of Israel—yet it was in some respect an honourable one. He is guided by God himself to the place where his last sleep is to end in everlasting refreshment; his eye is opened by God to gaze upon the wide and glorious panorama that spread before him, unveiling all the Land of Promise; and with his eyes upon that land, the burden of so many promises, he could say in the spirit, if not in words, what Simeon said long after—" Lord, now lettest thou thy servant depart in peace, for mine eyes have seen thy salvation." And as God gave Moses in his dying moments the brightest and the most gratifying sight of that land into which he would not permit him to enter; so God often gives, to Christians on the eve of death, the brightest insight into the splendours of the approaching inheritance. The eye becomes clearer, the ear becomes more sensitive; and such see and hear what eye hath not seen, and ear hath not heard; and the soul, disentangling and extricating itself from its earthly bands, and bonds, and imprisonment, seems—from all that has been written and expressed of human experience at that hour—to see more clearly, to feel more acutely; and to find the veil—the veil that intercepted the future from the present, either withdrawn, or so thinned that it can see through and hear what is transacted beyond, and on earth have a prelibation and foretaste of the joys and blessedness of the better Canaan.

I notice, however, that Moses, as we are told here, was buried; and no man knows his sepulchre unto this day. The reason of this was that if the Jews had known his sepulchre, they would have exhumed his bones, would have put then in golden chests or in silver shrines; stored them as precious relics, and given them—as people that ought to be more enlightened than Jews do still—the homage, and even the adoration, that is due to God alone. There was therefore infinite wisdom in thus secluding his sepulchre from the ken of the Israelites; and that single sentence so quietly stated, "But no man knoweth his sepulchre unto this day;" and, seeming to the careless reader a very unnecessary or a very worthless remark, is really full of the deepest philosophy, the richest wisdom; and teaches us and shows us, that God foresaw what men would do with the body of a distinguished leader, if these remains that contained as a shrine the soul that had fled into the presence of God should ever be intrusted to their care and keeping. In all probability he was raised from that sepulchre; in all probability the resurrection in his case was anticipated; because we read in the Gospels, that he appeared with Elijah; that Moses, and Elijah, and

Christ, were together on the Mount of Transfiguration; the bodily presence of each clear and unmistakable. And the very fact, therefore, that his sepulchre was undisclosed may, perhaps, have been in order that, raised from the dead *a* first-fruits, though not *the* first-fruits, of the resurrection of Christ, he might appear on the Mount of Transfiguration; and that the law, through Moses, and the prophets, in Elijah, might lay down their mission, and testify that Christ is the Priest, the Prophet, the Legislator of all.

And one cannot but feel, in remarking upon this subject, that all must desire that nothing should survive them that can do injury to anybody. Moses himself must have foreseen what the Israelites would do with his remains, were those remains intrusted to their keeping. And every Christian still desires that nothing that he says, nothing that he has written, that shall survive his transient and temporal span, shall ever be productive of temptation to evil, or mislead any, or prove a stumbling-block to the weakest or the worst of mankind. Moses desired that not even his very bones should be a stumbling-block to Israel; and we should desire that nothing that we leave, no, nothing that survives our brief span, should, if it be possible, be perverted into evil, or made an incentive to that which ruins souls and occasions dishonour to God.

When God removes one earthly leader from the midst of his people, he does not therefore leave them desolate. He removed Moses that Israel might see that he was not dependent for the accomplishment of his great plans upon any one, however wise, illustrious, or powerful; and he substituted for Moses another—that is Joshua—that it might be seen that when he takes from us one blessing, he will compensate with a better, or at least another. When Jesus ascended, and left his disciples sorrowing, the Comforter descended, and gave them those consolations that the world could not give.

We see, in the last place, that sin is sin even in a believer just as it is in a worlding. You will hear persons of what are called Antinomian or high Calvinistic views, tell you that sin is not sin in a believer. That is unscriptural; it is untrue; it is inconsistent with common observation and common sense. Sin is sin, whether perpetrated by the highest saint or the greatest sinner upon earth. And one sin, openly and publicly done in the sight and presence of all the hosts of Israel, on the part of the most illustrious leader, and eminent saint, and meekest spirit that ever dwelt in a tabernacle of clay, needed to be signally and publicly visited, that Israel should see that even sin in Moses would not be without its legitimate and its inevitable issue. Israel should thus be taught to fear that God who hates sin and loves righteousness, and so hates sin, that even in the case of that distinguished leader, that meek-hearted legislator of Israel, it could not be allowed to exist without being visited with just and righteous retribution.

Do we find Moses leading us to Christ? Does that law which Moses carries in his hand show us that by its deeds we never can be justified? Does he become our schoolmaster to lead us unto Christ? Have we accepted Christ as an atonement that Moses could not make as a priest that Aaron could not be;

and as a king and leader that Joshua could not equal? Is He to us king, and priest, and prophet? And do we regard Moses, and Aaron, and Abraham, and patriarchs, and prophets, and saints, and evangelists, not as standing in his place or dimming his glory, but all pointing to Him? And while they point to Him, do we too go to Him, saying, "To whom can we go but unto *Thee?* Thou hast the words of eternal life." If so, our life shall be lightened by this truth; our death, wheresoever it be, or whensoever it be, shall be Christ's; living or dying, we shall be His.

CONCLUSION.

" For whatsoever things were written aforetime were written for our learning, that we through patience and comfort of the Scriptures might have hope."—*Romans* xv. 4.

IT seems impossible to receive one part of the Bible without receiving all; every book in the Old Testament is so linked with every chapter of the New, and the predictions of the one with the facts and fulfilments recorded in the other, that he who rejects the one must necessarily repudiate and reject both. The New Testament is the complement of the Old; the one the development of the other: in the Old Testament the gospel is taught in material signs, visible smybols, ceremonies, types, and shadows; in the New Testament it is set forth in all its clearness, without shadow, symbol, or type; so that he that reads may run while he reads it. But the Old Testament was necessary to the infancy of the Church; the New Testament is fitted for the maturer manhood and more enlightened experience of the Christian Church now. But nothing can be more absurd than to say, We receive the New Testament, but we cannot receive the Old; or the New Testament supersedes the Old. It is not so: both are full of the gospel; both, like the wings of the cherubim, touch each other, whilst they look down upon Christ, the glory that is between; both, like the lips of an oracle, utter one testimony; and he that rejects the one as of no use will most logically reject the other; for the one is inexplicable except in the light of the other. How delightful is that statement of the apostle in this verse, " Whatsoever things were written aforetime were *written* for our learning." No one can exaggerate the value of this fact, that the Bible is not the transmission of oral testimony, but the fixed and imperishable record that it now is. Nothing is more precarious than oral transmission; nothing more precious than the fixture and the stereotype of a permanent record. In antediluvian days, in the lapse of two thousand years, all flesh had utterly corrupted its way; and under the reign of oral transmission there were only eight persons left out of the mighty multitude who retained the knowledge, and exhibited the spirit and the practice of the gospel. And so prone is human nature, even when the best intentioned, to pervert and to misstate what has been given out purely, simply, and intelligibly, that we find at the very close of the Gospel of St. John, when Peter asked a very impertinent question, and one that he had nothing to do with, " What shall this man do?" " Jesus saith, If I will that he tarry till I come, what is that to thee? Follow thou me."—Now, mark what tradition did; the moment Jesus said so, tradition began its havoc; seized a precious truth, and perverted it into a corrupt tradition. "Then went this saying abroad" —that is, the tradition—" among the brethren, that that disciple should not die." But how beautifully Scripture steps in the instant that the cloud of tradition has begun, and dissipates it: " Yet Jesus said not

unto him, He shall not die ; but, If I will that he tarry
till I come, what is that to thee ?" You see how soon
then tradition began ; and how happily Scripture has
appended its corrective. Now, if we were dependent
upon the transmission of great doctrines from minister to minister, or people to people, Christianity,
starting in its purity and simplicity at the beginning,
would be now what it became in the middle ages—an
aggregate of all corrupt and heterogeneous things,
dishonourable to God, and contributing in no shape
to the holiness, the happiness, or prospects of mankind. But we rejoice to know that what the Spirit
said is now written ; and that the frail parchment of
old, and the frailer paper of to-day, retains, by the
wondrous, providential discovery of printing, the everlasting record more surely than if it were written with
Job's pen of iron upon the rock, or with diamond,
ineffaceable apparently for ever. And were all the
impressions of the Bible in England to be swept away
to-day, you could have thousands of impressions scattered throughout the world from which to take fresh
ones, and restore the lamp taken from off the everlasting throne to its lofty and its supreme position. It
is a very interesting fact, that suppose the whole New
Testament were by one mysterious stroke to be extinguished, that not one copy were to be left in any
tongue or in any country upon earth ; you might take
all the writings of the first five centuries, the works
of scholars and divines, of enemies of the gospel
and champions of it ; and out of the writings of the
first five centuries you might collect every text in the
New Testament, beginning at Matthew, to the close
of the Book of Revelation. It is only curious that

God should have thus overruled the very opposition and hatred of his enemies to the greater safety and clearness of his truth. And it is also very instructive to notice that, if you open the writings of any one of the Fathers of the first five centuries, you will find the texts in your Bible quoted exactly as you find them still. The fact that every text was discussed seventeen centuries ago is a standing protest against the possibility of corrupting that text now, and evidence to you that the Bible that you hold in this year 1856 is just the Bible—I mean the New Testament— as it was inspired by the Spirit, written by evangelists, preached and addressed by apostles; without the mixture of a verse, the omission of a paragraph, or any deterioration whatever.

All this Scripture which was written was written "for our learning,"—let us see what plain lessons that suggests. "For our learning." To whom is he writing? Not to a college of apostles, but to the laity of Rome,—the soldiers, the sailors, the shopkeepers, the merchants, the lawyers of Rome; and to them simply as men; and, through them and by them, to us. Now then, he says, "The Scriptures were written for our learning." Then it is implied that we ought to possess the Scriptures, and that we have a right to possess them. How can we learn from them unless we have them? Every allusion to the usefulness of Scripture contained in the New Testament is a silent protest against the tyranny that would snatch the Bible from the people, and make it the monopoly and the possession only of the priest. The very fact that we are to learn from the Scriptures, and to draw patience, comfort, hope, from what, they say, involves and implies the prior fact that the Bible is in our hands. It implies too, that the Bible is to be read. What is the use of a book? Surely it is something to be read. And the very fact that the Spirit raised up men to write the Bible, teaches us that the Spirit meant there should be men that needed and had a right to read the Bible. Why write it, unless it was meant to be read? And why have it in our possession, unless we are at liberty to read it? It is not a book for the consecrated eye of the few, but for the joyous perusal of all mankind. The Bible is addressed to the people; it is the special property of the people; the New Testament consists of letters addressed to Roman people, to Corinthian people, to Galatian people; and because the human heart is always the same, and human nature always the same; and variety of circumstance only variety upon the surface; it is addressed to the British people, and the French and the German people, and to all mankind; as long as there is a soul that needs to be enlightened in the knowledge of the truth, or a heart to be saved, by its saving and its precious doctrines.

Do we not gather from this, that the Bible is also an intelligible book? You are told by some it is so dark and mysterious, that the laity are better without it; that it is so obscure a document, that you can never understand its meaning. Now, is this fact? I venture to assert, and every one's judgment will confirm what I say, that, notwithstanding the sublimity of its lofty themes, notwithstanding the instinctive enmity of the unsanctified heart to its pure and uncompromising morality, that there is no book more extensively understood; and other books that are

2 D

most popular are so because they are the closest reflexions of the magnificent and majestic simplicity of the Old and New Testament. There are depths in it, as some one said, in which elephants may swim, and shallows in it in which lambs may wade. There are portions of it too abstruse, because pictures of the infinite, that cannot be comprehended by finite minds; but in all that relates to our duties, our privileges, our obligations, our hopes; in all that relates to the way of acceptance to the way to heaven; there is no book that is so plain; in which the same truth is placed in so many lights, set forth by so varied imagery; and impressed and reiterated with so remarkable and effective emphasis. Take the Bible, therefore, as a whole; and it is the most intelligible book that was ever written. It is no objection, I answer, that there are great difficulties in it; because whilst it describes man, and man's duties and man's privileges, it delineates an infinite God; the very definition of whom is to be above, not contrary to, the grasp of the human mind. If you were to bring a peasant from the country into a royal palace; that peasant would understand, this is an entrance hall; this is a dining room; this is a drawing room; this is a sleeping room; but he would see twenty other rooms the end and use of which he could not understand. But you would not blame the architect; what you would blame, would be the inexperience of the peasant; whose mind is not enlightened, and whose habits are not such as to enable him to appreciate and understand all that the genius of the architect has originated, and the requirements of the palace have brought about. It is so with this blessed book;

because there are in it texts, allusions, dimensions, too vast for us to understand, it is not because it is imperfect, or its language is obscure; but because our minds are not yet initiated in the truth, able to comprehend the truth; and perhaps throughout everlasting ages we shall see truths beyond the horizon which we cannot clearly apprehend, and read records too magnificent for us fully to grasp.

Now "whatsoever things," says Paul, "were written," therefore permanent; written "for our learning;" therefore to be possessed, and therefore intelligible; were written for us specially for a great practical purpose. They were written not to gratify the curiosity of any, but to teach, instruct, and sanctify the hearts, the consciences, the understandings of all. You open a human biography, and you find a character sketched for the purpose of amusement; you open divine biographies, and you find every character sketched in the Bible, from Cain and Abel, onward to the last of the apostles, not to satisfy your curiosit as to what he was, but to be to you in some shape a model you are to imitate, or a beacon you are to avoid, or to impress some great lesson, or to illustrate some precious and practical truth. The history of Abraham and Isaac, Jacob and Joseph, was written for a very different end from the history of Alexander, or Cæsar, or Napoleon. You will find, for instance, Adam's position, character, and ruin, underlying all the doctrines of the New Testament. You will find Moses appear on the Mount of Transfiguration; his lessons in the teaching of Jesus, his character in the discussions of Paul, and his song amid the hundred and forty and four thousand who sing in heaven the song of Moses and of the Lamb. In the case of Abraham, he lives, though dead, in the New Testament. He speaks in its parables, he appears in its doctrines ; he is presented as a model of unswerving trust ; as an instance of a pure, lofty, and unfaltering obedience. The cloud of witnesses envelops us everywhere, each with his lesson in his hand ; showing that from Adam and Eve, onward to the last whose name and life are recorded in the inspired record ; all were written not to amuse the idle ; not to satisfy the curiosty of the inquisitive ; but to enlighten the mind, to sanctify the heart, to mould the life ; that through patience and comfort of the Scriptures we might have hope.

If now it should be asked, in looking at all these characters, and all that is written for our learning, What do we chiefly learn ? What are some of the leading truths that we learn ? First, in the very best of circumstances none were perfect before God. It is a singular fact, that there is not a perfect character in the whole Bible, except one great Original, approximation to whom is the measure of perfection, opposition to whom is contrariety to all that God requires, and that dignifies and beautifies man. Abraham was imperfect, Joseph and David were imperfect ; every one of the ancient patriarchs and prophets had their imperfections. Christ alone is the holy, harmless, perfect One. You learn that there never were more than two classes of men since Adam fell to the present moment. There were rich and poor ; learned and ignorant ; but the two classes that underlie all, that remain through all ; that are really the two distinctions that endure for ever, are the company of believers and the company of unbelievers; those that are born again, and those that are dead in trespasses and in sins. There never have been but two classes among mankind, really distinguished the one from the other; sinners by nature, and saints by grace. All other distinctions are extrinsic, adventitious, evanescent; these distinctions are coeval with time, will project into eternity, and last in heaven and in hell for ever and for ever. And we shall see next, in the course of reading this blessed book, that there was one great requirement made of every character from first to last; and that is, that he should be born again. One needed to conform to this ceremony, another to that; one to be circumcised, another to be baptized; one to worship in the temple, another in the synagogue, another in the Christian Church ; but in all these, and in spite of all these, there was one great requirement, never dispensed with in any, essential to the happiness and safety of all. Except Abraham be born again; except Paul be born again; except Joseph and Abel be born again; except Peter and James be born again; except we be born again, we cannot see the kingdom of heaven. That great revolution occurred in every case ; that great change was essential from the beginning until now. Justification alone by faith in the righteousness of Christ was preached amidst the ruins of Paradise ; and " Except a man be born again, he cannot see the kingdom of heaven," was experienced by Adam, as it must be experienced by us, in order that we may be numbered with God's saints in glory everlasting. And another great lesson that we learn from these things that were written for our learning, is, that the cross of Christ is not the discovery of recent times, but a revelation from the beginning. The same cross to which we look back in the exercise of retrospective faith, to find there the ground of our acceptance before God, was that very cross to which Adam, and Abel, and Enoch, and Abraham looked forward in prospective faith, to find the ground of their acceptance before God, and their right of admission into heaven. Abraham gloried in the cross as truly as St Paul; both were saved by the same name, washed in the same precious blood, clad in the same glorious righteousness. There never were but two ways to heaven ; one by law, which was shut and sealed for ever when Adam fell; the other by Christ, which was opened in Paradise; and, blessed be God! remains at this day open so wide that the worst and the greatest number may tread it; and yet so holy that the least known, deliberate, and wilful sin is not permitted to be perpetrated in it. And the reason why all this was written, and these precious truths personated in illustrious characters, was that we, through patience and comfort, taught by these Scriptures, might have hope. The word "written" is the very same as the word "scripture." And hence this verse might be read, "For whatsoever things were written aforetime were written for our learning, that we, through patience and comfort of these 'things.'" These things ; what things? Those things that were written aforetime for our learning; "might have hope." We are are to learn patience· But what does patience mean? Wherever there is patience, there must be suffering. And if patience be a lesson supremely impressed in the biography of the ancient worthies, then suffering must have been their previous personal experience. And when we open the record of what they were, we find that suffering was their lot; that what the apostle mentions in the Acts was the experience of patriarchs of old. "Through much tribulation we must enter into the kingdom of God." For, says Paul, "others had trial of cruel mockings and scourgings, yea, moreover of bonds and imprisonment: they were stoned, they were sawn asunder, were tempted, were slain with the sword: they wandered about in sheepskins and goat-skins; being destitute, afflicted, tormented; (of whom the world was not worthy); they wandered in deserts, and in mountains, and in dens and caves of the earth." And then, he adds, in the chapter that follows, "Wherefore seeing we also are compassed about with so great a cloud of witnesses, let us run with patience the race that is set before us." Now the lesson, you observe, that he draws from his catalogue of illustrious martyrs, is a lesson of patience; and that is, because they suffered, and suffered so poignantly because of their faithfulness to Christ, and endured their sufferings with such magnanimity and patience; that we, seeing how painfully they suffered, how patiently they endured, may, with greater light, greater privileges, greater mercies, far, far less suffering, exhibit greater patience than we now do; that we may through patience and comfort of the Scriptures have hope. But if we learn patience, where do we learn comfort? The whole Bible is written to give comfort; the author of it is the Comforter. "I will send you another Comforter." His promises are words that overflow with comfort; his prophecies were inspired, giving so bright and glorious a picture of the close, in order that we might have comfort. And all in the Bible tells us that amidst all the complications of events, amidst all the shakings of the kingdoms of the earth; God reigns, rules, regulates, restrains; out of evil still educing good, and compelling all, either as sacrifices freely given, or irresistibly exacted by himself, to contribute to his praise, and to the good of his own people. And thus this blessed book, carried into the midst of all the events of the world, of all the experience of the church, of all the contingencies that befall the individual Christian, casts light and harmony upon all, and exhibits the end and the issue of all, and teaches the presence of God, curbing, regluating, meting out, according to his love and his wisdom; and as we look at things in the light of what is written, we patiently endure the severest trial, knowing it is only for a season, and we imbibe the most precious comfort, because God is in the world working out his own great designs. Thus, through patience and comfort of the Scriptures, we have not a guess, not an expectation, but hope; that is, a confidence of future issues based upon God's immutable promises, satisfied that evil shall not gain the day, that the world shall not finally be cast off; that Christ's church shall not finally perish; but on the contrary, that the whole earth shall be filled with his praise and glory; that he shall reign from sea to sea, and from the river to the ends of the earth; and that the heathen shall be his inheritance, and the uttermost parts of the earth his possession.

GENERAL INDEX TO THE PENTATEUCH.

The numeral figures, i. ii. iii. iv. v., *refer to the Books of Moses, in their order.*

1981-82 TITLES

TITLES CURRENTLY AVAILABLE